How to be a Travel Writer

- DON GEORGE WITH JANINE EBERLE -

Contents

1

So you w
a travel

ant to be

writer...

Travel writer. Those two words are among the most alluring in the English language. No less a luminary than Mick Jagger has said that if he couldn't be a rock star, he'd like to be a travel writer. Drew Barrymore has claimed the same.

It is an enticing image. There you are, lying on a chaise longue on a white-sand beach by an aquamarine ocean, describing how the palm trees rustle in the salt-tinged breeze. Sipping a café crème in a Parisian cafe, scribbling impressions in a battered notebook. Bouncing through the African bush, snapping photos of gazelles and lions, then ending the day listening to spine-tingling tales over gin and tonics in the campfire's glow.

If you love to travel and you love to write, the dream doesn't get any better. But how does it tally with the reality?

The rewards of travel writing

Every year a few dozen people around the world make a living traveling and writing full-time – and if that's your goal, go for it! This book will give you all the information and inspiration you need in order to try to reach that dream.

But you don't have to get paid full-time or even part-time to profit from your travel writing. Whatever your goals as a traveler and writer, the rewards of travel writing – and of approaching travel with the travel writer's mindset – are numerous. First and foremost, you become a better traveler. You arrive at your destination having already learned something of its history, culture and important sites, making you far better able to explore and appreciate what it has to offer. Also, because you are on the lookout for trends, unique places to visit and essential hot spots, you gradually build up a store of knowledge, becoming more and more of a travel expert.

When you are on the road, traveling as a travel writer will force you to pay attention. You will look more closely, listen more clearly, taste more carefully – and continually reflect on what you're experiencing. As a result, your travels will be deeper and richer. In addition, you will often be able to go behind the scenes at a restaurant, store or hotel, to take advantage of special access to a historical site or museum exhibit, and to speak with intriguing people – from archaeologists and curators to chefs and shamans – whom everyday travelers would not be able to meet.

Finally, after you have returned home – or if you're blogging, while you're still on the road – you will be able to relive your journey over and over in the course of writing about it. And when your account is published, sharing your travel experiences with others – whether in a magazine, newspaper, travel website or personal blog – will further multiply your pleasure, forging connections with others who share your passions. All these effects will broaden and extend the significance and depth of your travels.

These riches come with a corresponding responsibility, of course. As a travel writer you will have a fundamental commitment to your reader to explore a place deeply and fully, and to report the information your reader needs to know by writing an honest, fair, objective and accurate portrayal of that place. Integrity is the travel writer's compass and key.

What do you want to write?

The travel-writing trail is long, and there are numerous destinations along the way, from Just-Blogging-My-Journal and Writing-as-a-Hobby to Trying-to-Make-a-Living and Want-to-be-the-Next-Bill-Bryson. Travel publishing today presents an unprecedented wealth of mentors to learn from and outlets to target.

If your principal goal is to share your travel experiences with others, without necessarily receiving compensation, that's easier now than ever before. You can create your own space online where you can post your writings and photographs. In thousands of blogs, everyday travelers are sharing their wanderings with the world. There are also community websites where you can post your experiences and opinions. If you just want to create and communicate, these options are for you.

If you want some compensation for your creative communication, you'll want to target websites that pay, as well as newspapers and magazines. Starting a blog and building it to the point of making money is an option for entrepreneurial writers, or it can act as a stepping stone to other opportunities. Writing books, whether guidebooks or travel literature titles, is another option.

Writers dedicated to making a living from their travel writing will consider all of these and aim for a mix that makes best use of their skills and experience to maximize exposure and earnings.

Do you have what it takes?

While travel writing can be one of the most enjoyable professions on the planet, it's not for everyone. In fact, trying to make a living as a travel writer can be extremely demanding and daunting, requiring a particular temperament and setting some harsh limits on your lifestyle.

A (very) short history

Travel writing is an ancient impulse: people have been sharing accounts of their journeys ever since they first began to wander. The earliest wall paintings present the prehistoric predecessors of Bill Bryson and Paul Theroux recounting their adventures in the larger world. The Greek historian Herodotus is generally credited with writing the first travel book, *History of the Persian Wars*, with its vivid depictions of exotic sites, rites and fights, in 440 BC. Through the ensuing centuries, traders and explorers from Marco Polo and Christopher Columbus to Henry Morton Stanley and Charles Darwin wrote diaries and dispatches describing their adventures and discoveries in far-flung lands.

In the 20th century, travel writing came into its own as a flourishing independent genre with the emergence of such extraordinary writer-travelers as Patrick Leigh Fermor, Wilfred Thesiger, Eric Newby, Colin Thubron and Jan Morris, and continued to evolve into the 21st century with the work of such masters as Paul Theroux, Bill Bryson, Pico Iyer, Tim Cahill, Stanley Stewart, Kira Salak, Anthony Sattin and Rory MacLean.

The digital revolution has allowed travelers everywhere to publish hitherto personal travel journals online and created a brand-new breed of travel writer: the travel blogger. Writers and content creators with access to video, instantly updatable content and massive online communities have ushered in a new age of travel communication. Next stop? Absolutely anywhere you want to go.

Of course, you need to have a way with words and an impulse to express yourself – the urge to fill an empty page. But beyond that, what are some of the quintessential qualities you need?

Be flexible

One of the hallmarks of the travel writer's life is its general instability and spontaneity. This is equally true both at home and on the road. At home, you have to be able to drop everything and take off for a far-flung destination at a moment's notice. Your life is dictated by the whims of editors and printer deadlines. To a certain extent, you can negotiate timelines with editors, but often their deadlines just cannot be adjusted – and then, if you're not flexible, you risk losing the commission (or assignment, as it is called in the USA). You might also risk building yourself a reputation for saying 'no', which you definitely don't want to have in the close-knit travel editorial world.

On the road, you also need to leave room for the unexpected. You may need to alter your itinerary to take in a once-every-seven-years festival you hadn't known about, or to spend an impromptu afternoon with the winemaker who promises to make a fascinating subject for your article.

Be adaptable

The second quality is a corollary to the first. If you want to maximize your chances as a travel writer, you have to be just as ready to explore the heart of Paris and the heart of Papua New Guinea. This means that you need to have a closet full of suitable clothing and gear but, even more important, you have to have a head full of suitable attitudes. Are you equally at home on high seas and low roads? Can you keep your cool in hot situations? Is your stomach strong or are you susceptible to illness? Could you hop from an expedition ship in the Antarctic to a $15-a-night hut on an isolated South Pacific island and then to a five-star hotel in London? To take the maximum advantage of such opportunities, you have to be adaptable.

Live modestly

Let's get this out of the way right now: it's not likely that you're going to get rich as a travel writer. Not in terms of money, anyway. You will certainly accumulate an uncommon wealth of experience, but to be a travel writer, you need to be able to live on a precarious income. If you are a freelancer you never know how much you're going to earn in a year, and you don't know when the money you have earned is going to come in. Some publications will pay you on acceptance of a piece, while others may not pay you until your piece has been published – and that could be many months or even years after your initial outlay. Some publications will pay automatically and on time; others will have to be reminded many times before you finally receive your payment.

As a result, the commitment of significant, regular, ongoing expenses – a mortgage or school fees, for example – does not fit well with the freelance travel writer's life. Generally speaking, the travel writer's lifestyle is a frugal one – and you need to be content with that.

Have an understanding family
The 'here today, gone tomorrow' nature of the travel writer's life takes a significant toll on friendships, and of course on more permanent and intimate relationships. You have to have an extraordinarily understanding and supportive partner who is able to carry on without you virtually at the drop of a hat, for uncertain – and sometimes prolonged – periods of time. If you have children, the situation is further compounded. This complaint by a UK travel journalist's wife is telling:

> In one year my husband managed to be away for my 40th birthday, our sixth wedding anniversary (he was also away for our fifth), our first daughter's third birthday and my brother's wedding. These are all dates he'd had in his diary for months and months, but we just can't afford to turn down work due to prior family commitments.

Even friends can become irritated by your comings and goings, and feel that they can't rely on you – they'll complain that they just don't know if you'll be there for them. In addition, when you are there you seem to be working all the time – working long hours is one of the only ways you can make travel writing pay. All in all, in committing yourself to the travel writer's lifestyle, you relinquish a certain amount of control over your own life – and the people in your life have to be satisfied with that.

Be curious
Curiosity is one of the prime characteristics common to all great travel writers – they are constantly studying the world around them, asking how

things work and why they appear the way they do. They always observe and absorb, and they always talk with people – waiters, taxi drivers, sales assistants, fellow travelers. It is essential to have a passionate and insatiable curiosity about the world, and it is equally essential to keep recharging this curiosity so that you bring a fresh eye and renewed enthusiasm to each new place and story. It is this that will set your research, reporting and writing apart from the pack.

Be tenacious

Travel isn't easy, especially when you're on a mission to track down information and experiences that will make good travel stories. No matter how exhausted and overwhelmed you may be, you have to keep plugging on, overcoming cultural differences, leaping over language barriers, smoothly swallowing stomach-tumbling foods. You have to find the courage to talk with people you've never met, and to learn to trust the kindness of strangers.

Time after time, place after place, you can't give up until you've got your story and then you can't give up until you've written it down and the editor has accepted it. And then it's time to start the next story.

Be motivated and disciplined

If you are a freelancer, you are your own and only boss, and procrastination is your enemy. You have to make yourself sit down at your desk every day, organize your material, plan your story and write. You need the self-motivation to repeatedly rework and resubmit your articles, and the organizational skills to manage travel schedules, workloads, deadlines, finances and networking. On the road you need the discipline to be continually researching, interviewing, taking notes and gathering information. Wherever you are, travel writing can be a relentless, ongoing, time-consuming balancing act that requires unstinting dedication.

Don't be easily discouraged

Think of your favorite travel writer. Whoever they are, at some time in their life they were unknown, struggling to get a foothold in the writing world, just as you are today. They faced rejection, probably many times, but they always persevered, continuing to send in their proposals and stories to editors. To survive as a travel writer, you too need the confidence, ability and just plain thick skin to bounce back from rejection after rejection. You need a tenacious faith in yourself and an inventive tenacity. The same applies for temporary setbacks on the road. If an avalanche has closed the route to your destination, you hire a horse. If the local tourism office doesn't have the information you need, you track down the long-time resident who is happy to spend an hour telling you neighborhood tales. Somehow you find a way to accomplish what you need to do.

Have passion

Finally, and fundamentally, you have to have passion – passion for people, passion for the world, passion for the whole business of traveling and for exploring and integrating your discoveries into precise and palpable prose. Travel writing is essentially a lonely profession, and it is your passion that will sustain and reward you.

Getting published

The world of travel publishing has experienced a kind of accelerated evolution over the past decade. The technological development and popular expansion of the internet as a publishing platform has profoundly affected its traditional media siblings. Traditional publishers have adapted their print publications to fit the age of the internet, in some cases expanding their presence on the web while simultaneously cutting back on their printed pages.

At the same time, the network of online-only publishers has expanded exponentially. This digital proliferation has mirrored the historical evolution of media: while it started with predominantly text-centric websites, the internet is now largely video-driven in an echo of the explosion of television, and podcasts have come into their own as the modern equivalent of radio broadcasts.

Where this media convergence/divergence, expansion/contraction is heading is unclear and ever developing, and is something that every travel writer needs to monitor and respond to so they produce material that is current, relevant and that will sell. But it is clear that today's travel writers can choose from a greater range of potential subject matter and a more extensive and varied range of publishing opportunities than ever before. Here is a brief overview of these possibilities; we will cover them in detail in chapters 3 and 4.

Online

This is where most budding travel writers will start out, even if it's just through a too-long Facebook post about their last holiday or a restaurant review on TripAdvisor. The opportunities for self-publishing online are limited only by your imagination and technological sophistication (and that can be easily learned). For some entrepreneurial travel writers, blogging becomes a source of income. If you don't want to start your own blog, there are countless places where you can submit your writing for publication – though making money from such opportunities is challenging.

Newspapers

Many newspapers in the USA, UK and Australia publish separate sections devoted exclusively to travel. While some of these, particularly in the USA, have shrunk in size over the course of the decade, they continue to represent a significant market for both beginner and established writers. In the USA, major newspapers' travel sections are usually published on Sunday and range in size from four to 40 pages. In the UK, most quality newspapers have travel sections of between four and 40 pages on Saturday and Sunday, and some also feature travel during the week. Major Australian newspapers also feature separate travel sections on Saturday and Sunday, ranging from four to 24 pages. In addition to these, local newspapers often include some travel coverage.

Magazines

Magazines focusing on travel continue to flourish, and lifestyle/general-interest magazines regularly include travel coverage in their pages. Virtually every airline has its own in-flight magazine, which publishes articles about the destinations to which it flies, and niche publications that focus on specific subjects, activities or regions often feature travel pieces. Subcategories within the travel world have also developed audiences and publications of their own; for example, family travel, business travel, gay and lesbian travel, and adventure travel, and there is a healthy niche in publishing high-end literary travel writing.

Travel literature

Many major publishers produce works of travel literature on a regular basis; these tend to come from writers with already established reputations, but some newcomers break into the ranks every year. Smaller publishers represent much better opportunities for writers who are not already well known. Travel anthologies are an excellent market for narrative travel writing.

Guidebooks

Travel guidebook publishing has sustained a significant blow to its bottom line as travel information has made its way online in greater and greater volume and the book industry as a whole has ridden the wave of the digital revolution. Despite that, guidebook publishers continue to publish their traditional titles while also looking for new ways to grow their piece of the travel pie. Publishing updates to a wide range of books every few years is a high-energy operation requiring a lot of writers, so guidebook publishers are constantly on the lookout for excellent writers and particularly for travelers who know particular destinations really well.

The journey starts here...

Being a travel writer is not all palmy bungalows, Parisian cafes and safari sunsets. It's hard work. But Mick Jagger and Drew Barrymore had it right: travel writing is one of the dream jobs. That doesn't mean it's beyond your reach. The world of travel writing is open to everyone; if you love to travel and you love to write, it's a natural. No one can guarantee that you'll be successful, but it is guaranteed that you'll never be successful if you don't try.

The aim of Lonely Planet's *How To Be A Travel Writer* is to get you started – wherever you may be and wherever you may be traveling.

While **chapter 1** aims to set the lay of the land and pose the key questions, **chapter 2** focuses on the 'writing' part of the equation, with a short course in the strategies and tools you need to identify your best story subjects from your travels, and then to evoke each of those subjects in a transporting and compelling account.

In **chapter 3** we'll cover the traditional publishing opportunities in print, with hard-won advice on how to break into the business of newspaper, magazine and book publishing – and get paid for it.

In **chapter 4** we'll look at how to launch yourself online with your own travel blog. From the technology you'll need to grapple with, to that big and important word 'monetization' (which you'll need to get your tongue around if you want to make a living as an online travel writer) – we'll cover it all here.

Chapter 5 deals with the tin tacks – what life is like on the road, and what are the tools and tricks you need to make it work day to day as a travel writer.

Chapter 6 is a bonus extra: how to add travel photography to your repertoire. This is your travel-writing box of tricks.

Chapter 7 provides an extensive compilation of online, UK, US and Australian resources, from travel websites and publications to publishers and writers' groups, reference books and travel literature classics.

Throughout the book you'll also find a treasure trove of top tips and real-life insights, including interviews with prominent travel writers, bloggers, editors and agents, to help guide you on your journey.

One last point about that journey. This book is intended for writing travelers of all kinds – from aspiring professionals to dedicated journal jotters. In the end, you don't have to make money to profit from travel writing; sometimes the richest rewards are in the currency of experience. The goal of this book is to reveal the varied possibilities that travel writing offers, and to inspire all travelers to take advantage of those opportunities. That's where the journey begins; where it takes you is up to you.

② A short in travel

course

writing

What makes a wonderful travel story? In one word, it's place. Successful travel stories bring a particular place to life through a combination of factual information and vividly rendered descriptive details and anecdotes, characters and dialogue. Such stories transport the reader and convey a rich sense of the author's experience in that location. The best travel stories also set the destination and experience in some larger context, creating rings of resonance in the reader.

The goals of good travel writing are to present an accurate and compelling evocation and assessment of an area, to bring that place and the writer's experience to life so vividly that the reader is transported there, and to enhance the reader's understanding of the world (whether the reader is moved to plan a journey to that spot, or simply content to visit it vicariously). In some cases, a secondary goal is to present the essential information the reader needs to visit that place and duplicate the author's experience.

So how do you write a good travel story? The journey begins well before you set finger to keyboard.

Finding your story

Find the right subject

The very first step in writing a good travel story is finding the right subject. If the topic is right, the chances of writing a compelling piece – and of getting that piece published – will be maximized.

A good topic is usually a marriage of passion and practicality. As a writer, you want to choose a subject that will allow you to infuse your story with a sense of connection and conviction; at the same time, you need to write about a topic that will capture an editor's attention and will fit well with the publication you've targeted.

Today's publishing world offers a bountiful variety of outlets for travel writing, so it is critically important to know the market. Study the publications and websites that you'd like to write for, reading several editions of each to analyze the focus, tone, approach and length of the articles they publish.

At the same time, it is equally important to know yourself, and to focus on subjects or places that especially interest you. Are you particularly drawn to food, crafts, festivals or nightlife? Do you prefer five-star resorts or no-frills guesthouses? Do you like to explore the heart of a city or far-flung hinterlands? Finding your passion will help you narrow the publication targets for your stories – but don't narrow your field too much. Think outside the box. If you love luxury resorts, you may think that you couldn't possibly write for a budget travel magazine – but what about a story on finding luxury for under £50 a night?

If you're not passionate about food, you probably wouldn't think of approaching a food and wine magazine, but a humorous piece on surviving a week in Tuscany with a ferocious foodie could be right on target.

Understanding travel trends

As you try to marry passion with practicality, it's critical to stay abreast of travel trends. Identifying one can become the nucleus for a story. You may create a story about the emergence of the trend itself – or you may be able to adapt that trend to a place you want to write about. For example, if you see that an editor has published a cover story on farm stays in Portugal, consider if there is a version of the farm-stay experience in New Zealand or Argentina that might interest the same editor. If the publication routinely features articles on extreme adventures, come up with an adrenalin-charged story in a destination they haven't covered yet.

It's also important to remember that most newspaper travel sections are inundated with stories on hard-to-get-to places halfway around the globe, but are desperate for great writing on easy-to-visit places closer to home. Try proposing a long-weekend story – they're easier and cheaper to research, and your odds of getting published are considerably higher.

There are three kinds of trends you should monitor in order to find good story ideas and get to know your market.

Objective travel trends reflect traveler behavior: where people are going, how they are getting there and what they are doing when they get there. Are ski resorts in North America suddenly all the rage with Europeans? Are more Americans barging their way along European waterways than before? Is Austria a hot destination for Australians? Does camping have a new cachet for Canadians? Is train travel booming around the globe? Are airlines or tour operators opening operations in any new and exciting destinations?

Whenever possible, anticipate these trends. If you read that a country is planning a major tourism campaign in six months' time, pitch a story about that country right now. When a city is chosen as a future Olympics site or European Capital of Culture, you know that travelers – and editors – will be interested in knowing more about them as their time in the spotlight approaches.

Subjective travel trends are anecdotal and often qualitative. Are the travelers who once flocked to Thailand now heading to Laos? Do luxury travelers consider the spa resorts in the Maldives passé and, if so, where are they going instead? Is Belize the new Costa Rica, Brno the new Prague? (Somewhere is always the new somewhere else.) Are baby boomers turning to volunteer vacations to add meaning to their lives? Are eco-cruises suddenly in vogue?

Exercise 1

What are your travel passions? Think about your three most recent trips. What activities were common to all three? What are the things you seek out when you travel, the experiences that really move you? Why? Make a list of three things you love to do. Consider each of these. Why do you love it and what have you learned by doing it? Could this be the nucleus for a story?

Editorial travel trends are indicated by changes in the weight of coverage given to different regions or types of travel. For example, these days almost every serious British newspaper regularly devotes coverage to European city breaks – a sharp contrast from the past when such coverage was patchy (this, of course, is driven by the objective travel trend that low-cost flights have radically opened up inter-Europe travel since the early 2000s). Stories on luxury spas might be on the decline while articles touting green travel options are on the increase.

Keeping up with travel trends
Finding fresh material, spotting travel trends and keeping up to date with industry and consumer changes are essential practices for all travel writers.

Chapter 7 of this book contains a wealth of online, global and regional information sources, and is a great place to start.

Scanning newspaper travel sections, travel magazines and websites will give you a feel for what your competitors are writing about, and will provide you with ideas for new stories. If you follow this practice you will also avoid the embarrassment of offering an editor a story similar to one that has just been run. Reading one or two industry magazines or websites a week will keep you informed about what airlines, tour operators, hotel groups and others in the travel industry are up to, and there are plenty of tourism facts and stats available online. Government and NGO sites are also useful.

Another useful way of finding out about what's happening in the travel world is by joining the press mailing lists of several travel companies. Ring up the companies you're interested in and speak to their PR departments, but try to be selective because you don't want to be flooded with press releases. Jaded travel writers or editors will tell you that 99 per cent of what you will be sent will go straight into the rubbish bin, but if that remaining one per cent forms the basis of a fresh travel article that you can sell, then it's worth it. And don't discount the fact that perusing a press release and learning about a new travel initiative adds to your overall body of travel information and may well be valuable one day.

Become a specialist

To make a decent living as a travel writer, you need to be able to turn your hand to a variety of travel articles. However, it can be very much to your advantage to find the niche that best fits your expertise as a writer. By narrowing your field, you can focus on a particular slice of the travel world and become an authority on it. Travel editors, and possibly broadcasters, will begin to recognize your skill, and will think of you when they are looking for a story or comment on your subject. Specializing in this way should mean more paid work, not less, because your particular expertise will be acknowledged. In addition, writing on something that you already know about means less research, and less research means more time to write – and in the end, writing is what you're paid for.

Choosing a niche will involve looking for a decent gap in the market – there's very little point in specializing in a subject that everyone else has chosen as their particular topic. Obviously, you also need to select something that truly interests you and fits your lifestyle; it might be travel with children, low-cost airlines, a particular form of transport or a specific part of the world.

Writer's tip: Staying on trend

To keep on top of what's happening in the world of travel, sign up for regular updates from sites like Travel Mole (www.travelmole.com) in the UK, and Skift (skift.com) and Travel Industry Wire (www.travelindustrywire.com) in the US. Professional organizations like the Association of British Travel Agents (ABTA; abta.com) create annual trends reports which are available on their website. Follow (and join) travelers' conversations about what's happening on the ground in your favorite destinations on Lonely Planet's Thorn Tree forum (www.lonelyplanet.com/thorntree).

Travel guidebook writers are in a great position to become experts on a region or country and its beliefs, customs and lifestyle. In addition, many journalists who are successful at being acknowledged as an authority in their area have done so by writing a book about their subject. Creating a specialist blog or website can also help to get your expertise recognized. Of course, you may change your niche over time, as you adapt to changes in the world and in your own life.

The advantages of specialization are that it cultivates expertise in a particular area, subject or style, and that it can accordingly help establish you as the 'go-to' expert for editors and producers who are looking for content on your specialty. The disadvantage is that you might work yourself into a professional pigeonhole; if you get known for writing about Southeast Asia, for example, your editor may scoff when you propose a piece on Paris. Or if you establish yourself as a consummate humorist, you may have difficulty getting outlets to publish a serious essay or destination piece. As with most things in travel writing and life, specialization is a question of balance. Developing a specialty in one area may be your springboard to articles on the wide world; your success will ultimately depend on your flexibility, imagination, perseverance and skill.

Writing about food

Food travel has become a genre unto itself, as countless studies show that these days we spend more time consuming food-related media than actually cooking our own meals. From a practical perspective, the beauty of specializing in food is that you considerably widen your market – there are as many magazines, newspaper supplements and websites devoted to food as there are to travel, and if you specialize in food travel, you can appeal to the audience for both.

Here is an example from *Gourmet* magazine, written by Jonathan Gold, that vividly brings a see-worthy site in Seoul to life:

Tsukiji in Tokyo and New York's late Fulton Fish Market may have more of a hold on the popular imagination, but the Noryang jin Marine Products Market is one of the greatest food spectacles on earth. A yawning structure in central Seoul, as large as several football stadiums laid end to end, it's crammed snout-to-elbow with exotic sea creatures from every conceivable aquatic locale: acres of stingrays aligned precisely as roof tiles; gilt lengths of ribbonfish; regiments of pike; oceans of halibut; endless trays of pickled clams; and more kinds of jacks and mackerels and anchovies than could be identified with a libraryful of reference books. As you weave through the 700-odd stalls, dodging the blasts of frigid water that the merchants occasionally sluice through the aisles, and the very small men charging through bearing very large bags of ice, you may notice the absence of anything resembling a fishy reek, replaced instead by the fresh smell of the sea.

Koreans favor species toward the bottom rungs of the food chain, so while you will see the occasional bluefin or salmon at Noryang jin, they are far outnumbered by croaker and corvina, bubbling clams and giant octopus whose arms extend further than Shaquille O'Neal's. You will also pass miles of live-seafood tanks, many of them filled with the usual lobsters, prawns, and crabs, but also finfish of every description, and a disconcerting array of bottom-of-the-sea stuff whose uses are difficult to contemplate. (It's hard to know which sea squirts are more alarming – the ones that look a little like warty, pulsing pineapples, or the pink ones resembling throbbing uncircumcised phalluses, right down to the undulating slit at the business end.)

There is a big auction area on the second floor of the 24-hour market, but almost all of the downstairs stalls are prepared to slice any one of their fish into sashimi for you on the spot – or better yet, to put your purchases into plastic bags and point you toward one of the cavelike seafood restaurants that line the north end of the complex, where they will serve up your sashimi in the traditional Korean style with sesame leaves, bean paste, sliced chiles, and raw garlic, and transform the rest of the creature into a seething cauldron of spicy, bright-red fish soup. Throw in some steamed Korean blue crabs, a few grilled prawns, some kimchi, and a bottle or two of soju, and you've got the greatest Korean breakfast in the world.

The stalls are unnumbered and unnamed, but I like the crab stall toward the extreme north-west corner of the market run by Robert, who spent much of his life in Wichita, Kansas – you will spot the phone number 813-9780 above his stall.

This piece is lively, quick, picturesque, and to the point. Without wasting a word, Gold captures the look, feel and smell of the place for the armchair traveler and conveys the essential information for anyone visiting Seoul who might be moved to stop by. With fishy pith, he serves up a tasty combination of food, culture and practical advice.

Now consider this can't-stop-reading lead from a *Guardian* piece by Jane Dunford on mushroom hunting:

Sitting at a table in an antique-filled dining room in the New Forest, I'm trying to identify a series of objects laid out before me. On one plate sits what looks like a dried human liver. It's big and red, but underneath it's the pale color of naan bread.

'When it's really fresh there's jelly on top and it seems to drip blood if you cut into it,' says Jackie, my host.

This is a beefsteak mushroom, she reveals, very popular with London chefs and delicious when thinly sliced and fried with garlic. The large, fluffy-looking ball turns out to be a Chicken of the Woods – which does indeed have a headless hen-like appearance – and then there's a plate of more mushroomy-shaped mushrooms, 'spongy underneath' boletes and dimpled chanterelles.

I'm on a seminar at Gorse Meadow Guest House near Lymington with 10 other fungi fans, delving into the fascinating world of mushrooms. There are, I learn, around 3000 types in the New Forest alone, but we're only interested in identifying about 10 edible varieties.

This is a good example of a story that uses food as a portal to a deeper understanding of a place. Dunford's mysterious mushroom lead immediately draws us into her subject and sets us up for an entertaining and illuminating introduction to a corner of England through its fungi.

Writing about culture

Culture can take many forms. You might carry readers deep into the soul of Bali by exploring its local dances, evoke Aboriginal values and beliefs on an Australian outback odyssey, or illuminate one side of the New York aesthetic by investigating its booming gallery scene.

Here's how Tahir Shah, in the *Guardian*, introduces us to the soul of Morocco through the city of Fes:

Abdul-Lateef sits in the shade at the front of his shop, a glint in his eye and a week's growth of beard on his cheeks. With care, he weighs out half a dozen dried chameleons, wraps them in a twist of newspaper, and passes the packet to a young woman dressed in black.

'She will give birth to a handsome boy child,' says the shopkeeper when the woman has gone.

'Are you sure?'

Abdul-Lateef stashes the money into a pouch under his shirt. He scans the assortment of wares – mysterious pink powders, snakeskins, live turtles, bundles of aromatic bark, and he smiles.

'We have been helping women like her for five centuries,' he says slowly, 'And never has a customer come to complain. Believe me, I speak the truth.'

Walk through the bustle of Fes's medina and it's impossible not to be catapulted back in time. It is as if the old city is on a frequency of its own, set apart from the frenzied world of internet and iPods and all the techno clutter that fills our daily lives. Abdul-Lateef and his magic-medicinal stall are a fragment of a healing system that stretches back through centuries, to a time when Fes was itself at the cutting edge of science, linked by the pilgrimage routes to Cairo, Damascus and Samarkand.

A writer's view: Rory MacLean

Canadian Rory MacLean (www.rorymaclean.com), long-time resident in the UK and now living in Berlin, is the author of more than a dozen travel and history books, including the UK bestsellers Stalin's Nose *and* Under the Dragon *as well as* Berlin: Imagine a City, *a* Washington Post Book of the Year.

I'd always dreamed of being a film director. To that end I wrote dozens of movie scripts, following every trend, choosing 'saleable' subjects rather than stories that moved me. The result was a series of flops, tame thrillers and busted blockbusters. But after each movie, to regain my sense of self, I went travelling. And soon I realised that I loved journeying into territory unknown (to me) and writing about the people and places met along the way.

The best way to establish yourself when you're starting out is to win a prize. I'm not being flippant. There are dozens of travel writing competitions run by newspapers and magazines. Researching and writing a travel article forces you to focus. Winning a competition opens the door to agents and publishers. I won the *Independent* newspaper's first travel writing competition. That enabled me to approach publishers with an idea for a book on Eastern Europe. Then Gorbachev was kind enough to knock down the Berlin Wall, making the subject matter of my book highly topical.

It usually takes me just under two years to write a book: three months' preparation, three months' travel and about 15 months bent over my MacBook.

An agent is vital. To find one, scan the *Writers' & Artists' Yearbook* or look up the name of your favourite travel writer's agent and approach him or her. Books submitted directly to big publishers often go unread.

Common mistakes? First, many first-time travel writers choose subjects because of their perceived popularity. Second, some of them don't engage their imagination or sense of wonder. Third, many don't check their spelling.

Write. Write. Write. Then write some more. And if you feel you've had enough, it'd probably be a better idea to do something sensible like becoming a dentist or raising rabbits.

These days the low-cost airlines shuttle the curious back and forth to Europe. And everyone they bring is tantalized by what they find. Fes is the only medieval Arab city that's still absolutely intact. It's as if a shroud has covered it for centuries, the corner now lifted a little so we can peek in. Once the capital of Morocco, Fes is one of those rare destinations that's bigger than mass tourism, a city that's so self-assured, so grounded in its own identity, that it hardly seems to care whether the tourists come or not. Moroccans will tell you that it's the dark heart of their kingdom, that its medina has a kind of sacred soul.

Doesn't this make you want to wander into the very heart of Fes, with Shah as your guide?

Using humor

Humor is exceedingly tricky because it is so subjective and often so culture bound, but humorous travel pieces are always in demand. Travel humor tends to work best when it contains at least a dose of self-deprecation; making fun of others is not nearly as engaging or entertaining as making fun of yourself. Some great humorists whose work rewards close scrutiny include Mark Twain, Bill Bryson, David Sedaris and Dave Barry.

Here are a couple of examples from the last two. First, David Sedaris writing in the *New Yorker* about an unfortunate incident on a plane:

On the flight to Raleigh, I sneezed, and the cough drop I'd been sucking on shot from my mouth, ricocheted off my folded tray table, and landed, as I remember it, in the lap of the woman beside me, who was asleep and had her arms folded across her chest. I'm surprised that the force didn't wake her – that's how hard it hit – but all she did was flutter her eyelids and let out a tiny sigh, the kind you might hear from a baby.

Under normal circumstances, I'd have had three choices, the first being to do nothing. The woman would wake up in her own time, and notice what looked like a shiny new button sewn to the crotch of her jeans. This was a small plane, with one seat per row on Aisle A, and two seats per row on Aisle B. We were on B, so should she go searching for answers I would be the first person on her list. 'Is this yours?' she'd ask, and I'd look dumbly into her lap.

'Is what mine?'

Option No. 2 was to reach over and pluck it from her pants, and No. 3 was to wake her up and turn the tables, saying, 'I'm sorry, but I think you have something that belongs to me.' Then she'd hand the lozenge back and maybe even apologize, confused into thinking that she'd somehow stolen it.

These circumstances, however, were not normal, as before she'd fallen asleep the woman and I had had a fight. I'd known her for only an hour, yet I felt her hatred just as strongly as I felt the stream of cold air blowing into my face – this after she'd repositioned the nozzle above her head, a final fuck-you before settling down for her nap.

And here's Dave Barry managing to make fun of himself and a venerable Japanese art form without really offending anyone:

When it comes to the classical arts, I'm basically an unsophisticated low-rent Neanderthal philistine kind of guy, which is why I'm probably just revealing my own intellectual limitations and cultural myopia when I tell you that Kabuki is the silliest thing I have ever seen onstage, and I have seen a man juggle two rubber chickens and a birthday cake.

For one thing, all the actors were wearing costumes that made them look like John Belushi on *Saturday Night Live* playing the part of the samurai delicatessen clerk, only with funnier haircuts. For another thing, since all Kabuki actors are male, a man was playing the role of the heroine. According to the program notes, he was a famous Kabuki actor who was extremely skilled at portraying the feminine character by using subtle gestures and vocal nuances perfected over generations. What he looked like, to the untutored Western eye, was a man with a four-year supply of white make-up, mincing around the stage and whining. It was Belushi playing the samurai whining transvestite.

In fact, everybody seemed to whine a lot. It was all that happened for minutes on end. Kabuki has the same dramatic pacing as bridge construction. It's not at all unusual for a play to last 10 hours. And bear in mind that one hour of watching Kabuki is the equivalent of 17 hours spent in a more enjoyable activity, such as eye surgery.

From time to time, a member of the audience would yell something. This is also part of the Kabuki tradition; at key moments, audience members, sometimes paid by the performers, yell out a performer's family name, or words of appreciation. Our guide, Mr Sato, had cautioned us that this yelling had to be done in a certain traditional way, and that we should not attempt it.

It was a good warning – although I'm not sure what I would have yelled anyway. Maybe something like: 'NICE HAIRCUT!' Or: 'WAY TO MINCE!'

While gently poking fun at his subject and at himself, Barry also manages to slip in some key facts about Kabuki.

Researching your story

Whether you specialize or widen your view, each new trip poses the same question: how do you develop a story from scratch? You've researched the publications that interest you, the passions that arouse you and the subjects that are currently popular. Now it's time to put your research to work.

A fundamental issue, particularly for aspiring newspaper and magazine writers, is the question of timing. Should you come up with story ideas before you travel or after you return? In the beginning you may find it easier to pitch articles from trips you've already taken – you know the place, and know exactly what you want to write about, making it infinitely easier for you to write a convincing proposal, or query letter, for that article. (We'll talk more about proposals and query letters in chapter 3.)

As you develop a collection of published articles (known as a clip file or a portfolio) and a reputation, you may want to try pitching ideas for subjects and trips you haven't yet made. The difficulty is knowing what exactly you want to write about before you've made the trip. To be convincing, you'll need to do a good deal of research so you can paint a compelling portrait of your subject and of its relevance to the publication in question without having experienced it. (A more advantageous situation is when you have visited a place in the past and are returning to update your impressions and experiences.)

Pre-trip research
Whether you're hoping to pitch your story pre- or post-trip, in order to get the most out of your journey, you'll need to do some research. Start by buying a few good guidebooks and thoroughly studying the place you're planning to visit – everything from history and cultural background

to specific events and attractions. These days, many destinations have English-language newspapers or magazines. You may be able to track down copies before you leave home, depending on the destination, and you can find and read many of them online. Studying these publications will give you a sense of local flavor and help you discover what news stories and events are capturing residents' interest. Reading travel literature set in the country you're planning to visit can also open up story ideas and offer deeper insights into the character of the place.

After you've done all this research – studied the markets, the trends, yourself, and the place you're preparing to visit – you should have a well-grounded idea of what you're likely to find in that place and what experiences or topics are most likely to impassion you. One more factor to consider, however, is that the best travel stories are often the unanticipated ones that you stumble upon when you're actually in a place. The best practice is to have a story idea in mind before you take your trip, and at the same time be open to discovering an even better story while you're there. Having a preconceived idea will give your trip preparations and itinerary a focus and framework. Of course, if you've interested an editor in a particular story pre-trip, you'll usually need to write about that. But if you find something extraordinary on the spot, all the better – your article possibilities will have doubled.

Researching on the road

Of course, all that pre-trip research is just the prelude to the journey itself. Once you're aboard the train, bus, ferry or plane, the real work begins. As you travel, stay alive to the world around you. Cultivate encounters. Ask questions. Gather brochures and other printed information. If something catches your fancy, follow it. When you can, let serendipity be your guide.

Use your camera to capture the look of a place; use your cell phone or audio recorder to capture conversations, evocative sounds and snatches of your own impressions when it's impractical to write them down; use your journal to record on-the-spot notes that will bring your experience back to you later. (For more about these essential tools of the trade, see chapter 5.) Absorb as much as you can, but remember to constantly filter what you're absorbing, so you retain and focus on the aspects of the trip that most appeal to you and offer the best potential story subjects.

Exercise 2

Play traveler for a day in your own backyard. Visit a local museum and pick up all the information you can. Is it open on holidays? Are there any special days when admission is free? What are the upcoming exhibitions and their dates? What artwork moved you the most, and why? Have lunch at a restaurant and take notes. What's the atmosphere like? What were the other diners like? What was the best dish? How much did it cost? When is the restaurant open? Does it take reservations? Walk around a favorite neighborhood and take notes. After you've finished your visit, write three 300-word descriptions – one of the museum, one of the restaurant and one of the neighborhood – in a way that evokes them for someone who's never been there.

Finding your focus

We have already discussed a number of ways to help you narrow your focus before and during your trip, but now let's consider the aftermath of the trip. You've just returned from three weeks in France and everything was great – every day brought new discoveries and treasures, and you want to write about them all. Tempting as that may seem, writing about everything you did on holiday should be kept strictly between you and your diary; you need to find the theme that will interest an editor. If you sounded out a few travel editors before you set off, you'll already know which stories might be of interest. But if you didn't, or if you want to try contacting other editors now that you've returned, how do you decide what to write about?

Ask yourself this simple question: what most impassioned you? When you meet people and they say, 'So, how was France?', what's the first story that comes to mind? Focus on that story, because for some reason your internal filter has decided that that particular one captures something special about your trip. Analyze why the story especially appeals to you, and ask yourself if other people would be interested in reading about it. Also ask yourself why you are choosing to describe that particular aspect of your trip. Think about the connection and resonance your focus has created. Does it capture an illuminating characteristic of French culture or French manners or French food? Does it tie in neatly with something that's highly topical today or with something that will be news in the future, such as an anniversary or event? Or is it so unusual that it stands out simply as an extraordinary travel experience? This is the seed of your story: seize it, explore it, look at it from different angles, draw it out. Think about what it means to you, but remember that the story isn't about yourself. A very common mistake that inexperienced travel writers make is to put too much of themselves into a piece; your job as a writer is to be the reader's portal into a deeper understanding of the place and of the experience of being a traveler there.

Now, think about other experiences from the trip that support this particular aspect or in some way complement it. You can begin to fashion your story in this way, establishing a central theme and then building upon it. Your final piece will be an exploration of this theme and how it was present in your trip, and ideally you will lead up to it step by step. If you feel you've got many seeds from your trip, then that's great – you'll be able to write a variety of different articles covering each one for a range of different outlets.

This process should help you avoid one of the most common traps for travel writers: the fear of the known. Writers often feel paralyzed when trying to write about a familiar subject. How can I write about Paris, they may say, when a million stories have already been written on the subject?

Writer's tip: Sidebars

Most destination articles include a fact box or fact file (also called a sidebar or a break-out box) that presents essential travel information: how to get there, where to stay and eat, etc. An editor will tell you if they are planning to publish a fact box with your story, but if you are not working in advance with an editor, it is always a good idea to include one. Ask yourself what readers need to know in order to duplicate your experience. If you're writing about food stalls in Singapore, you'll want to tell them how to get to the stalls you mention, the days and times they are open, and particular specialties. If you're writing about discovering the riches of Riga, your editor will most likely want to tell readers the best way to get there, and places to stay and eat.

A million stories have been written about Paris, it's true – but there could be a Paris you experienced that no one else has ever known. Let's say you love puppets and you stumbled upon a dusty puppet-maker's shop in an alley in the 14th arrondissement. You spent an hour talking about puppets and puppetry with the white-haired owner, who looked a little like a puppet himself. Here's the perfect subject for your story, one nobody else could write about with as much authority, presence and passion as you.

Ultimately, travel is all about connections – connections outside us and connections inside us. If you can bring those connections to life in your work, readers who may have never been to Paris or who may not care a whit about puppets will be brought in touch with similar connections they have made in other countries, in other places. They will connect with your sense of connection, and so the piece will in some metaphorical way build a powerful bridge and remind us all over again of one of the great and fundamental joys of travel: the stretching of personal boundaries, the flinging of bridges across cultures.

Exercise 3

After your next trip, or thinking back to your most recent trip, finish these sentences: I've just returned from _____. My most memorable experience there was _____. It was memorable because _____. The experience taught me _____. Think about how you could expand on this to build a personal and compelling anecdotal bridge to that place.

Interviewing and note-taking techniques
Central to the success of your travel research and writing is the ability to take good notes and to carry out efficient, effective interviews.

Taking notes
Notes taken on the spot provide reliable and vivid building blocks for your story. They are also poignant keys that can unlock a flood of images and details from a particular place and experience – even when you're writing your story half a year later. Fragments often do the job just fine. You might write 'red poppies, white columns' or 'pine scent, silvery sea'

or 'grandmother in blue fur, lilac perfume, Mozart from window'. You just need a few words that capture the essence of the thing you want to remember. At other times you'll want to write a more complete portrait of a moment, as the words written on the spot are inevitably the most vivid depictions of all.

One of the secrets to good note-taking is simply paying attention. Slow down and take the time to stop, absorb and reflect on your surroundings and on the things that have happened so far on your journey.

Interviewing people

Effective interviewing is an art of a different kind. Before you begin, you need to know what you want to get out of the interview. In many cases you will simply be trying to gather hard information, and so these interviews are not likely to be particularly controversial or confrontational. But since the interview will most likely be your only opportunity to talk with this particular individual, you need to make sure you have thought out in advance everything you want to learn from your meeting.

Basically, your interviews will fall into one of two types: the official and the unofficial. The official, or expert, interview involves anyone who represents a place. This might be a museum curator or the director of an archaeological site; a tourism official or guide; a hotel owner or chef. In every case, your job is to glean as much relevant information from this expert as possible. You want to be friendly and non-threatening, but you also want to be sure to get the information you need. If you ask a question and don't get a satisfactory answer, ask it again.

In this kind of formal interview it's vital to record the conversation. This will liberate you from note-taking so that you can focus on the answers and your questions. Whenever possible, get contact information so you can follow up if a question occurs to you long after your meeting.

The unofficial interview is usually a conversation with a fellow traveler or a local, often used to provide a different perspective and voice for your story, or to fill in background information. Your interviewing technique can be more indirect and conversational. You may decide not to record it, so the person you're talking to will feel at ease and converse freely. (Writers who are just starting out may feel that using an audio recorder or notebook will make them seem more 'professional'. This isn't necessarily the case, and if it makes your subject nervous or self-conscious, you may not get the free-flowing stories, information and quotes you're hoping for.)

Writer's tip: Exploit serendipity

Never underestimate the power of serendipity – and of being open to serendipity – to hand you a wonderful story. Early in my travel-writing career, I was talking with a Japanese friend in Tokyo about my upcoming visit to Kyoto. He casually mentioned that a friend of his had just visited Kyoto and had stayed in a temple rather than a hotel. A temple, I thought – what a great idea for a story! So I arranged to stay at Myokenji Temple in the heart of Kyoto and subsequently wrote an article about my stay for *Signature* magazine.

Ask for anecdotes that illustrate a point. Ask for memories. If you are not recording or taking notes during the interview, write down all the important points from your conversation as soon as you possibly can.

If you are planning to name and quote your interviewee you should let them know before you begin the interview. In an informal situation where you won't be naming the speaker, you don't necessarily need to say that you're interviewing them for publication, but sometimes it's easier to approach someone if you say you're gathering information for a story. If you're recording the conversation or taking notes, you'll certainly want to explain why. And, of course, there are times when you will be interviewing people by phone or by email, as many travel pieces these days are researched and written from home. Finally, if you do quote someone (without naming them) in a story on a sensitive topic, be very sure that they cannot be recognized from your writing. You do not want to inadvertently imperil someone because they gave you important information or freely expressed their views to you.

In all cases, it is absolutely essential for you to be accurate in quoting people you've interviewed, and it is important to have records from your interview – either audio or extensive notes – that you can give to an editorial fact-checker, if asked, to verify the authenticity of your quotes.

To achieve this connection we move to the next stage: the writing. You've done your research, analyzed the market, studied yourself and found a subject that marries publishability with passion. Now you need to write to that passion. Explore it, savor it, draw it out in your prose – paint such a complete, compelling, sensually full description that your readers will experience it just as you did.

Shaping your story

As a writer, you are a sculptor working with words, molding the clay of experience. An essential part of your job is to give that experience a shape that makes it accessible and understandable to a reader who hasn't shared it. The way you introduce and evoke your experience, the structure you give your story, is key.

A good travel article is structured, or shaped, like a good short story, with a clear beginning, middle and end. Broadly speaking, and of course varying according to the overall length of the story, the beginning is made up of approximately the first two to seven paragraphs. The aim of the beginning is to create a thematic or narrative lead (spelled 'lede' in the USA) that immediately interests and engages the reader, drawing them into the article. Often the beginning will set the story's scene, and sometimes it will hint at why the writer is there, but the prime purpose of the beginning is to grab the reader's attention. The middle is the long and winding road of the story, where the destination is brought alive for the reader, using your experience there as a filter. The end – and again, this is usually no more than the last two to seven paragraphs or so – wraps up the story and offers a kind of closure, tying the story back to its beginning but with a larger, enhanced sense of the whole.

A compelling start

How do you create a compelling hook to capture your readers' attention and propel them into your story? A few writers I know refuse to write any other part of their piece until they find that attention-grabbing introduction. I've sometimes found that a beginning will occur to me as I'm shaping the piece in my mind. When that happens I write it down immediately, as it can be a key that unlocks the rest of the story.

In most cases you'll only find the beginning in the process of writing the story. So my advice is to move on, and not get stuck on the start. You can, as Douglas Adams said so memorably, 'stare at a blank piece of paper until your forehead bleeds' but, if you're waiting for the perfect beginning, you may never get your story written. So just start writing.

You'll find that as you write, all sorts of ways to start your article may pop into your mind. Write them down and leave them at the top of your screen or page until they become so compelling that you feel forced to stop writing the body of your article to start writing its beginning.

Remember the serendipitous Kyoto temple stay I described on page 37? To set up that story, I wanted to show the importance of temples in Kyoto – and then suggest the value of a temple stay. How to do that? Here's the beginning I came up with:

Perhaps more than any other place in the world, Kyoto is defined by its temples. There are 1650 temples in this city of 1,480,000: more than one for every 1000 residents. Imagine New York City with 7000 churches! The grand temples – Kiyomizudera, Kinkakuji, Sanjusangendo, Ryoanji, Kokedera – are known throughout the world, but if you wander the thoroughfares and back alleys, you will come away convinced that there is one temple – with its attendant scruffy dog and potted plants carefully tended by neighborhood women – for every block.

On earlier visits to Kyoto, I had always done what most visitors do: toured the temples by day and retreated to a Western-style hotel at night. Then a Japanese friend told me that I had not really experienced

Writer's tip: Getting the quote you need

If you have a particularly intransigent interview subject, one trick is to turn off your recorder, put away your notes and prepare to leave. Then stop and say, 'You know, one more question has just occurred to me.' This may be the question you walked into the interview most wanting to ask, but if you had asked it directly during the formal part of the interview, you would not have received a useful response. Now, in that unguarded setting, you may get just the candid answer you need.

Kyoto if I had not stayed overnight at a temple. Staying in a temple, he said, revealed an entirely different face of the city, a place of ancient rites and rhythms hidden from those who confined their explorations to day. It was only after the visitors left that the temples truly came to life, he said. I was instantly hooked.

By the end of this 184-word lead, the reader should have a good idea where this story is going: we're going to stay at a Kyoto temple and discover the riches of this off-the-typical-tourist-path experience – and gain new insights into the quintessential spirit and character of Kyoto along the way.

In 'The Wonderful Thing about Tigers', published in *Wanderlust* magazine, William Gray describes a jungle expedition in India. To begin that description, he chooses to pull us immediately into an electric moment, and to keep us there:

It was almost as if the tiger had flicked a switch in the forest. One moment it was quiet and calm – the trees swathed in webs of early morning mist – the next, the air was charged with tension. Gomati had heard the distant alarm calls – the shrill snort of a spotted deer, the indignant bark of a langur monkey – and her mood suddenly changed. She blasted a trunkful of dust up between her front legs, then shook her head so vigorously that I had to clutch the padded saddle to keep my balance. Gomati's mahout, sitting astride her neck, issued a terse reprimand

Writer's tip:
The moment of connection

If you can't find your beginning, one strategy is to think of the moment when you first felt a connection with the place you are describing, when you were first drawn into that place. (But avoid: 'My plane landed on the tarmac at _____.' That lead was already stale in the time of the Wright brothers.)

before urging the elephant into the tangled forest. There was no path; Gomati made her own. Soon the air was infused with the pungent aroma of crushed herbs and freshly bled sap. Spiders and beetles drizzled from shaken trees; our clothing became wet with dew and stained by moss and lichen. We sounded like a forest fire – crackling, snapping, trailblazing. But through all the noise came a single piercing cry. Gomati stopped and we heard it again – the tell-tale alarm call of a spotted deer.

Manoj Sharma, my guide, leaned toward me. 'When the tiger moves, the deer calls,' he murmured. 'We must be close.' I nodded slowly, my eyes chasing around the shadows of the forest. Sunlight sparked through chinks in the canopy, but the understorey was still a diffuse patchwork of muted greens and shadows-within-shadows – the perfect foil for tiger stripes. Apart from an occasional rumble from Gomati's stomach, the forest was silent. No one spoke or moved.

Gray's beginning offers an effective example of a literary technique called *in medias res*, which sets you right 'in the middle of things'. This technique has a long and honorable literary pedigree – Milton employed it in *Paradise Lost*, beginning the epic in the middle of the story. Without warning, we readers are plucked from our easy chairs and set in the middle of the jungle, tensely wondering what will happen next.

Former US Poet Laureate Robert Hass employs the same technique to riveting effect in his powerful story about Korea, 'The Path to Sokkuram', which originally appeared in *Great Escapes* magazine. Hass takes a couple of notable risks in his opening. He begins with a very long first sentence that propels the reader into the story with a stream-of-consciousness momentum, and he begins his narrative with a character in mid-speech:

'The thing you need to understand about Korea,' said the dissolute, cheerful-looking British shipping agent I had run into at six in the morning in the fish market in the harbor at Pusan – we were drinking coffee at an outdoor table in the reek of fish and the unbelievable choral din of the fish merchants, beside tanks of slack-bodied pale squid and writhing pink and purple octopus – 'is that it's Poland. I mean, as a metaphor it's Poland. Caught between China and Japan for all those centuries like the Poles were stuck between the Russians and the Germans. The Japanese occupied the place from 1910 to the end of the war, and in the '30s they simply tried to eradicate Korea as a nation. Outlawed the language.

the Korean language was forbidden.'

An old woman pushed past with a cart full of fist-sized reddish-green figs. McEwan, the shipping agent, called her over. 'Try one of these,' he said. 'Damned good.' They were, red-fleshed, packed with seeds. McEwan was waving down a waiter with one hand, clutching a torn-open fig with the other. 'They demand soju, don't they?' Soju is a transparent, fiery, slightly sweet Korean brandy, perfect with figs, I was sure, but beyond me at that moment. I had been out the night before with a surprisingly hard-drinking lot of professors from Pusan National University, and wandered afterward rather aimlessly through the night market. Just before leaving America I had come to the end of a long marriage, and I had spent my first few days in Korea, when I did not have to concentrate on a task, in a state of dazed grief. In the night market the families had fascinated me, at one in the morning shutting down their produce stalls, loading up their boxes of fennel and cabbage and bok choy, moving swiftly in and out of the arc of light thrown by a hanging propane lamp, husbands and wives and drowsy children, working easily side by side. I drank beer at a stall and watched the market close down, and then went back to my hotel and couldn't sleep, and so got up again and walked down the hill in the pre-dawn coolness to the wharf.

Exercise 4

Considering the trip you wrote about in Exercise 3 (page 35), try to write an *in medias res* (in the middle of things) lead for your story. Think of the pivotal or most emotionally intense moment in your piece. Describe the prelude to that moment – the instance before the tiger, literal or figurative, appeared. Write two to four paragraphs – 400 words maximum – that place your reader right there with you in that scene. Could you begin your story this way?

In just two paragraphs Hass imparts a wealth of information about Korean history and culture – and about himself, an essential context for understanding his subsequent perceptions of and experiences in Korea. We are immersed in the Pusan fish market, ready to explore.

Not all travel stories need to begin so dramatically. Here's a good example of a thematic beginning from an article that UK author Stanley Stewart wrote about rodeos in the American West for *The Sunday Times*:

At the rodeo you notice that horses and cowboys are kind of alike. Horses stand around a lot, flicking their tails, breaking wind, doing nothing in particular. Cowboys are like that. They lean on fences, looking at horses. Sometimes they spit, sometimes they don't. With their hats tipped down over their eyes, it is never easy to tell if they are asleep, like horses, on their feet. The similarity disguises a major difference of temperament. Cowboys are soft-spoken mild-mannered fellows. In the West it's the horses that are the outlaws.

To the newcomer, cowboys are the surprise of the American West, like finding Romans in pleated togas waiting for the trolley buses on the Via Appia. Towns like Laramie and Cheyenne and Medicine Bow and Kit Carson are full of people who seem to have wandered off the back lot at MGM. They wear boots and ten-gallon hats and leather waistcoats. In town they drink in saloons with swing doors and stand around on street corners in a bow-legged fashion. Back at the ranch their nearest neighbors are miles away. The men are lean laconic figures with lopsided grins. The women look like their idea of a good time would be to rope you and ride you round the corral awhile. The women are rather chatty. With cowboys there is a lot of silence to fill.

The West is America's most vibrant subculture with its own music, its own fashions, its own political orientation and its own folklore. They care nothing for the suburban world that is the American mainstream. They talk of Washington and back east as if they were part of Red China. It is one of the pleasures of Wyoming to find Americans who are as cantankerous and as skeptical as the regulars of any Yorkshire pub. If the West is the spiritual home of America's ardent individualism, it is the landscape that is to blame. Between the Missouri River and the Rocky Mountains lies a vast swathe of country that early cartographers called the Great American Desert. They were wrong but you can see where they got the idea. The West is a landscape of skies and infinities. In the loneliness of this place, self-reliance becomes a kind of religion. When the first settlers tried to farm this land, it broke their hearts. The West did not take kindly to the idea of fields. It was a vast sea of grass, a landscape for horses.

The rodeos that are held in small towns all over the West are like church fetes with Budweiser tents and bullriders, a chance to meet the neighbors and complain about the government. They are also the moment for the big showdown between the cowboys and the horses.

With this beguiling beginning, Stewart introduces a multifaceted theme: visiting rodeos is a singular method of developing an appreciation for the history, quintessential qualities and contemporary culture of the American West. Through five spare paragraphs he paints a vivid and compelling portrait of the ensuing tale's main characters: cowboys, horses, and the infinite landscape they inhabit. By the end of that beginning, Stewart has already given us a good notion of where he's going – in search of rodeos – and a seductive sense of the riches and mysteries we'll find if we accompany him on the ride.

The article 'Las Vegas', by British travel writer and editor Simon Calder, published in the *Independent*, begins with this quirky angle on that city:

Neon: you need to know two things about this gas. The first is that it is, in elementary terms, a relative newcomer; even though it is present in small quantities in the air we breathe, it was identified only a century ago by a French scientist named Georges Claude. The second is that, being inert, neon is intrinsically dull. Oh, unless you pass an electric charge through it, as M Claude did. Do that, and it can light up the desert and dazzle the world.

Las Vegas was just a flicker in the eye of the San Pedro, Los Angeles and Salt Lake City Railroad when M Claude announced his discovery. The first neon sign in North America was sold in 1923 to a Packard dealership in Los Angeles.

At the time, the Mormons mistakenly thought they had discovered a promised, and morally safe, haven in the middle of the Mojave Desert. By the Thirties, they had lost faith with Las Vegas – and the rest of the world had lost interest in the fact that neon glows red in the dark and that, when mixed with a little mercury, its elementary cousin argon turns bright blue. But Las Vegas had barely begun to experiment with the extreme right-hand side of the Periodic Table of Elements.

Helium radiates a lurid magnolia when suitably fired up; krypton issues a steely silver; while xenon emits the palest blue. These elementary truths helped Las Vegas find its place in the world.

By presenting Las Vegas in this unexpected light, Calder prepares us for – and entices us into – a new appreciation of this much-described city.

Adventure writer and novelist Kira Salak begins her powerful article 'Libya: The Land of Cruel Deaths', published in *National Geographic Adventure*, with these simple, compelling sentences:

> 'You come, Madame,' the man says to me.
>
> He wants to show me something – something 'special.' And maybe it's the sincere look in his eyes, the supplication, the knowing, but I follow this complete stranger across Tripoli's Green Square and through the stone gate of the ancient medina, or historic Arab quarter. It's my first night in Libya; I arrived only three hours ago in a country that's still a mystery of culture shock and conjecture.

Who could resist following her – and her mysterious guide – into the medina?

Exercise 5

Consider a recent trip. What was the first moment you really felt drawn into the place you were visiting? How did that happen – was it a person who drew you in, or a scene? What was the first connection? And what occurred when you, like Kira Salak, took those first steps into the metaphorical medina? Write a 200–300-word lead, drawing your reader into your story by depicting the way you were drawn into a particular place.

Finally, an example of a beginning that combines the narrative and thematic approach. This comes from a story of my own, published in *Signature* magazine:

> There are no tavernas, no discotheques, no pleasure boats at anchor. Nor are there churches, windmills, or goatherds. Delos, three miles long and less than one mile wide, is a parched, rocky island of ruins, only 14 miles from Mykonos, Aegean playground of the international vagabonderie. Once the center of the Panhellenic world, Delos has been uninhabited since the first century AD, fulfilling a proclamation of the Delphic oracle

that 'no man or woman shall give birth, fall sick or meet death on the sacred island.'

I chanced on Delos during my first visit to Greece. After three harrowing days of seeing Athens by foot, bus and taxi, my traveling companion and I were ready for open seas and uncrowded beaches. We selected Mykonos on the recommendation of a friend, who also suggested that when we tired of the Beautiful People, we should take a side trip to Delos.

On arriving in Mykonos, we learned that for under $3 we could catch a fishing trawler to Delos (where the harbor is too shallow for cruise ships) any morning at eight and return to Mykonos at one the same afternoon. On the morning of our fourth day we braved choppy seas and ominous clouds to board a rusty, peeling boat that reeked of fish. With a dozen other tourists, we packed ourselves into the ship's tiny cabin, already crowded with anchors, ropes and wooden crates bearing unknown cargo.

At some point during the 45-minute voyage, the toss and turn of the waves became too much for a few of the passengers, and I moved outside into the stinging, salty spray. As we made our way past Rhenea, the callus-like volcanic island that forms part of the natural breakwater with Delos, the clouds cleared, and the fishermen who had docked their caiques at the Delos jetty greeted us in bright sunlight.

At the end of the dock a white-whiskered man in a navy blue beret and a faded black suit hailed each one of us as we walked by: 'Tour of Delos! Informative guide to the ruins.' A few yards beyond him a young boy ran up to us, all elbows and knees, and confided in hard breaths, 'I give you better tour. Cheaper too.'

This approach is more purely chronological than the *in medias res* method. It provides a thematic framework for the piece, promising that the rest of the story will detail how my experience in Delos offered encounters and lessons that deepened my appreciation of Greece.

Each of these beginnings successfully draws the reader into the story and induces them to keep reading because they are intrigued by the possibilities and want to know what happens next. Each hook promises that the reader will be entertained if they continue reading, and introduces questions that can only be answered by plunging deeper into the text.

What beginning will work best for you? Think about where you want the reader to be at the start of your story. How do you want your tale to unfold? What is the main point of your story? What's the best way to get that point across?

However you structure your beginning, remember that it is the doorway to your story – and that in the eyes of an overworked editor, it's also your calling card. The beginning is your one chance to inspire the editor to read more. Many editors read hundreds of submissions a week; in effect, when they take your story in hand, they are looking for a reason to reject it as quickly as possible. If your beginning doesn't work, the editor will not read any further.

Organizing the middle section

Most travel stories are structured by following either a thematic or narrative strategy. If your story is thematic, you will develop the middle section as an ascending succession of examples leading to your overriding point. If it's a narrative, you will most likely develop the central section of your story as a chronological sequence of anecdotal incidents that embody and reveal the main points of your piece.

In stories that are organized along chronological, narrative lines, the author will focus on selected moments in their travels to draw out the most important aspects of their tales. Along the way we will often be presented with portraits of people and places, history and culture, all interconnected in the unfolding of the author's experience, and culminating in unexpected revelations and resolutions. The result, done well, is a moving and multi-layered travel tale.

Let's say I want to write an article expressing my conviction that Croatia is the next big destination for travelers. First, I'd ask myself why I feel this way. Well, let's see: it's beautiful, it has a rich history, the people are warm and it's great value. I've isolated four salient points to support my theme, so the next question is order of importance.

To organize my story in terms of accelerating emotional connection, I'll lead with the point about value for money as it's the least emotional and most practical or logical consideration. History begins to involve the heart but is still fundamentally intellectual, so that would be second. Beauty is a more emotional consideration, drawing readers into the story via their soul. The people connection represents what I think is the climax of my trip, and the climax of travel itself, so that would come last. My final point is the top of the pyramid, but every step along the way contributes to my story's overall resonance and effectiveness.

Next, I'll search through my notes and draw out the experiences that brought these points to life. The hostel in Dubrovnik that cost just £15 a night, or that extraordinary meal under the stars that was £5. That's where I learned how inexpensive the place was, relatively speaking.

The historical richness of the country came to life in Dubrovnik, when I walked along the walls of the old city and saw roof tiles shattered during the war lying side by side with new roof tiles built to replace them – a poignant reminder of the constant presence of the past, but also an inspiring example of how tourism can help rebuild a place.

Croatia's beauty was obvious: the rocky coast and the shadowing cypresses, the wildflowers in bloom and not a person in sight.

And then it all came together for me on my last night in Dubrovnik, when I went out to dinner with a local tour guide and she told me about how her family had suffered during the war, how the entire country had suffered, but there was now new hope blooming in the land.

On reviewing these experiences, I realize that the historic part of the piece has more emotional resonance for me than the beautiful landscape. And so, I rearrange the segments. I start with the prices, then move on to the beauty and the history, and end with my meal with the tour guide. I'll have to make sure I pay attention to the transitions between the sections, but the piece is already taking shape in my mind. I've figured out how to structure the middle, and now it's just a question of bringing the individual examples to vivid life.

Exercise 6

Considering the trip you wrote about in Exercise 4 (page 42), list the eight most important events that occurred during that journey. Order them by their importance to your understanding of the place or the impact of the place on you. Do you see a thread connecting at least some of these events? Does this thread lead to some conclusion or revelation? Does it illuminate something important about the place, or about yourself? If so, you may hold the itinerary of your story right there in your hands. Choose the four most important events and write 300-word descriptions of each.

Writer's tip: The emotional hierarchy

If you're having difficulty starting, try making a list of the most important experiences you had on your trip, and then organize them in terms of their effect on you. I employed this method when struggling to begin an article about the South Pacific island of Aitutaki, and instantly a framing connection appeared: on my first night I'd attended an island-wide event to choose candidates for the annual Cook Islands dance competition, and the climactic experience of my stay was dancing a traditional Cook Islands dance on stage with local performers. So I began my story this way: 'Four drums pounded a deep, incessant rhythm through the sultry South Pacific night. A ukulele plunked plangent notes into the air. A smiling-eyed young beauty with copper skin and flowing hair, wearing a palm-frond skirt and a coconut bra, took me by the hand. "Will you dance with me?"'

Building blocks

One fundamentally important element to consider when shaping your story is its structural development. Think of each story as a set of building blocks. The beginning lays the foundation, and the middle builds on that foundation. It is essential that each part of the story builds upon the part that came before. This building up needs to be logical – that is, the progression of ideas and events in the story has to make sense – but it should also be thematic and emotional.

When you are editing your own article, ask yourself if each section advances the story in the direction it needs to go, and whether each section builds upon the one before. In order to answer these questions, you need to be clear about your article's overall aim – this is fundamental to a successful travel article. As long as you know your story's goal, you'll be able to tell if your story is proceeding clearly and powerfully, block by block. With each new addition, ask yourself: does the reader need to know this? Does this take the reader one step closer to the overall point? If you stray from your overall aim, you'll lose your reader.

49

Making transitions

In crafting a story, transitions are one of the writer's most important tools, linking one paragraph to another, and one section of a piece to the next. If you think of your article as a journey, the transitions are the stepping stones or tiny bridges that help the reader along – without them, the reader would fall into the chasm of incomprehensibility. Transitions give your piece coherence; they make sure your story follows logically from one step to the next, and they make sure you don't lose your reader along the way.

Transitions from one paragraph to another usually pick up a detail, image or theme from the last sentence in the preceding paragraph. In a chronological description, the sequential rush of events generally provides its own transitions, but when you leap from one event to another, you need to make sure that the reader leaps with you. Occasionally, you will find that there is no appropriate transition at a particular place in a story, or that you don't want to craft a transition – you want to make a clear break in the narrative.

This is the place to use a section break, indicated in the text by a line break or a graphic element, which signals to the reader that you have ended one sequence and are beginning another. The reader will leap with you over the break, but without that visual cue, the reader will expect you to lead them along by the hand.

Achieving narrative closure

The end of your article needs to do three intricately related things: bring the focus of your piece to a satisfying conclusion; tie the story back to its beginning; and deliver the reader back to the world.

The article about Las Vegas by Simon Calder quoted earlier in this chapter (page 44) concludes with a reference that nicely brings the piece full circle:

> Thanks to the physical properties of neon, a trip to Las Vegas can have much the same effect as expensive designer drugs.
>
> The hometown of indulgence looks and feels like Toytown for tycoons. But beware staying here too long. On my last evening I got so lost trying to find a way out of Binion's Horseshoe Casino that I had to ask for directions back to real life.

In the Aitutaki article mentioned earlier (page 49), I began by describing the dance invitation, then went on to explain the reason I had come to Aitutaki:

> I longed for quietude, simplicity and a sense of things as they used to be. I was pining for qualities I associated with islands and with the South Pacific: a lush, slow, wild beauty, a barefoot tranquility, a balmy, palmy, sea-scented sensuality.

Writer's tip: Highlight events

When making a list of highlight events, it's helpful to jot down a few notes about the significance of each. For example, here's the list of events I made for the Aitutaki article mentioned on page 49, along with the qualities each one represented, or illuminated, for me:

1. Dinner at Café Tupuna (island cuisine using all local ingredients, friendliness of people).
2. The Cook Islands dance competition (culture).
3. Island driving tour (landscape, history – marae: pre-Christian ceremonial site).
4. Meeting local woodcarver and pareu-maker (culture, arts).
5. Visit to One Foot Island (beauty, tranquility).
6. Church service in Arutanga (history, island spirit and tradition).
7. Dinner at Samade restaurant (cuisine).
8. Dancing on stage with performers at Samade (dance, tradition – climax of stay).

I ordered these events in terms of their chronological order and emotional impact, and that order became the 'roadmap' for my article.

To end that piece, I returned to the dance and the quest:

> After we had feasted, a half-dozen musicians trooped in bearing ukuleles and wooden drums, then young dancers stepped onto the floor in pandanus skirts and coconut bras. Their passion and energy were infectious, and with the warm, caressing air, the delicious food, the music mingling with the stars, and the dancers' supple limbs and exuberant smiles, it was easy to get lulled into the spirit. I found myself on the floor, hips swaying.
>
> Time slowed, and the discoveries of my five-day stay coursed through me: the island's slow, stately pace, the warmth of the people, the soul-soaring beauty of the place, the bountiful humor I had encountered, the sense of plenty in mango and pawpaw, the sense of peace in palm tree, lagoon and beach. The leg-thumping and heart-pumping rhythms reached my deepest core like a key, turning and turning, unlocking mysteries that seemed even older than me.
>
> Suddenly I found myself in a place I'd never been but knew instinctively. Drums pounded, hips swayed, gardenia perfumed the scene. In an instant I recognized this South Seas culmination: I had found the island of Salvation.

In the article about my Kyoto temple sojourn (pages 37 and 39), I described the highlights of my stay – first impressions of the temple and my room; meeting the master of the temple, and discussing the temple's history and his own hopes; and then wandering around the grounds late at night, when that history seemed to come magically to life.

Exercise 7

Think about a travel experience or destination that you passionately want to write about. What is it about the experience or destination that you want to convey to your reader? What is the fundamental point of your piece? Try to reduce that point to one sentence. For example: 'Spending a night on the Greek island of Delos offered life-changing lessons in the history and character of that sacred island.' Write that sentence at the beginning of your story. As you write your story, this sentence will be your compass and map; refer back to it continually. Is every building block in your story leading toward conveying this point to your reader?

To conclude the piece, I wanted to find and describe one all-embracing moment that would embody the effect the temple had had on me and at the same time would allow me to prepare readers for re-entry into the world outside the article – just as I was preparing for re-entry into the city beyond the temple. In evoking this threshold moment, I wanted to be sure that the temple impression lingered – like a pebble dropped in a pool – in the reader's mind. Here are the two final paragraphs that comprise the end:

> The next day I arose at five to join the monks' morning service.
> The garden was obscured in a rice-paper mist, and the floor chilled my stockinged feet.
> I followed the six resident monks and nun in their rustling robes to the main hall, and sat as they did on the tatami mats. Yamada-sensei, sitting in front, began to chant – a low, deep, long wail – and the monks took up the prayer, breathing in, bellowing out, filling the hall with sound. One monk slowly tolled a huge gong; all around gold and red lacquer and deeply polished wood gleamed, incense spiraled into the air, and the chants and gongs surged and subsided, rose and fell, rose again – until the temple seemed one huge vibrating voice, and we its chords. Ahead was the Kyoto of day, of trolleys and tourist buses, but for me, just then, there was only this Kyoto of incense and chant and gong, of stone lantern and paper screen, of priest and monk and nun, this place of waking dream.

A similar effect informs the Delos story. The extract reproduced earlier in this chapter (pages 45–6) ended with the introduction of an old man and a young boy, both of whom offered a tour of the island. The story goes on to describe how I spontaneously decided to miss the boat back to Mykonos in order to spend the night on the island, and depicts a raucous dinner with a Hungarian physicist who is also spending the night there, concluding with this description of the following morning:

> Streaming sunlight awakened me. I turned to look at my watch and disturbed a black kitten that had bundled itself at my feet. In so doing, I also disturbed the ouzo and retsina that had bundled itself in my head, and I crawled as close as I could to the shadow of the wall – 6:45. I pulled my towel over my head and tried to imagine the windy dark, but to no

The accordion theory of time

Students often ask me how to craft a description of an entire trip in a few words. Say you have between 1500 and 2500 words to write about a five-day journey. If you tried to write about everything that happened on that journey, you would have the travel equivalent of *War and Peace*. (You would also end up with a piece that was more suited to your personal travel diary than the very public pages of a newspaper or magazine.) So what you have to do is edit your reality. You have to think about all the pertinent experiences in your trip and then you have to choose those very few – three or four – that embody and illuminate the main points you want to make about your journey.

In order to do this well, you are going to end up focusing very precisely on those four experiences, and skimming over all the other experiences of your trip. This is where the accordion theory of time comes in. Your narrative focus moves in and out, in and out. You expand the accordion to full arm's length in order to focus closely on a moment in time, then you push it in to skim over whole days; then you draw it out again to focus on the next significant experience, then push it in to jump over more days.

Study almost any travel narrative, and you'll see that the author is playing the accordion of time. The writer isolates the cardinal events in their experience, analyzes how they fit into the pattern of meaning they are trying to evoke, and focuses on the details of those events to render them in a way that will enable the reader to live them just as they did. They may lavish three pages on an incident that happened in five minutes, then summarize the next five days in five sentences. The narrative proceeds in this way – in and out, in and out – singling out for scrutiny and expanded description the events that form the building blocks of the story. The full meaning and impact of the story is created through the accumulation, organization and integration of these event blocks.

avail. The kitten mewed its way under my towel, where it took to lapping at my cheek as if it had discovered a bowl of milk.

I stumbled down the stairs and soaked my head in tepid tap water until at last I felt stable enough to survey the surroundings. Behind the pavilion a clothesline led to the rusting generator. Chickens strutted inside a coop at the curator's house. Rhenea stirred in the rising mist.

Again I wandered through the ruins, different ruins now, bright with day and the reality of returns: the tourists would return to Delos, and I would return to Mykonos. I ate a solemn breakfast on the terrace with the physicist, then walked past the sacred lake and the marketplace to the Terrace of the Lions. Standing among the five lions of Delos, erected in the seventh century BC to defend the island from invaders, I looked over the crumbling walls and stunted pillars to the temples on the hill. Like priests they presided over the procession of tourists who would surge onto the island, bearing their oblation in cameras and guidebooks. As the trawler approached, a bent figure in a navy blue beret hurried to the dock, and a boy in shorts raced out of the curator's house past the physicist, past me, and into the ruins.

You can see how the story circles back to its beginning – the old man and the young boy rushing to meet the new day's potential clients – but everything else has changed. The reader has spent 24 hours on Delos with me, and so now has an entirely different impression of the island. At the end of the story, readers are led back to the world outside Delos and outside the article – but with an enhanced understanding of Delos and, ideally, with a renewed appreciation of the planet.

Finally, it's critical that you pay special attention to the last word of your story. This is where you leave the reader, literally and figuratively. It is your – and your story's – last point of connection with the reader, and the reader's threshold to the world outside the story. Where do you want to leave the reader? What do you want their last – and lasting – impression of your story to be?

Exercise 8

Re-read the beginning you wrote in Exercise 4 (page 42) and the descriptions you wrote in Exercise 6 (page 48). Now describe in 250–300 words what happened right after that moment you wrote about in your lead, and what you learned as a result. Is this the climax of your story, the place where all the pieces of the puzzle come together? If so, you have a natural ending to your account. And by combining Exercises 4, 6 and 8, you have a first draft of your story. Well done!

Bringing your story to life

How do you bring your story to life with the kind of lively prose that editors want? Here are some of the most important tools and principles.

Writing dialogue

Dialogue helps to enliven a piece aurally, varying its rhythm. On another level it can be used to humanize a story, injecting characters into your article in a way that creates warmth and resonance for the reader. It can also help to illuminate a place. Remember how Robert Hass began 'The Path to Sokkuram'? He employed dialogue to push the story thematically along. His account ends at another cafe with dialogue of a different kind:

> The waitress returned with a little paper packet of roast silkworms.
>
> On the house. She pointed at a shy boy at the next table and bit her lip before proceeding very deliberately. 'My friend is so exciting only to have this opportunity to speak practical English and having sharing Korean culture.' I understood. He was treating me to the silkworms. We were going to argue about politics. I ordered another bottle of wine and gestured him over. He sat down opposite me. Two of the waitresses joined us. The silkworms tasted vile, and I smiled gratefully trying to get one down. The girls laughed and the wine came. 'Korea,' the young man began, and shook his head. He said the word as if it were a synonym for life. Then he sighed happily and said it again. 'Korea, Korea, Korea.'

Dialogue gives a piece human context and contact. It can also help supply critical information in a non-textbook way. For example, a local resident or museum docent can enter the story to reveal the history of the town or the special qualities of the painting on display. And dialogue can introduce human quirks – turns of phrase, colloquialisms, patterns of speech – that help warm a story as well. The key is to use dialogue sparingly, keeping it crisp and authentic.

An editor's view: Lyn Hughes

Based in the UK, Lyn Hughes is the Editor-in-Chief and co-founder of Wanderlust *magazine and website. She tweets at @Wanderlust_Lyn.*

Be as professional as possible, sending editors well-thought-out proposals that demonstrate that you understand their publication and what makes their readers tick. This might sound basic, but it's surprising how many people fall down at this first hurdle.

Know the market: which magazines and newspapers run travel articles, what style of article they go for and who they are aimed at.

Think laterally: about where to send your idea or article, and about the angle.

Read. Read travel articles of all types. Understand what makes a good piece.

Does your idea pass the 'so what?' test? You say you could write an article on Thailand. So what? So could thousands of other people. Why should we go for you?

What are editors going to be looking for? What's in the news? What is going to be a hot destination and why?

Don't claim to be 'funnier than Bill Bryson'. People who claim that invariably aren't.

Think ahead to what the trends and newsworthy topics will be in six to 12 months' time. Magazines like to think of themselves as setting the trends and influencing their readers. It is absolutely key that you understand who those readers are and what makes them tick.

Photographs are important to a magazine – they use more of them and usually in colour. So, even if you can't supply the photos, they are more likely to go for a story if it's going to be visually interesting.

If you want to make travel writing pay, you have to very much treat it as a job, cramming extraordinary trips into just a few days. Your idea of a dream trip might not involve inspecting every hotel in town or having a very boring dinner with the local head of tourism.

Once you're a travel writer, you might find it impossible to ever take a proper holiday again – the temptation to just knock up a piece in your notebook or on your laptop will be too much.

Exercise 9

Re-read the beginning you wrote in Exercise 5 (page 45). Now that you can look back on your finished journey, consider if there is another moment later in your trip that recalls this same experience and theme. Are you able to find a thematic circularity? Does the second moment complement and complete the first? Describe the second experience in 250 words. These may be the 'bookends' of your piece.

Dialogue should never be invented or embellished to suit your purpose. If you are altering reality in any way – compressing sentences spoken by three different people at three different times into one cocktail party dialogue, for example – then you have to make it clear that you are doing so. It's perfectly acceptable to clean up dialogue by removing repetitious pauses such as 'um' and 'ah', but you must adhere scrupulously to the truth of what the person is saying. You must not distort their words or misrepresent their meaning.

Exercise 10

On your next trip, near or far, engage someone you encounter in conversation. It might be a fisherman or a flower seller, museum guide or metro conductor. Afterward, in no more than 250 words, reproduce your dialogue as closely as you can, so that someone who wasn't there is able to 'hear' the content and flavor of your conversation. What essential information did they convey? Can you picture the person from their words?

Paul Theroux is a master at dialogue. Open any of his travel books and you'll quickly find economical, illuminating conversations, as in this excerpt from his wonderful book, *Ghost Train to the Eastern Star*. Here, Theroux recounts a conversation with a woman in Hanoi who had been a teen at the time of the infamous US Christmas bombing of that city:

'Do you remember the Christmas bombing?'
  'I remember everything. I remember the day the bombs fell on Kham Thien Street,' she said, drawing her silk scarf close with her slender

fingers. 'It was the nineteenth of December. A thousand people died there that day, and most of them were women and children. Every home was destroyed. It was very terrible to see.'

'You saw it?'

'Yes. My aunt and my mother took me to see the damage,' she said.

'We saw many *cratères* – yes, craters – big holes in the road. And the dead, and the fires. I was so frightened. But my aunt and my mother said, "We must see this. What has been done to us." There's a monument on that street now.'

'Were you living near there?'

'We were just outside Hanoi.' She hesitated, then, seeming to remember, said, 'We didn't have much to eat. In fact, we had very little food all through the war. We were always hungry. Even after the war was over we had so little rice. And it was stale rice – old rice.'

'Because of the destruction?'

'No. Because of the American embargo, and the Chinese invasion…'

'We were told that the targets were military bases.'

She smiled sadly at this and said, 'Everything was targeted. The whole city. Especially roads and bridges. Our bridge was bombed by the B-52s' – this was the Chuong Duong Bridge, across the Red River to Haiphong. 'But we repaired it. Factories were especially targeted, no matter what they made. The bombings continued for years. Everything was bombed.'

Here Theroux conveys not just essential historical information but equally essential emotional information – without having to do any analyzing or explaining himself. The dialogue says it all. This emotional context and connection is critical for the reader to understand how deeply Theroux will be moved by his experience in Vietnam – by the country's current prosperity and by its extraordinarily warm and open-hearted welcoming of him, an American.

Creating characters

The introduction of characters is often critical to the success of a travel piece. Characters can illuminate places, and often help to propel and enliven a story. The human connection is arguably the most powerful element of travel, spanning cultures and backgrounds. Conveying a sense of human connection through the effective introduction of character is a great and powerful art. So pay attention to characters and don't shy away from bringing local people – or fellow travelers – into your story. Their presence in a story creates a human bridge between the story and the reader, just as they themselves are a human bridge between their home and you.

A character can be memorably painted using just a few brushstrokes. Consider this figure from James D. Houston's heart-touching Hawaiian tale, 'Everything Come Round', published in the anthology *The Kindness of Strangers*. Houston is locked out of his car on an isolated island road:

> I turned and saw a huge Polynesian fellow, Hawaiian or, perhaps, from the size of him, Samoan. His dark features were etched and fierce. Black hair was drawn back into a stubby knot. His mouth arced in what seemed a permanent scowl, as he regarded me in the twilight of this otherwise empty parking lot…
>
> I glanced past him, wondering if there were others, though he didn't need any others. His brown arms, purpled with tattoos, were the size of my legs. His thighs were as thick as nail kegs. He out-weighed me by a hundred pounds, and it wasn't fat. If he came at me, I was finished…

That's all we need in order to see the hulking fellow and to feel Houston's fear. Happily, as it turns out, the gentle islander produces a coat hanger from his own car and proceeds to expertly unlock Houston's rental car – and to unlock some truths about stereotypes and human goodwill as well.

Writing detail and anecdotes

Details hold the key to a good description and can be full of meaning, embodying the most important characteristics you want to convey. The more precise you can be in identifying and isolating the right details, and the more fully you can evoke those particular details in the reader's mind, the more powerful, compelling and effective your description will be.

You can never squeeze all the details of a place into a description. If you tried to do so, you could write a book as long as *Ulysses* about the room you are sitting in now. You have to edit reality. You have to isolate the most telling details, asking yourself which ones most powerfully and precisely convey whatever it is about the scene that is most directly relevant to your story, which details will best establish the points you want to make.

Exercise 11

Describe one of the most memorable people you've ever met. Begin with this simple sentence: The most memorable encounter I've ever had was _____. Think of what the person looked like. What were they wearing? How did they act? What did they say? What made the encounter so memorable? What did you learn from it? Why does it live so vividly inside you still? Write a 250–400-word description of this encounter that focuses on the most telling, the most revealing, details and events. What does a reader need to know to understand the impact of this encounter on you?

In Simon Calder's description of neon, he didn't tell you everything he knows about neon, just the facts that pertain to his eventual point about Las Vegas. And in Robert Hass' depiction of his Korean pilgrimage, he doesn't add extraneous details about the country or his experience there – he focuses solely on the information the reader needs to know in order to relive his journey.

Consider this portrait of a table-maker named Pierrot from Peter Mayle's delightful *A Year in Provence*:

> We knocked and went in, and there was Pierrot. He was shaggy, with a wild black beard and formidable eyebrows. A piratical man. He made us

Writer's tip: Capturing dialogue

To help in capturing dialogue, I always carry a pocket notebook with me. Whenever I have a conversation I want to remember, I immediately jot down as much of the conversation as I can. It's often awkward to start writing in front of the person I'm quoting, so if I'm talking to someone over a meal in a restaurant, for example, I'll excuse myself and go to the restroom, then write feverishly. Paul Theroux once told me that he uses this same technique. Now, whenever I'm waiting interminably for someone to vacate a restroom, I imagine Paul Theroux is inside, scribbling.

welcome, beating the top layer of dust from two chairs with a battered trilby hat which he then placed carefully over the telephone on the table.

With just these few key details, Mayle masterfully conveys a sense of this impetuous, larger-than-life eccentric.

The same is true of places. You just need a few details, but the right details, to paint a persuasive scene. Here is how Kira Salak evokes the ruins of Leptis Magna in her Libya article:

> I'm not the kind of person who usually gets into Roman ruins, can only handle about a day of them. But here at Leptis Magna — Latin for the Great Leptis — the city is so well preserved that it allows you to dream. There are the marble-covered pools of the Hadriatic Baths, great Corinthian columns rising 30 feet. There is the nearly intact coliseum, three stories high, where you can crawl through lion chutes and explore the gladiators' quarters. They don't make cities like this anymore, every architectural detail attended to, no plan too lavish, no material too dear. Bearded gods gaze down from friezes. Maidens and warriors lounge among the carved porticos. Even the communal toilets remain nearly unscathed, the marble seats shined by thousands of ancient buttocks.

How wonderfully those bethroned buttocks bridge the centuries!

A few paragraphs later, Salak brings another scene — the remains of a caravan town — to equally poignant life:

> Ghadamis is less a town than a gigantic labyrinth of narrow passage-ways that cut around and beneath adobe homes. Living here is like living in a subterranean world, the sun and its heat cut off by the rise of centuries-old buildings, each built into the next and accessed by an interlocking tunnel system. Now deserted, the town has an eerie quality of being just unearthed. Feeling like an archaeologist, I explore the dark, empty passageways with my flashlight, coming upon dead ends and mysterious chambers built from Roman columns. I squeeze through an open palm-wood door, climbing dusty stairs to the highest floor. Part of the ceiling has fallen in, incongruous sunlight gleaming on white walls painted with cryptic red Berber designs.
>
> Maneuvering through crumbling piles of adobe bricks and debris, I reach the roof and gaze out on a scene out of Arabian Nights: countless

white-washed terraces spreading toward the setting sun and the distant sand hills of Algeria. Nearby, palm gardens resound with birdsong and the burbling of aquifer water. The call to prayer wails from the squat mud minarets of a nearby adobe mosque, and I can only take it all in silently, reverentially, like a devotee.

Anecdotes are simply a larger, expanded version of details. Just as a scene is composed of myriad details that need to be filtered, so a journey is composed of myriad anecdotes. Your job is to choose just those ones that capture, crystallize and convey the point of your piece.

Exercise 12

Situate yourself somewhere comfortable – a cafe, say, or an open-air market, a city square or a beach. Quietly and intently observe for 15 minutes or half an hour, then write as precise a description as you can in 300 words. What are the most important, defining elements of the scene – the points of the place? What are the things you need to convey to make someone else understand those points? Repeat the same exercise in the same place the following day. Refine your description, paring it to the essentials.

Descriptive accuracy

One especially critical element in recreating a travel experience is accuracy. Travel pieces must be accurate in two ways. First, they must be factually accurate in their reporting. This means getting the population of the African village right, precisely conveying the color of the church in Nova Scotia and getting the year that the Spaniards settled on the coast correct. There is simply no excuse for getting your facts wrong, and you should not expect sympathy (or future work) from an editor if you do.

The second kind of accuracy is in perception and description. It is far more difficult to capture, but is equally critical to the depth and success of travel writing.

Let's say you are trying to describe a field in France. You write: 'I saw a field in France.' Does this bring any image of the field into the reader's mind? No. So you think some more about the field and write: 'In France I saw a field the size of a football pitch.' This helps a little – at least we have a sense of size – but we still don't see the field. So you dig back into your memory – and your notes – and write: 'In France I saw a field the size of a football pitch, filled with red poppies.' Suddenly the image blazes to life. We can see the field, the poppies extending toward the horizon. Now you're back in the scene, remembering the morning, and you write: 'In France I drove by a field the size of a football pitch, filled with red poppies and bordered on three sides by rows of lavender, whose sweet scent so filled the air that I had to stop.' Now we're right with you. Not only do we have a sense of size and color, we now also have another sense involved – the sense of smell – as well as the action of you stopping. You have successfully engaged your reader.

Exercise 13

On your next trip, keep a record of your journey. At the end of each day, list the main events of that day – try for at least three different ones each day. At the end of the journey, choose the six most important events of the entire trip. These are your prime anecdote candidates. Can you see connections between them? A thematic or emotional development from one to the next and the next? Focus on this development. Where does it lead? What characteristics or lessons does it reveal? Recreate these anecdotes for the reader, striving to faithfully and precisely duplicate your experience, so that the reader learns what you learned, as you learned it.

A good travel story is basically the accumulation of such details of perception and description. But you can't put these descriptive details into your stories unless you experience them first. You have to observe the world with a fearless curiosity, and then render that curiosity and the discoveries it brings in clean, clear, compelling prose. Do that and you'll get somewhere. And you'll take the reader with you.

Tim Cahill presents a compelling lesson in accuracy in this passage from his extraordinary tale 'Among the Korowai: A Stone Age Idyll', about a river journey deep into the wild heart of Papua New Guinea:

William spent several hours teaching me to finally see the swamp. The tall trees? The ones over there that grow from a single white-barked trunk and have elephant-ear-size leaves? Those are called sukun, and the Karowai eat the fruit, which is a little like coconut.

Stands of bamboo often grew on the banks of the river, in a green starburst pattern that arched out over the water. Banana trees also grew in a starburst pattern of wide flat leaves. They reached heights of seven or eight feet, and yielded small three- and four-inch-long bananas.

Rattan, a long tough vine used to lash homes together, to string bows, or to tie off anything that needed tying – the local equivalent of duct tape – was identifiable as a slender leafless branch, generally towering up out of a mass of greenery like an antenna.

Sago, the staple food, was a kind of palm tree that grew twenty to thirty feet high, in a series of multiple stems that erupted out of a central base in another starburst pattern. The leaves were shaped like the arching banana leaves but were arranged in fronds...

So – sukun, rattan, bamboo, banana, sago – the forest was no longer a mass of unvariegated green. Naming things allowed me to see them, to differentiate one area of the swamp from another. I found myself confirming my newfound knowledge at every bend of the river.

'Banana, banana,' I informed everyone. 'Sukun, sago, sago, rattan, sago, bamboo...'

The more accurately we apprehend the world, the more deeply we can penetrate it – and it can penetrate us.

Using all your senses

Most travel articles include good visual descriptions of the places in which the stories are set, but writers far too frequently ignore their other senses in their depictions. Think of it: when you walk into an Italian restaurant, what are the first senses that are accosted by the environment? Not sight, but probably sound and smell. There's the raucous ruckus of the patrons, the waiters pushing through the crowd, the garlicky snap and sizzle of food being flipped in frying pans in the steamy kitchens. The aromas may be the first sensory impression of all: the garlic that insinuated itself into the preceding sentence's sizzle, the mozzarella and tomatoes wafting from the kitchen, the heady mingled smells of veal piccata and pasta al pesto. So if you are going to describe this Italian restaurant in your article, you could begin with its smells and sounds – not forgetting, of course, the tastes.

When we travel we experience the world with all of our senses – so why do we focus so exclusively on sight in our articles? Cultivate the fine – and rewarding – art of paying attention to all the senses. Let your ears and nose and taste buds and fingers do as much work as your eyes.

Exercise 14

Return to the scene-setting you did for Exercise 12 (page 63). Rewrite the description, in no more than 350 words, using as many of the five senses as you can. What did the place smell like? What could you hear? What was the texture of the sand beneath you or the stone pillar by your side? Could you taste the sea salt in the air? Now read both pieces of writing aloud. See how using all the senses in your description brings the place to life? It's more satisfying for you and for your reader.

Show, don't tell

If you've ever taken a creative writing class, you will have had this maxim drilled into your head. Don't tell what your characters are feeling – show it. Reveal their inner selves through what they do and say. Let the reader draw the conclusions. The same is true for travel writing. Your piece will be much more powerful and successful if you engage the reader in the creative process of figuring out how the people in your tale are being affected. By the same token, don't spell out the fact that you were moved by an experience – make the reader feel moved by the way you describe it. Recreate the experience so that the reader is in your shoes – and is moved just the way you were.

Avoiding clichés

Clichés have a way of creeping into our writing – it's difficult to come up with something fresh every time. Sometimes, without our even realizing it, a well-worn phrase that we've picked up from who-knows-where slips surreptitiously into our prose. Reread your writing with your cliché-meter on high, and avoid those tired descriptions – land of contrasts, tropical paradise, bustling thoroughfare… Whenever you come to a phrase that sounds wooden, stop and ask yourself if there might be a better way of expressing what you want to say, one that more truly reflects your take on it.

One of the culprits editors most frequently cite when they talk about bad travel writing is the use of clichés. So be a vigilant self-editor. Always make your words and descriptions your own.

Finding your style

The following critical elements help to determine the success – or failure – of a travel story.

Your own voice

Travel stories need a warm human voice. Don't try to write like a fact-checker or reporter who is simply recording their surroundings, without any sense of engagement. You are undertaking a fundamentally human adventure – encountering new people and a new culture, whether it's in a different region of your own country or somewhere halfway around the world. Your humanity should be one of the fundamental strengths of your story.

Your voice should be a reflection of your personality and style, whether romantic, reflective, funny, sarcastic or informative. Over time you will come to be identified with the voice you project in your stories, so it's imperative to write in a way that feels natural to you and to the story.

Another aspect of voice is its use to express opinion and judgment. Readers – and editors – are relying on your expertise and discernment to steer them away from scams and disappointments, and to point them in the direction of the best on-the-road experiences. Informing your voice with opinion when appropriate is an essential part of your job.

Set your pace

What kind of pace do you want your story to have? It can be headlong and breathless or slow and measured. Make sure the pace fits your piece, and that you're in control of it. It's absolutely fine to speed up and slow down – it can make the reading a richer experience – just don't let the story careen out of control like a South American mountain bus crossing a snow-patched pass and then heading downhill when suddenly the brakes give out and the driver can't stop and the landscape is whizzing dizzyingly by and before you know it the reader is gone – pfff! – like the bus into the South American sky.

Play the language like music

Think of English as a musical instrument. You are using that instrument to create great music. Read your writing out loud, and listen to the music of your writing. What kind of mood are you creating? Are you keeping the pace lively or is it wooden? Are you varying the tempo in your writing? Are you using devices such as internal rhyme and alliteration?

Take any book by Jan Morris, open it at random and begin to read aloud. Listen to the way she modulates your journey through the story. Revel in her masterful use of the intrinsic music of our language.

Here's a luminous example of Morris' art from her essay 'Chaunrikharka', about a Sherpa home where she was nursed back to health when she fell sick in Nepal:

> Outside the house everything steamed. The monsoon was upon us. The rains fell heavily for several hours each day, and the gardens that surrounded Chaunrikharka's six or seven houses were all lush and vaporous. My room had no window, but the open door looked out upon the Sonam family plot, and from it there came a fragrance so profoundly blended of the fertile and the rotten, the sweet and the bitter, the emanations of riotous growth and the intimations of inevitable decay, that still, if ever my mind wanders to more sententious subjects, I tend to smell the vegetable gardens of Chaunrikharka.
>
> The taste of the potatoes, too, roasted at the family hearth, seemed to me almost philosophically nourishing, while the comfort of the powerful white liquor, rakshi, with which the Sonams now and then dosed me, and the merry voices of the children, frequently hushed lest they disturb my convalescence, and the kind wondering faces of the neighbors who occasionally looked through the open door, and the clatter of the rain on the roof and the hiss of it in the leaves outside, and the enigmatic smiles of those small golden figures in their half light at the end of the room – all built up in my mind an impression not just of peace and piquancy, but of holiness.

Study the musicality and modulation here. Those last two sentences go on and on – and yet you never lose your place in them. Morris builds them – and conducts us through them – phrase by phrase, detail by detail, until a sturdy, sensual and spiritual edifice is complete.

Writer's tip: Change things up

One of my first assignments for *Travel + Leisure* was a description of great places to go in Northern California, including famed Muir Woods. The most striking aspect of that sacred place – and an aspect featured in every article I'd read – was how the sunlight filters through the high branches of the trees, creating an effect like stained glass in a cathedral. As I approached the place, I wondered: how can I avoid writing the same description as everyone else? Then I came up with a solution – I walked around Muir Woods blindfolded. Suddenly an entirely different place – of rough-textured bark, crackling pine needles and crisp evergreen scent – came to life.

Make your words work hard

One of the biggest traps for novice writers is the urge to make prose powerful by overwriting, using high-flown adjectives and adverbs. You can feel the sentences collapsing under the weight of such words. Use active verbs, and don't use three words when you can use one. Rather than writing 'He walked as quickly as he could up the crater', write 'He raced up the crater' or, even better, 'He scrambled up the crater'. Reread your work slowly, and ask yourself if you really need each word. Remember that less is more.

Exercise 15

Choose a few paragraphs from your favorite travel writer and type them into your computer. Now edit those paragraphs. Analyze their choice of words, especially the verbs they use. Does every word do as much 'work' as possible? Are there any words you can delete or improve upon? Now type a few of your own paragraphs. Read those sentences with the same critical eye. Can you delete or strengthen any of your word choices?

Pay attention to verb tense

You would be amazed how many writers, even very established ones, mix up their verb tenses in their stories. Unless you're doing this on purpose and with a sure sense of control, you shouldn't begin your story in the present tense and then flip into the past tense, and then into the present tense and then back into the past tense again. You might think this is an obvious point, but just watch yourself the next time you write a travel piece. Reread it very carefully and see if at some point you too don't fall prey to inconsistencies of tense.

Writing in the present tense has become something of a vogue recently, largely due to more immediate prose style the internet has encouraged and cultivated. Somehow, online feels like a present-tense medium. But writing in the present tense can have its pitfalls. As a narrator you can have no more sense of what's coming than your reader. You cannot possibly know what happened two days after the day you're describing, and you need to take particular care not to let that knowledge color your narrative in any way. You have to recreate the ignorance you had at the moment you are describing, and never divulge more about your trip than you knew at that time. Writing in the past tense, on the other hand, liberates you. You already know what happened at the end of the trip, so in that sense writing in the past tense is a much more natural choice. But it's up to you – just be sure to be consistent and in control of your choice. If you're not, the reader will get lost – and your piece won't get published.

Writer's tip: Check your tenses

When I was starting out, I wrote a commissioned piece for a magazine. I was pretty naive about the business of travel writing, and fashioned myself an artist – a poet of the road. And so I purposefully crafted my work in the present tense. The editor asked me to rewrite it in the past tense. After initially exploding with righteous anger (note: this is not recommended as a way to impress an editor), I recast the piece and discovered that in fact it made hardly any difference at all. I had written it in the present tense because I wanted to convey a sense of immediacy; I wanted the reader to feel they were right there with me. But the truth is that the reader will still feel that way when the piece is written in the past tense – if it's written well.

Rewriting and self-editing

Different writers have different strategies for rewriting and self-editing. Some rewrite as they go along; others wait to rewrite until they've completed a first draft of the entire piece.

A good practice is to write three drafts of an article. In the first draft, try to get down everything that's in your mind about the story – all the important incidents, impressions and lessons. In this phase it's best to write as quickly as possible, rather than pausing to rewrite.

The second draft of your article is where you undertake the macro-editing phase. Read the story for flow and logical development, possibly looking to move sections in order to clarify and refine the movement and development of the piece. Also look to remove any sections that do not add to the story and identify any gaps that still need to be filled. Ask yourself if you've supplied all the information a reader needs to know in order to recreate that experience. Does the story build up coherently to its main point?

The third draft is the micro-editing phase, where you read very slowly and precisely, paying close attention to the style of the prose. Have you made every word count? Are you re-creating your experience as vividly and truly as possible? Are all the transitions there? How about the music of the piece?

Exercise 16

Choose a particularly compelling encounter, event or activity from a recent trip and describe it in 200–300 words in the present tense. Then write the same account in the past tense. Which one works better? Which is more powerful? Does one feel more restricting or liberating than the other? Keep these differences in mind as you craft your stories. The tense you choose can help or hinder your ability to tell your tale.

After you have finalized the third draft you should be ready to send the story to an editor. At this stage, many experienced writers show their work to a 'trusted reader', whether that be their spouse, a good friend or their agent, before they send it off to be published – sometimes even the

An editor's view: Jim Benning

Jim Benning (www.jimbenning.net) is the co-founder and co-editor of online travel magazine World Hum *(www.worldhum.com). He was deputy travel editor at BBC.com and editor in chief of SKYE on AOL. His writing has appeared in many publications, including* National Geographic Adventure, Outside *and the* Washington Post. *Find him on Twitter at @jimbenning.*

I launched *World Hum* with fellow writer and editor Michael Yessis. Our goal was simply to publish great travel writing, and we worked on it in our spare time for six years. It was a labor of love – we didn't make more than a few pennies from the site until the Travel Channel acquired it in 2007 and hired us to be the editors.

Travel is easy. Writing great stories takes a lot of skill and hard work. So work on improving your writing. Get critical feedback. It's hard to get that from friends and family, so reach out to others. Join a writers' group. Write multiple drafts. Revise, revise, revise. Narrow the focus of your stories. Rather than writing a general story about Paris, write about an aspect that's often overlooked. Or better yet, venture to places few others are writing about.

Anything you can do to hone your writing will benefit your travel writing. Beyond that, learn a foreign language or two. Take classes in history, literature, architecture – any topic that interests you. That's the beauty of travel writing: you can indulge your quirks and passions, and doing so can make for great stories.

Often, writers don't read the site carefully and they pitch stories we'd never publish. Or they send a generic pitch to us and dozens of other editors, hoping one might bite. That approach never works for us. We want to work with writers who are familiar with our site and have a specific idea about how and where their story might fit.

I love that travel writing requires action in the world – getting out beyond your backyard – and then retreating to your desk for reflection. They're two very different ways of being, and yet I think both are necessary for a rich life, as well as to make great travel writing.

More newspaper travel sections will shrink or disappear, sadly. Magazine stories will continue to get shorter. Travel websites and blogs will evolve. One thing, thankfully, won't change: a good travel story will always be a good travel story.

most capable writers are too close to their work to see something that an objective eye can pick up. Of course, after the editor has read it, you may be asked to rework the piece further, but that is an essential part of the process, too.

The editor will have their own view of the piece, and of where and how it fits into the puzzle of their publication. It is the writer's job to work with the editor to come up with a story that satisfies both parties. If you feel very strongly that you do not want to make an editorial change, you should state your case and discuss that point with the editor by all means, but you should be careful not to alienate them. Just as finding a great story entails a marriage of passion and practicality, so too publishing a story entails marrying the editor's and the writer's views of the story.

Writer's tip: less is more

One of my most memorable writing mentors is the great John McPhee, longtime staff writer at the *New Yorker*. I was one of the lucky students in his first groundbreaking non-fiction writing workshop at Princeton, called The Literature of Fact. One of his favorite assignments was to pass out 250-word pieces from the 'Talk of the Town' section of the *New Yorker*. Though these had been meticulously edited and re-edited by the magazine's staff, until they had been pared to the editorial bone, he would delightedly tell us to cut 10 words from each piece. We would groan, but the value of this exercise was immeasurable. It taught me to read each sentence word by word and to ask: is this word really necessary? Is this one? When I read my own pieces with that same mindset, any superfluous words stood out.

3

Getting

published

*We've talked about knowing your goals and about the riches
and requisites of the travel writer's life. Now let's focus on the
different markets that publish travel writing, and on how to
begin to get published in those markets.*

*Whether you are writing for newspapers, magazines or
online, you will follow one of two approaches: you can pitch an
idea or proposal to an editor before you write the actual piece,
or you can write the piece in its entirety and then submit it.
Generally speaking, if you are a beginner writer, it's unlikely
that a publication will commit to publishing a piece by you
based on the idea alone, without reading the finished piece. So
if you are starting out, the best advice is to write your story
first, with a particular publication (and so story angle) in mind,
and then submit it. The key to success in this process – and it
merits repeating, because it is so important – is to know your
market intimately and thoroughly.*

*Given the generally low rates for online publication (see
page 156), this chapter focuses mostly on print publishing. For
advice on starting your own blog, see chapter 4. For listings
of publications and websites that offer opportunities for
publication, see chapter 7.*

Breaking into print media

The three main print outlets for travel stories are newspaper travel
sections, travel magazines and lifestyle magazines with a travel component.
Become a regular reader of the publications you want to target, and
understand the types of stories they publish.

Are the destinations mostly short-haul, long-haul or a mix of the
two? Is family travel an important element, or do most stories target
the adventurous, independent traveler? Are articles tailored to bare-
bones, mainstream or luxury budgets, or do they cover a spectrum of
destinations and options? What is the tone, the approach and the length
of the stories? Are most of the articles service pieces, round-ups or
destination based? Are there any regular formats that appear each week?

In many publications you'll find, for example, features such as the
stopover destination piece called '48 Hours in…', and the short mini-guide

to a destination called something like 'A Complete Guide to…' All print publications run regular features each edition – you need to get to know the features in the publications you want to target. If you have good ideas that could fit these formats, you'll be offering copy that you know the travel editor needs each week or month. Conversely, if you offer a city-break piece that is not in the right format, it is not likely to be considered.

Detailed research will pay off. Keep brief notes about the stories your targeted publication has printed. Also, make use of the publication's online archives – you can search by topic and destination to find any stories similar to the one you're planning to pitch. Such research will enable you to begin a proposal for a piece on Swiss chocolatiers, for example, by saying, 'I'm aware that you published a story on Belgian chocolates a year ago, but…' At the very least, this research will help you tailor your articles to a particular publication. In addition, you'll never commit the cardinal sin of offering a travel editor a story that they have just run, and so risk taking a giant step backward in this tricky relationship.

Whether you're targeting a newspaper or a magazine, your first step should be to look on the publication's website for contributor guidelines or a style guide. If this information isn't available online, ring or email and request a copy be sent to you. These guidelines will usually spell out what the editors are looking for in an article and how they prefer to deal with freelance writers. They should also advise on how your submission should be presented, and whether they require accompanying photographs (this is less likely in the UK). Having these contributor guidelines will help to maximize your chances of giving the editors what they want. To give you

Writer's tip: How to get there

There are a number of different strategies you can follow to get started in your travel writing career but in essence, they come down to this progression of points: know your goals; know your markets; start local and start small; build up your clips, your confidence and your contacts; hone your craft and your expertise; keep your eyes – and your door – open for opportunities; and keep your focus on your goals.

some examples, we've reproduced the contributor guidelines for three publications at the back of this book (see pages 248–58).

There are broad differences in the ways writers need to approach and work with newspapers and magazines. There are also significant differences in practice between the UK and the USA, while Australian and UK working methods are generally similar.

Writing for newspapers

It's worth saying up front that worldwide, the newspaper industry has been well and truly disrupted by digital media, resulting in changing business models, downsizing and even closures. Some newspapers have folded, others have become purely online business. While most papers still carry a (usually weekend) travel section, times are tough, and budgets are small. This is not to say you shouldn't set your sights on print publication in your local broadsheet – but do your research to understand how they're putting their travel section together. Is it mostly syndicated content? Have they combined operations with another paper under the same ownership? If you want to work for travel media, it's worth keeping your finger on the pulse of the media landscape.

Newspapers in the UK

At the base of the UK's complex newspaper pyramid are the 'freesheets' – local newspapers distributed to every home in a particular area, or distributed on the street and at Underground stations. These rarely carry travel editorial (or, indeed, much editorial copy at all).

At the next level are more than 70 local and regional newspapers, which are more likely to carry travel stories. Often these papers will be syndicated, but they are always interested in local people doing interesting things, so travel writing opportunities shouldn't be discounted.

The highest circulation newspapers, and therefore those with the highest profile and (usually) rates of pay, are the 'nationals'. These are split into three categories:

The 'red-top' tabloids: the *Daily Mirror*, the *Star* and the *Sun*, and their Sunday counterparts, the *Sunday Mirror*, the *People* and the *Sun on Sunday*. Distinguished by their traditionally red mastheads and comparatively downmarket sensibilities, these papers offer relatively slim travel coverage, and that coverage is most commonly handled in-house or by regular freelancers.

Middle-market tabloids: the *Daily Mail*, the *Mail on Sunday*, the *Daily Express* and the *Sunday Express*. These have larger travel sections, but are usually written in-house or by regular freelancers – or by celebrities.

'Quality' newspapers (previously more commonly called 'broadsheets' because of their larger format, until they began downsizing in 2003): the *Guardian*, the *Daily Telegraph* and *The Times*, as well as the *Financial Times*. (The *Independent*, once a broadsheet, then a tabloid, moved to an online-only model in 2016; it still publishes lots of travel content.) These papers publish their main travel issue on Saturday, sometimes adding a minor travel section during the week. Their Sunday equivalents – the *Observer*, the *Sunday Telegraph* and *The Sunday Times* – also have substantial travel sections (except for the *Financial Times*, which has just one weekend edition).

A daily paper and its Sunday equivalent are usually compiled by totally different staff; this means that *The Times* and *The Sunday Times*, for example, have separate travel teams and travel editors for you to target. The size of these travel sections or supplements ranges from four to 40 pages. Wales, Northern Ireland and Scotland also have national newspapers that publish travel stories tailored to their readers' interests.

Newspapers in Australia
Australia has 20 national and metropolitan newspapers, and more than 120 regional and community papers. The major capital city papers publish the best travel content – *The Australian*, *The Advertiser*, the *Melbourne Age*, the *Sydney Morning Herald*, the *Brisbane Courier Mail* and *The West Australian* – and there are travel features in Sunday editions of these papers too. However, many of these papers are actually separate arms of the same large media company, and they combine their resources – for example, the *Age*, the *Sydney Morning Herald* and the *Canberra Times*, all owned by Fairfax Media, share their travel content. What may seem to be a proliferation of opportunities is actually merely two outlets.

Travel sections range from four to 24 pages; see below for details of various papers' travel 'special section' schedules.

Special sections
Most travel sections feature half a dozen to a dozen 'special' or 'theme' sections a year, presenting an exceptional opportunity for freelancers.

In the UK, special sections often concentrate on a particular part of the world – more often than not it's somewhere in Europe – and are produced in conjunction with the local tourist board. Typical special sections in the USA include Cruising, Mexico, Hawaii, Family Travel, Europe and the Caribbean. In Australia, the sections focus on regional and seasonal fare such as snow- or other activity-based holidays, mid-winter breaks and European, Asian and domestic destinations.

The themed sections are planned a year in advance, in conjunction with the papers' advertising sales staff – if the sales team knows that a specific section will be devoted to Hawaii, for example, they will have extra leverage to try to persuade a Hawaiian hotel owner to buy an ad in that section. The editorial content in these sections is not directly linked to the specific advertisers (that is, if a particular resort purchases an ad, this does not oblige the editor to publish a story about it), but the editor is obliged to put together a package of stories around that section's theme.

This is where your opportunity comes in. If you know that a particular newspaper will be publishing a special section on a particular date, you'll also know that the travel editor will be sourcing content specific to that destination or theme. In the UK, you would contact the travel desk two to three months before publication with a proposal for a couple of articles; in the USA, you would send in two or three of your best relevant stories three months before the section's publication date.

Themed sections offer particularly good opportunities to publish niche, off-the-beaten-track or reflective essay pieces – an article on studying the hula, for example, or hiking a remote but rewarding trail.

Pitching to newspapers

Travel editors are very busy people. In addition to traveling and writing (they often provide a weekly column and/or a few big stories each month), they also commission, edit and select the content for the weekly travel section; attend weekly editorial meetings; deal with advertising departments; process paperwork; read manuscripts; liaise with art and photography departments; and much more. The result of this hectic schedule is that although travel editors might like to deal in a humane way with freelance writers, they don't always have the time. The hard truth is that they are not going to call you up and offer advice on how to improve your submission. Basically, if you submit a story to them, they'll read what

Writer's tip: The editorial calendar

Travel editors should include a calendar of special sections in their contributor guidelines; if not, ask the editor to send you a copy. It's a good idea to request special-section calendars from all the newspapers you're interested in and take full advantage of the expanded editorial possibilities they offer.

you've written and if it is a good fit, they'll take it; otherwise, they'll reject it. Do not expect more than that.

It can be tricky to know how to go about contacting a travel editor with an unsolicited submission or a proposal, as each has their preferred way of being contacted. Some like to be emailed but might dislike attachments clogging up their inbox, so want the text to be in the body of the email. Very few travel editors want to be contacted by telephone, unless you have built up a relationship with them (and whatever you do, don't call on press day – usually Wednesday, Thursday or Friday – as you'll definitely get short shrift).

Read the contributor guidelines to see if there is a preferred method for submissions. If this information isn't available in the guidelines, make a phone call to find out. Once you're known to the travel editor or travel desk, you'll most likely be asked to submit your proposals and articles by email.

In the UK there are three main ways of pitching a story or a proposal to a newspaper, while for the vast majority of US newspaper travel editors, there is only one way: write it and send it in as an unsolicited submission. The only newspaper travel section in the USA that welcomes query letters rather than complete submissions is the *New York Times*.

Unsolicited submission

This is when you send a completed article to a travel editor or travel desk out of the blue, on the off chance that they'll publish it. You have little idea whether your story is of interest, whether it fits with future publishing schedules, or if a similar article is due to be run this week or is in the pipeline. For all these reasons, this method offers the least likelihood of publication.

For you, it is also the least financially astute because you've incurred all your costs up front with absolutely no idea if you'll be able to sell what you have written. In addition, you can send that article to only one newspaper at a time, unless you make it absolutely clear that you are offering it to more than one, and let the other(s) know once it has been accepted; this kind of multiple submission is usually only advisable for a time-sensitive story. Complicating matters further is the fact that travel editors often sit on submissions for months before you learn that it will never be used, or you open up the paper one day and discover that it has been published. On the other hand, there is always the extremely slight chance that your unsolicited article is just what the editor needs to fill an unexpected gap in the travel pages next weekend.

When you submit your story to a newspaper, enclose a cover letter pithily describing what the story is about and any special experience or expertise you may have that makes you better qualified to write this piece than any other writer (eg, 'The enclosed article about where to find and buy the best Japanese pottery synthesizes what I learned in the past five years living in Kyoto…'). If you have other writing credits, you should mention those in your cover letter as well. Some travel editors in the USA still prefer to receive submissions by post rather than email; others refuse to accept anything other than emailed submissions. Check the contributors' guidelines.

How long should you wait to hear about your submission? If you haven't heard back within three months, send a follow-up postcard or email checking to make sure that the editor received your piece and inquiring about its status. Some publications specify in their contributor guidelines how long you might need to wait to find out if it has been accepted; don't expect to ever hear anything back if your piece has been rejected.

On spec

To avoid many of the unknowns in the first scenario, you could submit your article 'on spec'. To do this, you need to contact the travel editor or travel desk before you travel (or at least before you write) with some story ideas. If the editor likes one of your angles, and can see where it might fit in their paper, they'll ask to see the article when it's finished, but with no obligation. If they like the finished article, they'll publish it. This is a good deal for you and a good deal for them. You know that the editor is interested in publishing your article, assuming your writing is up to scratch. They know that they'll get a story, and if it isn't what they want they won't have to pay you for it. Many freelance travel writers work this way until they've built up a relationship with a travel editor. Of course, after you've written a few articles on this basis, you become more of a known quantity and the travel editor will have enough faith in your abilities to give you a paid commission.

In the USA, the phrase 'on spec' does not carry the same weight as it does in the UK. If a US travel editor says, 'I'll be happy to consider your story on spec', it does not necessarily mean that they think your story has a good chance of being published. It means: 'If you send it to me, I'll read it, no strings attached.' Also, note that policies and practices regarding press trips and freebies in the USA are extremely different from those in the UK; see pages 98–100.

Commission

This is the goal of every travel writer: you come up with an idea that the travel editor likes enough to guarantee that they will publish your story and pay you for it. A paid commission also means that you will have little trouble arranging free facilities such as flights, rental cars and hotels, because the paper's travel desk will usually give you a letter outlining the arrangement. Sometimes, particularly if you have proved your reliability, the desk will contact you and ask you to write a specific piece, though this tends to happen only with the most regular contributors.

How newspapers are produced
The US production process

If an editor in the USA decides to use your story, you will most likely receive a phone call notifying you one or two weeks before the piece is scheduled to appear. The editor will tell you when your story is going to be published and how much you'll be paid. Depending on the subject, the editor may also ask if you have any photographs to go with the piece (for which you will be paid an extra fee). Do not expect a lengthy style discussion. Newspaper travel editors do not have the luxury of time or staff to go over minute editing changes; in the case of some especially overworked editors, you'll be lucky if you get the opportunity to go over editing changes at all. If editors want to make substantial alterations to your story or have serious questions about the content, they'll tell you.

Many newspapers require freelancers to sign a contract, so you should be notified – and you should sign a contract – before a paper publishes your piece. But not all papers require contracts, and at many of those that do, signing a contract once a year is sufficient, meaning that you may not be notified about your second or third published piece. Still, most editors make a great effort to notify writers before their pieces are printed. In the worst case, you will find out when you're paid. (Such 'worst cases' are rare; many newspapers now require writers to send in an invoice before they are paid, so at the very least, the editor or someone from the paper's staff will contact you to request an invoice.)

In general, weekend travel sections are edited on Monday and Tuesday and 'put to bed' by Wednesday or Thursday. Editing will be sharp, quick and usually minimal; fact-checking of only the most potentially troublesome facts – such as phone numbers and prices – will be performed. This is an important detail to note: travel editors in the USA rely absolutely on writers to get their facts straight. And if a writer's false 'facts' bring on a deluge of complaining phone calls and emails on Monday morning, you can be sure the editor won't be keen to use that writer's work again.

The UK production process

In the UK, the production process followed by most newspapers resembles a sausage factory. As soon as one issue has been sent to bed, production work begins on the next. But many of the ingredients for this sausage will have been chosen months ahead.

Most newspapers have an editorial schedule that can sometimes extend a year or more in advance. There will be certain topics coming up that the editors know they will want to cover – anniversaries, major events, holiday periods, etc – and these pegs are the building blocks around which each issue's contents are structured. In March, for example, a newspaper may include a city guide to Dublin for St Patrick's Day, plus a look ahead to Easter breaks in Britain. In addition to these 'time-sensitive' stories, most publications will also carry a range of articles that complement them: a long-haul beach holiday, for example, or an overland expedition in Africa. Space can always be made for late-breaking stories, however. If a dengue fever epidemic threatens travelers to Thailand, or an airline fares war creates incredible bargains for city breaks, many editors will want to replace a planned story with a fresh article. This is one reason why you may not be told that your piece is definitely being used; weary travel editors try to manage expectations, and a good way to avoid having to call a freelance contributor to say their story has been postponed is by never having made any promises in the first place.

Most of an issue's 'raw' copy will not be read in detail until the previous issue has been finished. Press day, when electronic images of all the pages are transmitted to the print site, is Thursday for travel sections published in national newspapers on a Saturday. For the Sunday travel sections, it can be anything from Thursday to Saturday, depending on how the newspaper prints its different components. Typically, the travel editor will start to look at the stories for the following weekend on Friday morning. They will probably begin with the longer and more prominent articles: the lead story; the comprehensive round-up (for example, a guide to the best Greek islands or beach destinations for young families); the city-break page. Even at this relatively late stage (as it will seem if you submitted your story months ago), you may be contacted for clarifications, embellishments or even a rewrite. If the editorial team cannot contact you, it is possible that your story will be replaced by someone else's – this is why it is essential to provide contact details (ideally your mobile phone number and an email address that you check regularly). If you plan to be away on a long trip, say so – and call the editor a few days before you leave to remind them that they have a limited window if they need any changes, so perhaps they should look at the story ahead of time.

Some editors merely tidy things up a little; others will restructure a story to their liking. But often they will have to cut back a story to fit the available space, and rarely will you get a chance to review their edit – this is a good reason to make sure you don't overwrite.

Most national newspapers have staff (or interns) who check telephone numbers and websites – and possibly hotel rates, admission prices and hours. Every writer is allowed a little leeway in getting the odd figure wrong, but if a check turns up more than a few errors your reputation could be jeopardized.

Once the editorial staff is confident that the story is in good shape, it is passed to the designers and sub-editors. They are professionals who are concerned with getting the story to look good and to match the house style. They will lay out the page, 'flow in' the story (usually a simple copy-

and-paste job), apply the house fonts and add the furniture: the headline, standfirst (sub-heading), captions etc.

When their work is done, a proof copy of the page is printed out. The travel editor, features editor and editor will usually look at it, though only the travel editor is likely to study it in detail. Last-minute changes are made, the issue is transmitted, and the whole circus begins again.

Writing for magazines

Travel magazines 101

Magazines with a market for travel stories fall into four basic categories.

Specialist travel magazines in the UK include *Wanderlust, Condé Nast Traveller* and *Sunday Times Travel*; in the USA *Travel + Leisure, National Geographic Traveler, Condé Nast Traveler* and Arthur Frommer's *Budget Travel Magazine*; and in Australia *Travel + Leisure Australia, Get Lost* and *Vacations & Travel Magazine. Lonely Planet Traveller* magazine is published in countries including the UK, the USA, India, Argentina and China.

Trade magazines include the UK and US versions of *Travel Weekly,* Australia's *Travel Week* and the UK's *Travel Trade Gazette.*

The majority of **corporate magazines** aimed at consumers of travel are in-flight magazines such as British Airways' *High Life,* United Airlines' *Hemispheres,* Delta's *Sky,* American Airlines' *American Way* and Qantas' *Spirit of Australia.* Leading hotel chains also publish lavishly produced magazines for their customers, as do most train operators, ferry companies and car-rental companies. A number of cruise lines – including Princess, Holland America, Royal Caribbean, Norwegian and Carnival – also publish magazines for their on-board and 'preferred' clientele.

Lifestyle magazines may not have travel as their sole focus, but their content includes a travel element. Examples in the UK include *TNT Magazine, Harpers & Queen* and even *Dogs Monthly.* In the USA this spectrum includes highbrow publications such as the *Atlantic* and *Harper's*; men's/adventure magazines such as *Outside, National Geographic Adventure* and *Men's Journal*; bridal and women's magazines such as *Modern Bride* or *Elle*; and subject-focused publications such as *Preservation, Gourmet, Smithsonian* and *Organic Style.* Australian lifestyle magazines with travel content include *Inside Out, Vogue Entertaining and Travel* and *Australian Gourmet Traveller.* There's also the internationalist *Monocle* (with its summer travel-specific offshoot, *The Escapist*).

The editorial requirements of these publications will differ sharply, and your approach should, as always, be clearly targeted. Specialist travel magazines provide the most promising opportunities, because of their robust appetites for travel stories. Trade magazines are much less useful, unless you have an inside knowledge of the workings of the industry; they would be far more interested in a story on new developments in Cuban resorts, for example, than in pursuing the trail of Che Guevara. Corporate airline magazines provide more encouraging opportunities, particularly for features on the destinations they serve – whether Asian beaches for an international airline, American festivals for a domestic US carrier or British cities located along a main railway line. Numerically, lifestyle and niche magazines take up the most space on the shelves, but they can be tricky to sell to – often their modest travel needs are looked after by a small team of regular freelancers or in-house contributors. However, the range of these publications does offer some alluring possibilities for freelancers, especially in the USA; as always, the better you know the publication, the better your chances of pitching the perfect article.

Magazine sections

In the trade, the three parts of a magazine are called the 'front-of-the-book', the 'well' or 'middle-of-the-book', and the 'back-of-the-book'.

The front-of-the-book refers to the section of the magazine that appears between the table of contents and the feature stories. In this section, along with all the advertisements, you'll find snappy reports of hot hotels, spas, restaurants, bars or boutiques that are just opening in a major city; new galleries or museums; inventive and useful new travel products; and noteworthy news such as a major museum moving to a new location or a change in a venue's status – a new owner, new chef or multimillion-dollar renovation. Slightly longer pieces might include destination news updates or issues-oriented reports.

The well, or middle-of-the-book, is where you'll find the juicy 2500–4000-word feature articles illustrated by lavish photographs. These are the high-profile stories that sell the magazine each month.

The back-of-the-book is reserved for promotions, a few round-up pieces and classified advertisements.

The best way to break into magazines is to start off by writing front-of-the-book stories. Some publications require proposals for these; others are happy to read the entire piece (after all, the proposal may be as long as the piece) – usually this will be spelled out in the contributor guidelines. These days the path to magazine writing success most often proceeds this way: you write a few of these front-of-the-book pieces, get your name published in the magazine, establish a relationship with an editor at the publication and lay the groundwork for further, possibly larger, commissions. You do these well and, after a year or two, you start working on a 'favored-writer' basis, which eventually results in a big middle-of-the-book feature. You do that well, and you're on your way. Many successful writers have followed this exact path to develop working relationships with different magazines. Never underestimate the power of the front-of-the-book story.

As front-of-the-book stories generally run from only 150 to 300 words, it's important to remember that the subject has to be just right. You have to hit the bullseye with your proposal or story, so it's essential to study the front-of-the-book pieces closely to see what the editor is looking for. Unfortunately, it's harder to write 250 words than 2500 words. Every single word has to pull its own weight, yet you need to use zingy language and precise, colorful details to convey some feeling for your subject and still get the essential information across. The answer is to edit, edit and edit some more.

Another point to keep in mind is that it's never too early to pitch a story to a national magazine. Editors know about most significant tourism developments before they even break ground. Don't wait until that great new resort or museum opens to propose a story on it; pitch your piece as soon as the plans are announced. Otherwise you're likely to be told, 'Oh yes, we know all about that. We've already commissioned it.'

Pitching to magazines

Magazines are usually published monthly, which means there are far fewer pages to fill each year in comparison with newspapers. However, there are literally thousands of magazines out there. As with newspapers, preferences for how to receive submissions vary from publication to publication and even from editor to editor. Check the magazine's contributor guidelines.

Pitching a story to a US magazine is done by writing a query letter. The query letter is your foot in the door, and as such it's your chance to impress the editor with your perceptiveness and your prose. In the UK,

Writer's tip: The new indie travel mags

Perhaps as a kind of backlash to the throwaway nature of much online content, a new breed of periodicals has emerged, sometimes quirky, sometimes self-consciously intellectual, usually style-obsessed and always finely crafted (mostly in vegetable inks by a local printer).

It's hard not to dub *Ernest Journal* (www.ernestjournal.co.uk) 'hipster travel' when it describes itself as being 'for those of us who appreciate a craft gin cocktail as much as a hearty one-pot supper'. The new indie travel mags are as much about sensibility as subject – for Ernest, the subjects include slow adventure, workmanship and wild food – and if you have an affinity with the feel, they could be the perfect market for your writing.

Some magazines are doing something quite radically different. *Boat* (www.boat-mag.com) is a 'nomadic' travel magazine that gathers a team of talented writers and photographers for each issue, moves them en masse to the city they're featuring in that issue, and covers their food, travel and living costs for five weeks (in lieu of payment) as they live together and create the content. *Collective Quarterly* (www.collectivequarterly.com) does a similar thing for regions of the USA.

Another Escape (anotherescape.com) is a beautifully photographed and designed publication going deeper than your traditional travel magazine, covering outdoor lifestyle, creative culture and sustainable living. It ranks high on the 'intellectual' side of the scale. *Lighter Smith Journal* (www.smithjournal.com.au), an Australia-based quarterly, welcomes submissions for unexpected, interesting, funny and complicated stories, including ones that fit the 'travel' genre, told with irreverence and style. Its crafty, girly counterpart *Frankie* (www.frankie.com.au) does too.

pitching a story to a magazine is a very similar process to pitching to a newspaper (see pages 80–3).

However, there are some critical differences between the two types of publications to bear in mind before you start shaping and submitting a proposal or story.

Lead times

Magazines work much further in advance than newspapers. Printers' and distributors' deadlines often dictate that the final page proofs are signed off a month before the edition hits the streets. As a result, most magazines have a much longer planning horizon than newspapers – some editors know the main ingredients of their magazines up to 12 months in advance, and most close their editorial pages three months before the date on the cover; for example, the contents of the April issue will have been finished in December/January. If you want to write an article with a Christmas angle, for example, you'll want to submit your proposal in February or March.

Because of these long lead times, it isn't a good idea to base an article around a subject that is highly topical at the time you're writing, since it won't be current by the time the magazine appears on the shelves. The reason that magazines appear to be up to date when we buy them is because their writers have become adept at predicting and anticipating travel trends.

Keep these timelines in mind when proposing time-sensitive stories, and don't be late with your proposal. The best rule of thumb is to send in your proposal as soon as it is finished; if you're writing about a once-a-year festival, the editor will determine when they want to publish it. Many magazines produce an annual editorial calendar that outlines the specific themes they will be focusing on, month by month; for example, March might be the Cruise issue, June the America issue, and November the Islands issue. As with newspapers, this schedule helps advertising salespeople target potential advertisers. This doesn't mean that an entire issue will be given over to a designated subject, but it does mean that the editors will be producing a substantial package of articles based on that theme. If a magazine you're interested in has such an editorial calendar (they all should), request a copy and propose stories based on the relevant monthly themes as far in advance as possible.

Writer's tip: Think local

Front-of-the-book stories offer an excellent opportunity to write about your local area. Keep your eyes and ears open, use your social networks, join a few local travel industry-related mailing lists to ensure that you know what's coming up in your region. And remember, a story that seems well known to you may be intriguing news to an editor at a publication in another part of the country or world.

Photography

Magazine publishing has a strong photographic component. At its most extreme this could mean that a magazine might turn down your piece on the best choices for changing money because it just isn't interesting visually. They might also reject a good story because the photography will be too expensive (words are cheap in comparison with the photo shoots that are needed for magazines such as *Condé Nast Traveler*).

Simultaneous submissions

It is virtually impossible – and definitely not recommended – to send simultaneous queries (that is, copies of exactly the same query letter) to more than one magazine. Your proposal should be closely tailored to fit an individual magazine, and if you are successful, the magazine will be buying exclusive North American Rights (if you're pitching in the USA). It is absolutely fine to propose quite different stories from the same trip to non-competing publications (a story on open-air markets for *Saveur*, a hotel review for *Travel + Leisure* and an adventure narrative for *Outside*, for example), but you should not propose the same or similar stories to editorially competing publications.

Presenting your pitch

Professional presentation is all-important when sending in proposals and submissions. The content must be logically set out, legible and neatly presented. It sounds obvious, but it's crucial that you spell the editor's name correctly. It's also vital to ensure that your grammar, spelling and punctuation are correct throughout, as obvious errors and sloppy presentation can lead to a knee-jerk rejection.

Don't try to use fancy fonts or fussy design elements; just present your story in a simple, clean manner, with ample margins (one inch is fine unless otherwise specified in the contributor guidelines). Some magazines prefer that you double-space your article submissions; again, check the contributor guidelines.

If you are submitting a completed story, include on the first page: the title (which in most cases will not be the title used if the story is published); your name and contact information (address, home and cell phone numbers, and email address); and word count. On subsequent pages, type your surname; one word identifying your story; and the page number (e.g., George/Delos – 2) in the upper right-hand corner of each page. For the sake of clarity, write 'The End' at the conclusion of the story.

Your query letter should be no longer than one page and should propose no more than three article ideas. It should be a pithy, provocative and compelling condensation of your story, illustrating how well you know the magazine you're pitching to, how vividly you can bring your particular idea to life, and why you are particularly suited to writing the best story on this topic. Your letter should always include details of any experience or expertise you might have that distinguishes you from other writers. It can also help to enclose copies of your previously published articles (known as 'clips') – especially any articles that are similar in style, subject or tone to the one you're proposing, and that have appeared in reputable publications.

When writing your pitch, it's vital to keep in mind everything you have learned about the publication you are targeting. What kind of tone, angle and subject do they prefer? In addition, think about what might actually help to sell the magazine – most editors will tell you that writers rarely give this all-important aspect any thought, proposing stories that interest them rather than stories that interest a particular publication's readership.

Addressing your pitch

You'll find a listing of a magazine's editorial staff on the publication's masthead, usually a couple of pages into the magazine (these details are often also available on the magazine's website). The best practice is to write to an editor three or four rungs from the top of the editorial ladder – this person's title will usually be articles editor, features editor, senior editor or travel editor. If you are unsure which editor to write to, address your submission to the editor-in-chief or managing editor, who will pass it on to their assistant to assess.

After the pitch

If you haven't heard back from a magazine after two months, send a follow-up note to check that the editor received your piece, and ask about its status. In as nice a way as possible, mention that if you don't hear something in the next month you'll assume that the editor is not interested and you'll send your proposal elsewhere. If you don't hear anything in the next month, just move on to the next publication. (Of course, you will probably have to rework your proposal in order to fit that next publication.)

When you do hear back from the magazine, the response will be either a rejection or acceptance.

Provisional acceptance

A magazine acceptance will take one of two forms: a provisional acceptance or a commission. In the UK, provisional acceptances are rare, since British magazines usually use writers who are known to them and who are respected in the industry to write their big stories – which is why it is recommended that you break into magazine publishing by writing front-of-the-book pieces.

In the USA, if an editor is unfamiliar with your work but intrigued by your idea – or familiar with your work and tempted by but not quite convinced about your idea – they may ask you to write the article without a guarantee that it will be published. The editor will go over the approach, length and deadline of the story with you, but will not offer you a firm contract. This is still an excellent opportunity and you should follow through on it.

Working on commission

This is what every writer hopes for. If an editor is convinced that they want to buy your story, they'll contact you by phone or email and discuss the story with you, then send you a contract with a cover or commissioning letter. If the editor doesn't send you a follow-up letter, it's a good idea to request one. The letter will reiterate what the editor went

Sample US magazine query letter

Here is a query letter I sent to the articles editor of the US magazine *Signature*, which resulted in a feature assignment:

Dear Ms Shipman

Every month *Signature* presents a mix of stories that takes readers beneath the surface and behind the scenes of countries and cultures around the world. One subject that I have not yet seen covered in your magazine – and that I think would intrigue and enrich *Signature*'s readers – is a new travel option in Kyoto, Japan: travelers can now spend the night at a Buddhist temple in the heart of the city. In marked contrast to staying at a hotel, spending the night in a temple can open up entirely new aspects – and bestow an entirely new appreciation – of this ancient capital.

I know this firsthand because I recently spent an exhilarating night at Myokenji Temple, about 20 minutes from Kyoto's main train station. This night was the highlight of my two-week journey through Japan this spring, and I would like to write about it for *Signature*.

The article I have in mind would focus on my own experience at the temple: I would describe first impressions of the clean, serene space; a meeting with the koan-quoting, baseball-loving head monk; a glorious evening encounter on the temple's grounds, when the past seemed to spring to life; and an enlightening immersion in incense and chants at a pre-dawn service the following morning.

This little-known alternative is open to all travelers, and I would detail the practicalities as well as the poetry of a temple stay, telling readers exactly how to arrange such a visit, and how to behave at the temple itself.

My own experience in Japan is extensive. I lived in Tokyo in 1977–9 and have visited the country every two years since. I have written about Japan for a variety of publications, including the *San Francisco Examiner & Chronicle* and *Winds* magazine, and I speak Japanese fluently. (This is not necessary to enjoy the temple experience, however.)

Thank you for considering this article proposal. I look forward to hearing from you.

over with you: the angle and approach your story should take, the length, your deadline and your fee.

Make sure that your deadline is reasonable, given the amount of research and writing you'll need to do and any other dictates of your personal schedule; it's far better to negotiate the deadline at the beginning of the process than to have to ask for an extension at the end. The contract will reconfirm the subject, length and deadline; the rights the magazine is purchasing; the fee to be paid for the article; the amount of expenses (if any) you will be reimbursed for; and the kill fee you will be paid if the article is not published.

When you score a commission, the real work has just begun. Your obligation and goal is to give the magazine what the editor wants. Every article is a compromise between the writer and the editor, but remember that in this relationship, the editor holds the final power to publish or reject your piece. So take the editor's guidance very seriously.

If you find that your story is deviating from what you had agreed upon, call the editor and talk it over. Don't surprise the editor by turning in a story that is completely different from the one they are expecting. The editing process may go smoothly or bumpily, but either way, your job is to work with the editor to make it as smooth as possible. If an editor asks for a major rewrite, make sure you understand why, and what changes the editor is looking for. Occasionally, an editor may ask for so many changes or so drastic a rewrite that you simply can't agree. In this situation you

Writer's tip:
The personal approach

Another strategy for addressing your proposal is to find an editor at the magazine who also writes, and whose articles you admire. Send in your article to them, with a note saying how much you enjoyed the piece they wrote for a recent issue – any writer who has struggled to produce a good story will be happy to hear that at least one reader enjoyed it, and this strategy will help get you noticed and read.

have the right to say you're not going to do the story after all, but this should be a truly last-case scenario. You'll forfeit the money you were supposed to be paid (including the kill fee and any expenses you may have been promised) and also effectively squander any chance of working with that editor again.

The kill fee

'Kill fee' is the rather aggressive expression used by the industry to denote compensation that is given when a commissioned article is submitted (or an article sent on spec is formally accepted) and the editor eventually decides not to publish it – that is, to 'kill' it. There can be many reasons for this. It could be because the subject has been overtaken by events – for example, the destination you wrote about has been devastated by an earthquake or disrupted by internal social upheaval. More often it is because of a change in personnel or policy, which means your story is no longer required. The kill fee is usually between 25 and 50 per cent of the fee agreed upon for your story. If you receive a kill fee, you are free to sell the story to another publication; you may sell the story just as it is or rewrite it to suit a different editor and readership.

How magazines are produced

When a magazine editor accepts a story, they will call you to discuss your article. Sometimes the editor will want a substantial rewrite, and will go over the article in great detail with you, paragraph by paragraph and even sentence by sentence, as necessary. At other times the editing changes will be minimal but, again, the editor will discuss them with you in detail. When your story has been reworked and edited to the editor's satisfaction, you will often be sent a copy of the edited version. This is a final opportunity for you to approve the changes or to raise any final concerns, because you will most likely not be sent a final proof of your story as it will appear on the page.

At some point in the editing process, depending on the publication, you may be contacted by a fact-checker or sub-editor. In the USA, the fact-checker will ask you to supply materials that corroborate your information – maps, brochures and pamphlets, pages from guidebooks and other source materials, tapes of quoted conversations and the like. The fact-checker or sub-editor will also contact all of the places mentioned in your story – every hotel, restaurant, store and museum – and will use independent resources to verify every cultural, historical and geographical fact in your story. So, to avoid humiliation and to cultivate an ongoing relationship with the magazine, be sure to do your own scrupulous fact-checking before you deliver your story. The more errors the editors find in your story, the less likely they will be to use you again.

Magazines have a much more elastic publishing timeline than newspapers. For example, your article could be accepted in May and a photographer sent to shoot photos to accompany your piece in June (photographic conditions permitting); the editor would then contact you about editorial changes in the piece in August, and then work on it with you until the end of September.

The magazine would go into production in October, close in November — and hit the news-stands in February or March. Because of the lengthy printing process, magazines work on issues many months in advance — and often on three editions simultaneously.

In another scenario, a piece may sit at a magazine for a year — or much longer — before it appears in print. This might be because the magazine is waiting for the appropriate season to publish your article or because the photographs needed to accompany your piece can't be shot until the following year — or quite simply because space is limited and other stories have higher priority due to the volatility of their subject matter or the celebrity of their author. If this is the case, you won't be contacted to fine-tune your work for many more months. In such cases it is wise to maintain a cordial relationship with your editor, periodically checking on the status

Writer's tip: Always read the fine print

Always read the contract you're signing. Don't get so overwhelmed or flattered by acceptance that you neglect to study the fine print or decide not to negotiate on points that make you uncomfortable. You may well regret this later. And if you breach your contract, even unwittingly, you will be legally vulnerable.

of your story and pitching new ideas. Above all, don't be precious about your work – once you've submitted your piece, allow the magazine staff to get on with what they need to do to make it publishable without interference. If the wait is sometimes great with magazine publishing, the rewards are usually great, too.

Press trips and freebies

Journalists will sometimes be offered an all-expenses-paid trip to a particular destination arranged by travel companies such as tour operators or government tourism organizations, usually in association with an airline. Such press trips can involve traveling with three to 15 journalists and a PR consultant: you all fly out together, you all stay in the same hotel, and you are all expected to follow the same pre-arranged itinerary (lunches, dinners, museum and carpet-store visits, etc.). A good press trip will build in plenty of free time for journalists to explore the destination independently, so that any ensuing articles won't be based on exactly the same experiences (although not all press-trip organizers are so imaginative or enlightened). The sponsors will be hoping that the writers will write favorable stories about the destination or tour for their various publications.

Press trips in the USA

This is a hot issue in the USA these days. Thirty years ago press trips were an accepted part of the business of travel writing. They were seen as ways to broaden editorial horizons at minimal expense, and as excellent perks for otherwise under-rewarded staffers.

Since then, however, acceptance of subsidized travel of this kind has changed dramatically because of the all-important issue of impartiality. Most publications do not allow their own staffers to take press trips or to accept freebies, and many do not accept freelance articles that have resulted from accepting such perks.

The development of a special discount rate called a press rate has further complicated matters. This is a reduced rate that sponsors will often offer to writers who want to participate in a trip but who have to show that they have paid for it. Essentially, it was developed as a way to get around prohibitions on press trips. Press rates can make an absurdity of the whole situation. For example, if you pay $25 or even

A writer's view: Andrew Bain

Andrew Bain is an award-winning Australia-based travel writer and author, specializing in adventure and the outdoors. His work is published around the world, and he writes online at www.adventurebeforeavarice.com.

Skip New York, London and Paris, and look for lesser-known places with appealing quirks. If you must stick to the blue-chip destinations, find a different way to look at them. Develop a specialty – food, spas, outdoor adventure – that will gain you a niche market, then supplement it with general stories.

It's a risky business. I determine how much a certain trip will cost me, then calculate how much I'll need to earn to justify the journey. I break this down into the number of stories required from the trip and then scurry about making certain I come up with at least that number of stories. Then comes the problematic bit: selling them. It's difficult at the beginning of your travel-writing career to make accurate forecasts on expenses and profit because you're not sure how much a certain story will bring in, but eventually you get a feel for the markets you're targeting.

Books are a long, slow process… and that's even after the writing's complete. As *Headwinds* was my first book, I completed the manuscript before making any approaches to agents or publishers. It's then a marketing battle – to convince a few people that this book will reap a profit to any publisher. I found an agent who thought the book had potential and she then found it a publisher.

Behind all things glamorous there's the everyday tedium: actors learning their lines, models waxing their backs, and writers spending hours wrestling with a sentence. It happens, and more regularly than we'd all like. And while everybody else at the Grand Canyon is oohing and aahing about the wonderful view, you're quietly fretting about how your story is progressing and wondering how you're going to express the scene in words – 'words cannot describe…' will never suffice. Everything you now see and do will be tainted slightly by the knowledge that you'll later be sitting at your computer recreating what you wish you never had to recreate.

$250 for a $2500 trip, is that more valid than getting it for free? It's a tremendously delicate and complicated issue – but the best thing is to be as honest and upfront with your editor as possible, and to be clear about the publication's guidelines and policies. Sometimes the publication's policies on press trips and freebies will be spelled out in their contributor guidelines, but if you are in any doubt whatsoever, be open about the situation before you find yourself in a predicament you could later regret. A few publications still rely on press trips to supplement their own meager travel budgets, so it is essential to know the position on this issue before you accept any travel offers.

It's not unheard of for sponsors to insist on reviewing any articles that result from the press trip, prior to publication. This is absurd and you should never agree to any such conditions. If a sponsor wants you to go on their trip, they need to give you editorial freedom. Equally, although you need to write your story based on your observations, you also need to ensure that your description isn't colored by any special treatment you may have received. In most cases, it's futile to write about experiences that would not be available to the general traveler.

Press trips in the UK
The press trip has long been an integral part of the UK travel journalism scene, and most travel editors receive a dozen or so such invitations each week, asking them to nominate a writer.

Many publications prefer not to use pieces based on press trips because they want their writers to take a more independent approach than is often possible on such a subsidized trip. Also, they don't want to run the risk that another publication – whose writer also accepted the press trip – might publish the story ahead of them. Regardless, hundreds of press trips are taken by staffers or freelance journalists each year.

Before a journalist agrees to go on a press trip, it is important for every party – the writer, the publication and the benefactor – to agree on the credit that will be given to the organizations that are providing facilities. This is often less of an issue for tourist boards (who are generally happy simply to see their country/region/city in print), but is of considerable concern to commercial firms. Some publications will mention that 'Joe Bloggs traveled as a guest of Soaraway Vacations, which has holidays to the Costa Brava from £299', but will then go on to suggest other companies. It is very unlikely that an editor will agree to an 'exclusive' mention, although some airlines issue formal contracts to this effect.

Free facilities

While UK publications rarely pay travel expenses, it's also true to say that very few UK travel writers pay for their own travel. When travel journalists receive a commission from a newspaper or a magazine, it is commonplace for them to negotiate free facilities with tourist boards, airlines, hotels, tour operators and car rental companies, on the understanding that some sort of credit will be given in print.

These freebies exist because travel organizations believe they will gain more of an impact from money spent on a journalist than if they were to spend the cash on advertising – there's an industry term, 'equivalent advertising spend', which means an estimate of what it would cost in advertisements to procure the same level of media coverage. The effect is to help the journalist make a living.

Press trips and objectivity

Both press trips and freebies introduce the thorny issues of objectivity and impartiality. If a hotel has given you a free room, how objective can you be in assessing it and writing about it? If an airline has carried you in business class, won't that prejudice the way you think about the company? Integrity is the editorial bedrock. If you take a press trip, or negotiate free or discounted accommodation or services, you must not feel obliged to write a favorable piece just because someone else is paying your way. Your story will be judged – and your reputation as a travel writer will be based – on your integrity; your primary obligation is to the reader.

Syndicating your stories

In order to augment their earnings, many freelance writers syndicate their stories, selling one article or story multiple times. This happy scenario is much more likely to occur in the USA than elsewhere.

Syndication in the USA

The USA has five 'national' newspapers, to the extent that they buy first national rights to the stories they publish: the *New York Times*, *The Washington Post*, the *Los Angeles Times*, *The Boston Globe* and *The Christian*

A writer's view: Mara Vorhees

Mara Vorhees has written about destinations from Costa Rica to Mother Russia, as well as her home in New England. These days she often travels with twins in tow. Read about their adventures at www.havetwinswilltravel.com

Develop a regional expertise: travel, learn the language, develop a network of contacts. Learn as much as you can about that place, so you can demonstrate that you are an expert. And by the way, you'll probably do better if your regional expertise is not France.

Guidebook writing comes in relatively big chunks, meaning that one assignment will keep you busy (and pay the bills) for several months. Assignments from newspapers, magazines and websites are usually much smaller, occupying a couple of days or perhaps a week.

Many guidebook writers are homeless: they crash with friends or family between assignments and avoid housing costs.

Good guidebook writing is accurate and informative, but it is also entertaining. It is insightful, funny and inspiring. It allows readers to make informed decisions about how they will spend their valuable travel time.

Travel always inspires learning – even more so for guidebook writers, who must become experts about their destinations. We go everywhere, we see everything, we have incredible adventures; then we come home with a suitcase full of notes and a head full of stories and histories to share with others.

It's very important for me to have a stable home, but it's hard to keep it stable when I am traveling all the time. Now that I have children, I am not willing to leave them for long periods of time. Balancing work life and family life is challenging.

Remember that life is trade-offs. This is not an easy job. The hours are long, the pay is short and the benefits (capital B benefits like healthcare and retirement plans) are non-existent. But the small-b benefits are infinite. We guidebook authors definitely have more than our fair share of once-in-a-lifetime experiences, and that's what makes it all worthwhile. That, and meeting our fellow travelers, who lug those books around, trust our opinions, share our adventures, forgive our oversights (hopefully), and make the planet a little less lonely.

Science Monitor. All of the nation's other newspapers buy local rights, which means that they want exclusivity within their circulation area but do not care if your piece appears in a paper outside their area. You would be ill-advised, therefore, to submit your story at the same time to the *Chicago Tribune* and the *Chicago Sun-Times*, or the *Sacramento Bee* and the *San Francisco Chronicle*, because their circulation areas overlap. However, you would have no problems sending the same piece at the same time to the *San Diego Union-Tribune* and the *San Francisco Chronicle*. This is called simultaneous submission and most newspaper travel editors in the USA recognize that, given the low fees they pay, simultaneous submission is a necessity of freelance life. It is a courtesy but not a necessity to inform an editor in your cover letter if you are simultaneously submitting a story.

The vast majority of freelance writers who sell their stories more than once practice self-syndication. That is, they develop a list of travel editors – anywhere from 10 to 50 – to whom they routinely submit their stories. A timely, well-written story may be published by 10 papers, or sometimes even more. Preparing and keeping track of these submissions is both time- and energy-consuming for the writer, and for every story that gets picked up by 10 papers, there are two dozen that may get published by one paper or by none at all. Still, writers who make significant earnings from their newspaper writing all practice some form of self-syndication.

The other syndication option that tempts freelancers is the notion of selling their work through one of the national syndication agencies. The top agencies include King Features Syndicate, New York Times Syndicate, Hearst News Service, Creators Syndicate, Universal Uclick, and Gannett (a list that has shrunk in recent years after a spate of closures and mergers that will no doubt continue). If you peruse newspaper travel sections, you will often see these agencies credited under the bylines of different writers. The truth, however, is that almost all of these agencies do not accept submissions from freelancers. When you see an agency credited, this means that the writer works for a newspaper that belongs to this syndication group.

If a syndicate accepts one of your stories, they will submit it to all of the newspapers that subscribe to their service. If any of these papers publish your story, you will receive a percentage – often 50 per cent, though terms vary – of the money the syndicate has been paid for your story. This arrangement will be specified in the contract you will have signed with the syndicate.

Writer's tip: Press trips and blogging

While the press trip has long been an expression of the symbiotic relationship between the travel industry and travel writers, that has exploded with the growth of blogging. It's a two-way street: travel bloggers want free travel to give them something to blog about and power their content (plus, free travel), and the industry, from destination tourist offices to tour companies to individual hotels and attractions, wants access to influencers with loyal followings – it's the equivalent of paid word-of-mouth, an advertiser's dream.

While there are arguments to be made about how this kind of marketing affects the trustworthiness of information in general – hello, post-truth world! – bloggers are not journalists and the wheels of the internet are greased with this kind of arrangement.

As a blogger, you need to be sure you maintain your integrity by being honest in what you report about your travel experiences no matter how you come by them, and upfront with your audience about how you travel. Remember, you primary value is the trust that your readers place in you – don't do anything to damage it.

• Tell the company in question that you will be writing the truth about your experience.
• Make it clear on any posts associated with the trip that it was sponsored, and by which company or organization.
• Don't accept trips that don't fit with your niche.
• Never accept any form of payment for positive tweets, posts or other coverage.

Syndication in the UK

It is normal for a freelance writer to offer an article to a UK newspaper with First British Serial Rights; this is also true for UK magazine submissions. This means that the writer is giving the publication the right to be first to publish their article in the UK. In theory this allows the writer to resell the piece later to someone else, either in the UK or abroad, in which case they might be selling Second British Serial Rights or Second EU Serial Rights.

In reality, however, if a newspaper or magazine publishes your piece, it will usually expect to retain syndication rights to your article for a specified period. Some publications will ask writers to sign a contract; others will either verbally, or merely on their website, say that you are bound by their conditions of acceptance. This means that they reserve the right to sell your article on to other publications in Britain or overseas and keep a percentage of the fee (typically 50 per cent). The prospect of earning more cash for no extra work in this way sounds attractive – but the arrangement is unlikely to be as lucrative as it sounds. Very often your article isn't resold by the original publication, and you are powerless to sell it yourself.

It is very rare for writers to resell their own travel articles in the UK. This is not only because of the rights situation described above but also for the following reasons:

• Most UK newspapers and magazines are national, and so their readership overlaps. You would not be able to sell a travel piece to more than one of them.

• Since most freelance travel writers tailor an article for a specific slot in a specific publication and its readership, the article simply wouldn't be appropriate for another newspaper, magazine or journal.

• In reality it is only regional newspapers that might be interested in a syndicated travel piece. However, this will only be worth your while in terms of payment if you have a regular, non-regionally focused column to sell. Reselling individual pieces just won't be worth the time it takes to do so. Moreover, there'd be few takers because international travel isn't usually a topic of interest to a regional newspaper, and local travel would be written by a staffer.

Writing books
Travel guidebooks

The two fundamental truths about writing for guidebooks seem contradictory. The first is that the pay you'll receive as a guidebook author, especially when you're starting out, will be dauntingly and even depressingly incommensurate with the energies and hours you put into your work. The second truth is that every year a number of people make a decent living as full-time guidebook writers. The bridge between these two seemingly conflicting truths is built out of experience. The more you hone your craft as a guidebook researcher and writer, the higher the fees you'll receive and the more efficient you'll become. At some point, the ascending graph-line of your payments received will intersect the descending line of your hours expended – and you'll be making money! Of course, that's assuming you persevere through the early years of little pay for lots of work.

What qualities do you need to be a good guidebook writer? First of all, you have to love to travel and, in particular, you should have a passion for exhaustive exploration of the logistical minutiae of travel – where to stay, where (and what) to eat, how to get there, what to see and do. You should be obsessed with accuracy. And you should be able to write with poetic precision and concision.

Guidebook writing is probably the most demanding branch of the travel writing tree. To make it work, you have to investigate multiple attractions, restaurants and hotels every day. You have to juggle your budget, your assignment and your deadline – making sure that you cover everything you need to cover as economically as possible (so that you maximize your earnings) but also as efficiently as possible (so that you have enough time to write up all your findings).

But if you're fascinated with a particular country and culture – or even better, if you're already living in a fascinating country and culture – guidebook writing can be just the ticket for you.

Getting started

The vast majority of work for guidebook writers involves updating already existing guides. A much slimmer slice of the guidebook pie is devoted to writing first editions – guides to an area or on a theme that the publisher hasn't covered before.

Whichever kind of work you're hoping for, the way to get started is the same as when writing for print and the web: study the markets. In this case, that means study all the different guidebook publishers' products closely. What areas do they cover? What audiences are they targeting? Examine where the publications intersect your passions. Do you hike in the Himalayas every year? See if there's a Himalayan hiking guide that you can update, or a publisher who has covered hiking in Europe but hasn't yet expanded to Asia.

Have you honed the fine art of surviving on 5 rupees a day? Perhaps there's a bare-bones guidebook line perfectly synched to your practice.

When you've determined the subject you want to pitch and the publisher you want to pitch it to, do further research to discover how that publisher works with first-time contributors. Follow their guidelines, and briefly but evocatively describe your writing and travel background, being sure to cover any particularly relevant experience and expertise you have. The unasked question you need to answer: what can you (the writer) bring to me (the publisher) that I don't already have? The answer

Writing for brochures and newsletters

Travel-related print materials are not restricted to newspapers, magazines and books. Virtually every travel-related company promotes its products in some kind of printed format. Travel agencies and tour operators, airlines and cruise lines, global hotel chains and family-run guesthouses, urban museums and rural galleries, government tourism organizations and regional visitor information offices – all of these organizations produce brochures, catalogues and newsletters, and all of these products need at least one writer and/or editor. It may not be *The Sunday Times* or *Travel + Leisure*, but it's an excellent way to put baguettes and Brie on the table while you're waiting for the big editors to discover you.

You may want to work as a freelancer with one of these companies to maximize your free time and flexibility, or try for a staff job to give yourself some financial stability and security. If you discover a travel company of any kind that intrigues you, contact them and see if they need anyone with your experience and abilities. Whatever your professional goal, stay alive to the possibilities all around you, and think outside the box.

may be your deep personal knowledge, your fresh perspective, your extraordinary writing skills or some combination of all these. Your job is to show the publisher that you understand their books intimately and that you can provide exactly what they need.

If you're pitching an entirely new idea, you'll need to sell the publisher on the value of the idea itself as well as your unique ability to realize it. In this case, you can bolster your argument with figures on the number of visitors to the area you propose to cover, or the growing popularity of the theme you're presenting. You need to make the business case that the book is worth publishing, that a sufficient audience exists to make the publication profitable.

What happens next? You may receive a rejection – in which case, move on to the next publisher and the next project. You may not receive any reply at all; in this case, after a couple of months, contact the publisher to inquire about the status of your application, noting the date of your original inquiry. If you still don't hear from them, it's time to move on.

A happier scenario is that you receive a response asking for more detailed information. In the case of Lonely Planet, you'll be asked to create a writing sample that shows your ability to write lively prose in the Lonely Planet style, and to pass a mapping test. If your submissions are accepted, you'll be made part of Lonely Planet's writer pool, from which virtually all the company's guidebook contributors are drawn. Typically, your first assignment will be small – covering a section of a city for a city guide, for example, or a second-tier city for a regional guide. If that's successful, you'll be given a larger assignment – more areas of the city you originally covered, or a major city for that regional guide. If all goes well with this assignment, you'll be given more responsibility with your next assignment, and in this way both your area of coverage and your remuneration will grow. Most other major guidebook publishers work in this same way.

Some smaller, more specialized publishers offer greater opportunities for beginning contributors. Depending on your experience and expertise, you may be asked to cover an entire city or region. The downside is that because sales tend to be lower with smaller publishers, your remuneration will probably be lower as well. As always, you must try to balance the opportunity for valuable experience with financial reality.

Whether you're employed by large or smaller publishers, your work should be based on an assignment or commission that clearly details the scope and content (including tone, style, audience and number of words)

What the experts say: Paul Clammer

Since 2003, Paul Clammer has written nearly 30 Lonely Planet guides, as well as guidebooks to Haiti and Sudan for Bradt Travel Guides. In a previous life he may have been a molecular biologist. He currently divides his time between England and Morocco. Find him online at www.paulclammer.com or on Twitter as @paulclammer.

I'd travelled in Taliban-era Afghanistan and written a website about it. After their ouster I added more travel information, so it evolved into a guide. In 2003, Lonely Planet was looking to send an author to Afghanistan for the first time since the 1970s, saw my site, and got in touch.

Develop an area of expertise, so you can really sell your skill set to editors. My foot in the door was Afghanistan, but it could equally be something like trekking or regional food. You need something on your résumé to help you stand out against the competition.

As a guidebook writer you're primarily an information provider, often writing in a very structured way – first the introductions, then the sights, then the hotel listings and so on.

It doesn't matter how beautiful your prose is, no reader will forgive you if you put the train station on the opposite side of town. Everything else flows from the accuracy of those facts that you collect in the field.

It's like being a journalist – you're going out there to get the story, and that's fantastic fun. And of course, all authors get a big kick out of seeing people reading their books. What's not to love about that?

No one gets into travel writing to make it rich. A lot depends on the type of guide and publisher. If your fees cover the research costs on top of actual income, fantastic. In some cases you can defray costs by arranging freebies, but that's dependent on the publisher – some encourage it, for others it's forbidden.

Work–life balance takes on a new meaning when you're away for months on the road. Throw in the financial uncertainty of never knowing where your money is coming from in a few months' time, and it's not always a bed of roses.

It's rewarding in so many ways, but it's not a job that really has a career ladder. You're always hustling, so if you get in, make sure you enjoy it. Oh, and never try to buy a house when you're in the middle of a research trip in the Indian Himalaya.

of your coverage, the deadline, and the pay and payment schedule. It is absolutely essential that you have a contract before you begin your work (unless you have so much money that you don't mind spending a few months and thousands of dollars researching a destination with no firm commitment that your efforts will be published).

Your assignment – or 'brief', as it's often called – is your roadmap. Make sure that you cover all the content requested, write it up in the required style, and submit it on time and to the commissioned word count. After this, you'll likely work through a number of drafts with your editor; the editor's goal is to make the book as lively and useful as possible, but also to make sure it conforms to the company's or the series' style. Making this as smooth a process as possible will help ensure that you continue to move toward the front of the author pool.

Travel literature

If you want to publish a book-length work of travel literature, in the vein of Bill Bryson or Paul Theroux, there are two possible scenarios to follow: you can write the entire manuscript and send it to an agent or publisher, or you can pitch the idea for your book to an agent or publisher and, if you're among the lucky few with just the right proposal, get a publishing house on board from the start. (The third option that has opened up in recent years is that of self-publishing; see page 111.)

The first option is full of uncertainties: you don't know if a publisher (approached directly or through an agent) will be interested in what you've written and you'll have to fund all the research and writing yourself. Pitching an idea seems a better choice, but it is extremely rare for a writer, especially a beginning writer, to pitch a book idea directly to a publisher and have it accepted. The most common – and desirable – path is to pitch your book idea to an agent, who will then aim to rouse the interest of a publisher.

A proposal for a book-length travel narrative is a much more ambitious package than a simple proposal letter to a newspaper or magazine. You will need to send a short covering letter and include a two- to three-page synopsis summarizing your book's themes and structure, a table of contents, a sample chapter or two (usually of around 5000 words) and a little biographical information. Your covering letter will need to establish why you believe your topic and perspective are compelling, why they should publish your book, and why you think your book will sell.

Should you self-publish?

You've written a travel memoir that you're convinced is a potential bestseller, but you can't find a publisher for it. Or maybe you'd just prefer to go it alone. Happily, there are now alterative ways you can relatively easily get your words into the impatiently waiting hands of your audience.

With the rise of ebooks (which account for around 30 per cent of all book sales in the USA) and Amazon, non-traditional authors can self-publish, self-market and self-distribute their books without spilling a drop of ink. And for anyone who doubts that it can work, there's an easy four-word answer: *Fifty Shades of Grey*.

So what do you need to consider before launching your own (perhaps less raunchy) travel blockbuster?

When you use a publishing service like Kindle Direct Publishing for Amazon, it's not like publishing with a traditional publisher. They take no responsibility for the quality of your work or for trying to achieve sales, but nor do they claim any rights to it. You're free to sell your work to another publisher without any obligation to the service you've used.

You don't need much technical know-how. Most services offer automated tools and free tutorials to get you through the process. And there are many companies offering layout, cover design and other services.

You're free to price your book as you wish, though in the case of Amazon (which accounts for around 70 per cent of ebook sales in the USA), your royalties will be 70 per cent of the list price only if the book is priced between $2.99 and $7.99.

Be prepared to become a one-person marketing machine. There's no high-powered marketing team doing the job for you. Self-published authors estimate they spend 90 per cent of their time promoting their books and 10 per cent writing them.

If you become a travel blogger, you can create a ready-made audience for your book – bypass Amazon, and take your product directly to your own market. Bloggers like Nomadic Matt (www.nomadicmatt.com/books) and ProBlogger (www.problogger.net/learn/) have successfully created their own book distribution networks online.

There are plenty of resources online to help you on the path to being a self-published author. Take a look at www.thecreativepenn.com for a step-by-step guide.

An agent's view: Lizzy Kremer

Lizzy Kremer is Head of the Books Department at David Higham Associates in London, British Book Industry Awards 2016 Agent of the Year, and Vice-President of the Association of Authors' Agents. Lizzy blogs at publishingforhumans.postagon.com and tweets at @lizzykremer.

Publishers usually prefer to commission agented authors because they know that agents provide invaluable advice and support to writers.

Agencies often indicate that they don't pay any attention to the manuscripts that are sent to them on an unsolicited basis, but my experience is that good writing stands out a mile and will be read.

Make sure your submissions are well presented, professional (no long chatty letters) and always enclose a two- to three-page book outline, the first few chapters and a self-addressed envelope. Work hard at getting yourself published in other ways. If you've had articles printed in papers, magazines or on websites, enclose those with your manuscript.

Take care when choosing an agent. Trust your instincts. Go with the one who seems passionate about your writing. Make sure the agency has a good reputation within the industry by reading up on them in the various writers' handbooks available.

If you have written something wonderful, the power is in your hands. I take on new clients when two things fall into place – when I love their writing and when I think I can sell the ideas they have. Apart from that I just have to get a sense we would work well together.

A good agent will work with you on your book proposal or manuscript prior to making submissions if she feels it could benefit from some editorial attention. Then she will draw up a list of editors she believes will enjoy your work and will want to publish you. Hopefully she will communicate with you effectively — letting you know who she is sending your work to, why she has chosen those people and what you can expect to happen next. She will encourage swift responses from the publishers and perhaps arrange for you to meet them, so that you have an opportunity to sell yourself in person and in order for you to gain a better understanding of the publishing team you might be working with.

She will negotiate the best possible deal for you. That deal might be the result of an auction between editors competing to become your publisher. Or it might simply be a nice deal with the one editor or publishing house who you and your agent believe will do the best possible job of editing and promoting your work.

Your agent will negotiate your contract, using all the precedents available to her from the other contracts she has negotiated with your publisher in the past. An agent might retain certain rights, such as translation rights or newspaper serialization rights, in order to make those further deals herself. Once your contract has been signed, the agent will continue to act as a middle person on certain aspects of your relationship with your publishers, from encouraging their publicity or marketing efforts to chasing moneys due.

Don't try too hard. Write from the heart. Don't list everything you did and saw. Remember the book has to have a dramatic arc just as a novel does. Once you think you have finished the book, go back to the start and review the first few chapters. Writers often 'write their way in' to a book, using the first few chapters to find their feet.

Books that offer a personal journey as well as a physical one have great appeal. When I pick up a book I want to be moved by it, I want it to change my life. I don't see why I should lower these expectations, even if sometimes it is enough to be entertained. I want to find out about a place but also something about life at the same time.

An analysis of any recently published books on a similar theme or covering a similar area is also essential, as is your own best indication of the potential audience for your book. You'll also need to send an SASE if you want to have your work returned. Your whole package should look as professional as possible.

Getting an agent

Only a very few publishers will consider book proposals and unsolicited manuscripts sent directly from an author. Most book publishers, particularly the larger ones, will only deal with an agent.

Initially, if an agent likes your book and agrees to represent you, they may work with you to strengthen your book editorially, identifying any narrative weaknesses or suggesting ways to smooth out rough spots in your story and prose. Once your manuscript is finished, your agent will target appropriate publishers. Agents know what interests different publishing houses, and also what different editors within those houses are hoping to find, since they develop relationships with editors over time. Rather than blindly sending your proposal into the vast editorial slush pile, an agent will send your book directly to the person who is most likely to be receptive to it.

If a publisher is interested in publishing your book, your agent's next task is to represent you and make sure the publisher's contractual terms are as fair and favorable as possible. If your book attracts interest among multiple publishers, your agent will oversee an auction, with a number of publishers bidding for the right to publish your work. They will also advise you as to which publisher is likely to promote your book the most robustly and generally treat you well. As any published writer knows, getting your book published is only half the battle. If the publisher doesn't

Writer's tip: Do you need an agent?

Or do you have the skills and knowledge to do all of this yourself? The answer is up to you, of course, but you will most likely save yourself a great deal of hassle and heartache if you can find a sympathetic and enthusiastic agent.

Publishing in travel anthologies

Another print outlet that deserves mention is travel anthologies, compilations of a mix of previously published and original stories by a variety of writers. San Francisco–based Travelers' Tales specializes in anthologies that are focused either geographically or thematically (women's travel tales, food, humor etc.). Seattle-based Seal Press publishes themed travel anthologies that feature women contributors. Lonely Planet also produces anthologies that draw on a wide range of contributors, from best-selling travel writers to never-before-published writers.

Most publishers of anthologies announce their upcoming projects on their websites, and post guidelines on the theme and length of the stories they require. While the monetary prospects are underwhelming, they do offer good publishing opportunities, especially for narrative pieces. It's good practice to periodically check the websites of the aforementioned companies – and other websites dedicated to writing opportunities – for updated information on forthcoming anthologies.

allocate any resources to promote it, your beloved tome can quickly sink into literary oblivion.

An important part of negotiating your contractual terms concerns the split of foreign-language publication or screen and other media rights. If you're lucky enough to attract the attention of a film production company, for example, an agent will help navigate you through the tricky waters of rights and fees negotiations.

If you do enter into an agreement with an agent, you will sign a contract. The agent will agree to represent you and your work and you will agree not to seek representation with any other agent and to pay the agent a commission (anything up to 15 per cent) if they find a publisher for your work. Usually, the contract will also spell out circumstances under which one or both parties may terminate the agreement and may include the time period of the mutual commitment.

Travel literature payments work on the royalty model. If your proposal is accepted by a publisher, they should pay you an advance, which will be deducted from your subsequent royalties. The advance will go some way toward keeping you financially afloat while you're working on your book, but as discussed earlier, this might not amount to much: roughly up to

How books are published

Depending upon their location and culture, publishing houses are apt to call their production processes and personnel by different names, but the following is a general overview of the book production process.

Once you have delivered your manuscript, meeting contractual obligations such as length, format and delivery date, your work will be assessed, usually by the commissioning editor or publisher. They will either return the manuscript for further work, discussing any problems in detail and setting a later delivery date, or they'll accept it for publication. On acceptance, you will be assigned an editor, who in some situations will be the commissioning editor you've already been dealing with, and it is part of your contractual obligation to work cooperatively with them, responding to suggestions and criticisms in an open and understanding manner. As Bill Bryson has said, 'Even the most experienced writers need an editor.' Your book may be your baby, but the editor is the midwife, delivering it to your readers.

The editing process includes a structural edit, which reviews your book's themes and narrative, chapter by chapter. The editor will work directly with you to fix any major editorial issues. Copy editing is sometimes handled by a different editor, who will ensure that all grammar, punctuation and spelling are consistent and correct.

Once the book has been edited, you will be sent a copy of the revised manuscript. This version will usually be submitted as draft 'page proofs', meaning that the book has been laid out by a designer: fonts and heading weights will have been imposed, and each page of the printout will contain a double-page spread (emulating the final printed book). Any major alterations, queries or problems should already have been discussed with you, and any remaining issues will be indicated for your attention in the edited text. At this point you will have a last chance to make corrections and changes, in consultation with your editor. Once this is done, the work will be proofread by a second editor.

You may be able to review the manuscript one more time at final proof stage, shortly before the book heads off to the printer, but any changes made at this stage are expensive and strictly limited. You should also be involved in the cover design process and be shown the back-cover text, summarizing your book for the reader – but do not expect that you will have final approval; that usually lies with the publisher.

£10,000 in the UK, $15,000 in the USA or AU$20,000 in Australia. For listings of publishers who produce travel literature, see chapter 7.

If your book is accepted by a publisher, either as a completed manuscript or as a substantially fleshed-out proposal, your authorial job from that point on is to give the company what they want – just as with a commissioned magazine article, only on a bigger scale. Your agent will stay in touch with you to monitor your progress, but in effect, once the contract is signed, they will hand you and your book over to the publisher's commissioning editor. This editor is your bridge to the publishing house, the internal champion for your work, as well as the person charged with making sure you deliver a publishable and marketable manuscript on time. Deal with your editor judiciously. Fight for what you believe in, but be as professional and easy to deal with as possible. In the long run, you both share the same goal of bringing out the best – and most successful – book possible.

(4)

Writing a

travel blog

In the digital age, there's a world of possibility for budding writers. Anyone – no matter your level of experience or talent – can relatively easily knock together a web presence and get their words out there.

But of course, there's more to starting your own travel blog than that. There are some technological hurdles to clear (although that just keeps getting easier and easier) but more importantly, and more difficult – what do you want to do, when you get there? What is your blog or website going to be, and who's going to read it?

There are lots of things to consider before you start – from your subject matter to your domain name to what blogging platform you use to the question of whether you want to earn money from your blog. This chapter will give you an overview of what it takes to conjure a travel blog from thin air, and then what it takes to get it out there – read, followed, and maybe even profitable. It's a broad overview of all the things you need to consider.

There's a lot more to say – and luckily, there are plenty of veteran bloggers prepared to share their hard-won experience. See chapter 7 for a list of our favorite blogging resources.

Why do you want to blog?

Blogging has boomed in the last 10 years, and travel is one of the blogosphere's most popular topics. Just type 'travel blog' into Google – you'll get a number well into the millions, and that number will be bigger than the one we got when we did it yesterday. There are new travel blogs starting up every day.

It's not surprising. The allure of finding a way to make money while traveling means that many, many people are prepared to give it a shot, even if it's a long one. That's not to say that you shouldn't try. But be under no illusions – when you start a travel blog, you are entering a market that's beyond saturated.

It's important that you're honest with yourself about why you want to start a blog and what you want to get out of it, because that starting point is the basis on which you'll make lots of decisions as you go. Think about which of the following categories you fall into:

1. I'm starting a blog to keep in touch with family and friends.

If that sounds like you, it makes things nice and simple. There are great, free options for building and hosting your site so you won't have any expenses, you can get your site up and running quickly, and you can write about exactly what you please. Do note though, that most bloggers say this is how their blog started, even if it went on to become a super-popular, branded travel blog…

2. I want to be a freelance travel writer, and my blog will act as a portfolio to showcase my writing.

If this is you, you might want to invest some time and effort in a more professional-looking site, and spend some money on your own domain name. If your site will be primarily a portfolio site, you might want to look at other options too, like publishing your work on other online platforms (either paid or unpaid).

3. I want to travel the world and be paid for it.

If you want a travel blog that ultimately becomes your full-time job (or at least a source of some income), think about it that way from the start – as a business, and not just a blog. It will influence your decisions about platform, domain name and hosting, but more importantly, it means that you'll have to be strategic before you start – about who your blog is for, and the kind of content you'll need to create for it.

It also means you'll need to develop a broader skillset beyond writing. Creating a successful blogging business means being entrepreneurial and multi-skilled – marketer, project manager, finance person, strategic lead… Are you ready for the challenge? Read on. Much of the information in this chapter is here to help you.

Finding your niche

In the old days (let's say, 2009 – this is a fast-moving world!), when there weren't hundreds of thousands of travel blogs around, it was enough to choose a broad subject area – family travel, for example, or adventure travel – and start a blog, and you could discover an audience who found that theme relatable. Over the years, many blogs have filled those broad niches to bursting point, meaning that the level of competition for readers is extremely high.

A blogger's view: Geraldine DeRuiter

Geraldine DeRuiter started her blog, The Everywhereist (www.everywhereist. com) in 2009. It made Time *magazine's list of the top 25 blogs of the year in 2011. Her first book,* All Over the Place, *was published in May 2017.*

For the first few years of my site, I put up a post every day Monday to Friday (sometimes publishing more than once a day). That became how I distinguished myself – I was the lady who blogged every single day. And when you do that, you have the chance to test a lot of things out.

I started narrowing it down to what felt most natural and most comfortable to me stylistically (if something feels natural to the author, it will resonate better with an audience. People like authenticity).

Oddly, the more personal the content of the blog became, the more it resonated with people. I think we all inherently latch on to personal stories. We want to read about what people are passionate about. For me, that wasn't exactly travel – but it was travel with my husband. Also, the acquisition and consumption of baked goods.

The big turning point was when I was listed on *Time* magazine's Top 25 Blogs of the Year in 2011. Everything sort of changed overnight. My blog traffic increased 20-fold, and people were actually reading my work. At the time that the article came out, I'd been blogging nearly every weekday for two years. There were a lot of posts out there, and some of them were getting attention.

I was creating content as though I had an audience. And that's one piece of advice I'd give bloggers – persistence is key. Keep writing. Write, even if no one is reading it. Write, even if it feels like you are screaming into the ether. Pretend that you have a dedicated audience, and one day you'll find that you actually do.

I'm going to be brutally honest: it is incredibly difficult to monetize a blog in a way that will make you enough money to live on. You should blog because you enjoy writing. Not because you want to make money. I have a really healthy audience, but I'd have to inundate the site with ads in order to make money.

The writers I know who manage to make a living off of it are constantly taking freelance gigs, snapping photos, doing research, and conducting interviews. But honestly, I feel like that falls into the freelance journalist category, and not blogging. And even after all that, they definitely don't make a huge amount.

The online travel writing community has helped me immeasurably – especially in the early days of my blog, when I was trying to get traffic to my site. I was fortunate enough to write a few guest posts and be interviewed by some reputable sites. I'd say that Twitter is predominantly how I interact with most people I know in the travel world. Honestly, though, they're a lot more hardcore than I am. They're the free-spirited adventurous friend; I'm the nerdy homebody.

I've written about a lot of difficult personal experiences, and the blog has helped me exorcise a lot of demons. I've had readers reach out to me with some of the kindest, most supportive emails anyone could hope to get. And I've met some incredible people, and had some wonderful experiences that couldn't have happened otherwise. It has led to some wonderful professional opportunities – including, of course, the publication of my book, which has been a lifelong goal of mine. It has, without hyperbole, changed my life in incredible ways, and I'm so grateful.

If, like Nomadic Matt (see page 111), you were there early, building an audience and creating a brand, now you're at the top of the search results for 'budget travel'. Because of the way Google search ranking works (we'll cover this in more detail later, see page 134–7), if there are already many popular blogs with the same search terms as yours, it will be very difficult for your blog to be discovered by an audience who may absolutely love it – if only they could find it.

You can respond to this by narrowing your appeal to a more specific audience – you'll appeal to fewer people, but they'll be ones who want to read specifically what you're writing about. Some bloggers narrow their niche further by going sub-niche. For example, you'll now find blogs on luxury family travel, ecologically sustainable budget travel, adventure travel for women.

You might decide to focus on just one region or country, so you're more likely to get results from people searching specifically for (for example) 'budget travel Greece'. Maybe the 'hook' of your blog is its humor. Maybe its super-chic design will appeal to an audience with a high design aesthetic. Maybe it's a particular, idiosyncratic story that you tell through your blog. The important thing is that you've thought about this and you have an idea of the audience you want to attract – so you can write the type of content that will appeal to them.

When you think you've come up with your niche, it's a good idea to brainstorm topics for blog posts – if you can't come up with 20 pretty easily, your niche may be too narrow.

Setting up your blog

Domain name and hosting
One of your first tasks will also be one of your hardest: choosing a name for your blog. Here are some tips that might help:

• Choose something that reflects yourself, your travel style and your blog's philosophy – something brandable and unique.
• Consider trying to include keywords in your name – we'll talk more about keywords later, but basically they're the words that, when typed into search, will direct someone to your site. If you can find the magic

Blogs that hit the mark

With countless travel blogs online and new ones starting up every day, it would be foolhardy to provide a list of our current favorites. If you want a good overview of the most popular or buzzing blogs out there today, sites like Fathom (fathomaway.com), the Huffington Post (www.huffingtonpost.com) and The Expeditioner (www.theexpeditioner.com) publish annual 'best blogs' lists – they're a good place to start.

But here are some examples of successful bloggers who have carved out a very clear niche in the crowded ecosystem of travel blogs.

www.nerdseyeview.com – A portfolio site with a focus on great writing; meet the blogger Pam Mendel on page 138–9

triphackr.com – The focus is squarely on the practical – how to get the best value from your travel dollar

theplanetd.com – Adventure travel with a healthy dose of inspiration and the benefits of traveling as a couple – Dave and Deb's personalities are front and center

www.nomadicmatt.com – One of the first budget travel blogs out there and still going strong; meet Matt on page 111

www.ytravelblog.com – One of the most popular family travel blogs, out there since 2010

www.everywhereist.com – A great example of a blog that uses humor to differentiate; meet blogger Geraldine on page 122–3

mrsoaroundtheworld.com – A well established blog in the luxury space, focusing on personal tips and great photography

expertvagabond.com – Adventure crossed with travel photography, two niches that are made to go together; learn more on page 130–1

name that combines your unique branded self with a keyword, you're almost there.

- Avoid hyphens, numbers and difficult spellings.
- Make sure that no one else owns the name you decide on. It's easy to search for copyrighted and trademarked names; in the USA search copyright.gov and uspto.gov.
- It's also worth checking whether your name is available as a handle on the social media sites you'll want to use: Twitter, Facebook, Instagram, etc. (though it's not the end of the world if you need to use a slightly modified version on these platforms).

There are some domain name generators online that, although the names they suggest will usually be too spammy-sounding for you to use, may send you off in some fruitfully random directions.

Your site will be hosted on a shared server (a large server that hosts many sites). There are hundreds of companies out there offering 'unlimited' deals for low prices – be aware that not all these companies have great reputations. Some of the big, popular names are bluehost, DreamHost, GoDaddy, HostGator and SiteGround. Do some research, read some unbiased reviews (be aware that hosting companies do a ton of affiliate marketing – see page 145), and choose the one that best meets your needs. Expect to pay US$5–10 a month.

As a beginning blogger, shared hosting will be perfectly adequate for your needs; if you hit the jackpot, acquire millions of followers and need more server space you'll need to upgrade.

Blogging platform and set-up

WordPress is the most popular platform for bloggers. It's free to set up, easy to use (once you've mastered the basics), gives you lots of options for tools and design, and there's lots of support available. Depending on which version of WordPress you use, you can have total control over your blog's content and how you monetize it.

WordPress.com vs Wordpress.org

At WordPress.com, you can create a site very easily, which is then hosted on the WordPress server. It's free, but you pay to upgrade different elements of it (for example, Your WordPress.com blog comes with a URL that goes like this: yourtravelblog.wordpress.com – if you want the

Writer's tip: Help is out there

Things can get a bit technical at this stage of the game, but don't worry – there are loads of great resources online to walk you through every step of the way. Most of them work on a 'freemium' model – there's plenty of content that's free to access, and if you want to take it to the next level you can buy a course or ebook to really enhance your skills. To get through the early stages of your blog set-up, you don't need to go any further than clicking on these sites:

ProBlogger.net One of the most respected blogging resources out there. Tons of invaluable free info, and the courses come highly recommended.

smartblogger.com All the free advice you need to get things off the ground, backed up with courses for the more advanced blogger

breakintotravelwriting.com Loads of articles and podcasts on all aspects of travel blogging

For more recommendations on good online resources to help you get your head around blogging, see chapter 7.

URL yourtravelblog.com, you'll need to upgrade). Your choice of designs is restricted, and there are limitations on monetization channels (for example, you can't use affiliate links). You also can't use custom plug-ins, and if you want to get serious with your blog, that's a serious drawback.

At WordPress.org, you download free software to create your blog, over which you have complete control. You organize and pay for your own domain and hosting (although many shared hosting services have deals with WordPress to make this straightforward). The software is open source, meaning there are thousands of developers creating templates, plug-ins and tools to which you have (paid) access. It's a fully-fledged CMS (content management system), which gives you flexibility and control over content, but also means it's more complicated than other solutions.

Your choice here comes down to how serious you are about this business of blogging. If you fall into category 1 or 2 on page 121, WordPress.com is probably going to meet your needs. If you're in category 3, you should start with WordPress.org.

Some other options

There are loads of other options out there and we encourage you to do your research before you make a choice. Be aware that, as you are soon to learn, one of the way bloggers earn money is to recommend things, and blogging platforms and other services spend millions on this type of marketing. Look for unbiased recommendations, speak to other bloggers and make an informed choice; see chapter 7 for our recommended resources.

If you're looking to build a portfolio site, Contently offers a free, simple portfolio platform. Medium, somewhere between platform and publisher, also works well as a portfolio builder, with its own established community giving you an instant audience. The writing interface is very easy to use, and there are no set-up costs; although you're within the Medium ecosystem, you can have your own URL. If you want to dip a toe in the water of writing online, it's a good place to start.

Google's Blogger is also free, easy to use and great for beginners. It's a simple blogging platform, which means your design choices are limited, as are your options for expanding what your blog does – if you get beyond 'beginner' stage, you may find it limiting. On the plus side, you can connect your Blogger account to your Google Adsense and Analytics accounts for seamless tracking – handy if you go pro.

For bloggers with a focus on images or video as well as words, Tumblr is free, with a minimal interface – great if you just want to get in and start blogging. Like Blogger, your options for tailoring the experience are limited – if you want to go further with your blog you may find yourself hobbled.

Squarespace, Weebly and Drupal are more advanced platforms to consider if you think your needs will go beyond the blog into a website with more complex features.

Designing your blog

The good news is that you don't need to know anything about coding to set up a blog. While most serious bloggers will end up getting their hands dirty with HTML at some point, when you're starting out all the hard work will generally by done behind the scenes with whatever platform you choose.

One of the reasons most bloggers build their blogs using WordPress is the huge variety of designs to choose from. This is achieved with the use of 'themes' – ready-made templates that allow you to do a little customization to create a blog that has just the look you want. The big question you'll hit here is: should you choose a free or a premium theme?

There are plenty of free themes built into WordPress, and if you can find one that meets all your needs, it's worth considering using one of them. These 'official' themes go through a screening process and are generally compatible with a lot more plug-ins than premium themes. Be aware, however, that there is generally no dedicated support for them.

Many bloggers recommend using a premium theme. There are hundreds of WordPress theme stores out there, offering thousands of creative designs – you should be able to find something that does exactly what you want. Choosing a premium theme will not only give you more chance of having a blog with a unique look that makes it stand out, but it will also usually be higher quality, have dedicated support, advanced functionality and better security than a free theme. However, themes can be expensive, and make sure you check whether the price is a one-time-only cost, or whether there is a monthly or annual licensing fee as well.

As with everything: do your research, read the experiences and advice of other bloggers (while recognizing that some of them may be paid to make certain recommendations), and keep in mind your blog's purpose and potential profitability when you make your selection. Choose a reputable theme store, read reviews, and go with someone with a track record for excellence and a healthy business.

Writing your blog

Your blog will reflect you. Your passions, interests and ambitions will direct the kinds of things you write about. With this book in your hands, you're already off to a great start – you're a writer, or at least on the way to becoming one. As any blogger will tell you: not all bloggers can actually write!

In chapter 2, you did a set of exercises to help you learn to write a great travel story. While your blog might be an excellent way for you to practice getting words on the page/screen, writing that kind of story

A blogger's view: Matthew Karsten

Matt Karsten packed up his life in 2010, bought a plane ticket to Guatemala for a one-year trip, and never stopped travelling. His blog, expertvagabond.com, is full of fantastic travel tips and advice on how to become a successful travel blogger.

It was during my second year of blogging that I began earning regular income from the site, and by the end of my second year I was earning enough to live on, as long as I lived in budget-friendly places like Southeast Asia or Central America. I've now been doing this for six years, and earn six figures annually.

When I first started, I didn't understand the importance of SEO. Or writing engaging headlines. Or encouraging conversation in the comments section. Or networking with other bloggers. It's been something I've learned with the help of books, tutorials, and websites. I always try to stay up to date on the techniques for increasing the reach of my content and growing my audience. But educating yourself about these topics takes a major time commitment, and it's not always fun.

It's been a constant game of trial and error to figure out what works and what doesn't work. I'm still adjusting the mix even today. In the beginning I'd try anything because I was desperate. These days, I prioritize income streams that are consistent, large, and that don't annoy readers too much. Affiliate income is a favorite part of my strategy. Once your articles receive steady traffic, the income from these links is pretty steady too. It's a long-term strategy that takes time to grow.

So-called 'influencer' marketing projects have become a big source of income too. These are when a nation's tourism board or a large international brand (car company, airline, etc.) invites me to highlight a destination or product through a mixture of blog posts, social media coverage, photography, and maybe video too.

Understanding the business side of blogging, and SEO, is incredibly important if you want to make a living from your blog. You could be the best writer ever, but if someone can't find your article when they type the topic into Google search, they won't be using your affiliate links either.

If you post high-quality content on a consistent basis, your blog's traffic will grow quicker. I think the key is building up a solid foundation of good content. Once you have that base, you don't have to worry as much about posting every week. I try to post two to four articles per month.

It's often the online travel community who is most active in commenting on, linking to, or sharing your content. We exchange tips and ideas with each other, so the whole industry can grow. I regularly attend travel conferences, participate in online forums, and share the content of other travel bloggers on my social media channels. I learn from others in the community all the time.

See what's out there now, and work to produce writing that fills the gaps. Make your writing more entertaining and more useful than what others have done. Focus on quality over quantity. Answer common questions. Figure out how to give readers what they're looking for, and they'll come back for more. Don't underestimate the importance of learning to market yourself and your writing. The writing part is only half the work!

The best thing that's happened to me due to my travel blog is gaining complete freedom and independence over my life. I can work when I want to work, travel when I want to travel, and have an excellent outlet for my creativity. I've invested a lot of time, sweat, and money, with no guarantee of success, but it's work that I absolutely love so I was willing to take the risks. I'm now able to pursue my passions with no restrictions, and share them with the world. A dream come true.

is probably not something you can do every time you want to post a blog. Blog posts are a different kind of writing – more journal-style, less polished, with a different set of rules and conventions.

If you're not already doing it, start reading lots of other blogs. Not just travel blogs, but all kinds of blogs. Think about what works and what doesn't appeal to you. Make a wishlist of the kinds of things you'd like your blog to do, 'borrow' ideas that you can tweak for your own blog, note down the things that inspire you. Just like any kind of writing, the best thing you can do to develop your own skills is to read and absorb what others have written before you.

How often and how long?

The million-dollar questions of blog writing – how often to post, and how long should those posts be? 'How long?' is relatively easy – it's generally accepted that longer posts do better. But what is 'longer'? It depends on what you're trying to achieve. Short posts (300 words) generally get more comments, longer posts (1000–1500 words) get more social media shares, and long posts (2000 words and over) will do better with Google search results.

If you aim for 800–1200 words as a general standard then you're hitting a good middle ground. Of course, the length should always be a function of the story you're telling or the message you're trying to get across.

Similarly, how often you post will depend on what you want to say and what you're trying to achieve with your blog. In the early days, if you want to grow your traffic quickly, you might want to post more often to build up a core of content to attract search results and readers. Most successful bloggers say that in the long run, two to three times a week is optimum, that once a week can be perfectly fine if your posts are longer and useful, and that every day is too much (unless, of course, your blog is called dailytravelupdates.com). Once you've established a routine, keep it consistent – both readers and search engines respond well to regular, fresh content.

Your blog's content

Only you can decide what you want to blog about – what you want to share with the world. Some travel blogs are amusing, some are full of useful information, some are inspirational. The best are a mixture of all three. What matters is consistently creating posts that are engaging, informative, and unique enough to build an audience and keep them coming back.

How to write killer headlines

It's sad but statistically true that 80 per cent of people will read your headline, and only 20 per cent will read the whole post. That headline is your one chance to grab attention and keep people reading. Click-bait headlines have become an internet cliché – be aware of how you're pitching your blog, who your audience is and how your headline style portrays your blog's personality. Keep it real.

Having said that, there is a tried-and-tested formula for an effective blog post headline that will help you construct effective headlines:

- Use a number, preferably an odd one, and not too big.
- Or, use a trigger word like what, why, how or when.
- Use an interesting or attention-grabbing adjectives.
- Include at least one keyword.
- Make a promise to your reader – what will they gain by reading this article?

Using this formula, you might for instance come up with '9 unexpected ways to earn money when you travel' or 'How you can effortlessly earn money while travelling'.

Calls to action

Every copywriter knows that the 'call to action' is a vital piece of any online content. It's an expression of what you want the reader to do next, as a result of reading your post. Do you want them to leave a comment below the article? Do you want them to sign up for your newsletter? Or perhaps you want to lead them to another post that they might be interested in?

You must be clear in your own mind what the call to action is (there should only be one per post), express it clearly and simply, and make it achievable. If appropriate – say, if you're promoting an affiliate product – you might want to offer an incentive. Many bloggers use ebook giveaways as an incentive for newsletter sign-up – it's a great way to help build an email list, and you can often create the ebook easily by repackaging useful content you've already created for your blog.

Non-travel travel writing

Whatever your niche and your travel schedule, you may find it difficult to write about an on-the-ground travel experience each time you blog, even if you have a good backlog of material. There will be times when you're at home between trips, and weeks where you're staying still, recharging. How to keep your blog's content fresh when you're not traveling?

Many travel bloggers get around this problem by having a good supply of non-travel subjects to blog about. These are posts that will be of interest to your travel-loving audience even if they aren't directly connected to a travel experience. Lists of great films to watch or books to read, 'how-to' guides, trends connected to travel – think about your niche and brainstorm the kinds of things you could blog about, without leaving home. The more of this kind of writing your niche allows, the easier it will be for you to keep a consistent, regular posting schedule.

As your blog matures, you'll also benefit from having 'evergreen' content that that can be enhanced and improved, brought up to date, and re-posted. That means that you won't have to write something brand new from scratch every time you post.

Understanding SEO

Over two million blog posts are published each day – and counting. If you want your blog to spread beyond your inner circle of friends and family, thinking a little about search engine optimization, or SEO, is step number one.

SEO is the science/art of increasing the number of people who come to your website as a result of typing words into a search field (through organic, rather than paid, results). Because Google virtually own the market for search (over 90 percent of organic search results came through them at the time of writing), most SEO is focused squarely on them.

The good news is, if your site is regularly updated, if you understand your audience and write clear, useful and informative content that's targeted to their needs, you're already doing a lot of SEO, naturally.

SEO is a book unto itself, or rather, 1001 ebooks, all available online for free when you sign up to 1001 'how to blog' newsletter lists. It's a big, complex and ever-changing subject. Here we'll give you a brief overview of two of the key elements to think about: keywords and links. When you're ready to go deeper, online markers Moz publish a fantastically comprehensive beginners' guide to SEO on their website at moz.com. (Plus, see chapter 7 for more of our favorite online experts.)

Writer's tip: Nine blog-writing tips you can't ignore

When you're writing your blog (or indeed anything online), think of your reader, sitting at their computer/tablet/phone, with the pressure of literally millions of other things they could be reading instead pressing down on them at every moment. You need to grab, and keep, their attention. How do you stop them from clicking away?

• Plan your post so it has a point, is well structured and builds toward a conclusion.

• Hook them with the first sentence – pose a question they have to answer 'yes' to, ask an intriguing question, say something unexpected, make a bold claim or promise – find a way to grab your reader's attention.

• Keep your style conversational – sound like someone they're sitting down having a coffee with.

• Write for scanners – short sharp paragraphs, broken up with headings and short sentences.

• Lists are easily digestible at a glance – there's a reason they're everywhere online. Can you structure your post as a list?

• Make your post unique – it's hard to find new subjects, but you can always find a new angle.

• Photos are vital – at least one for each blog, ideally your own, and ideally stunning.

• Be you. Relatability, sincerity and authenticity are the gold dust of blogs. Find your authentic voice – it might take a while, but your audience will respond.

• Don't be afraid to try things out – play, experiment, and learn from the results.

Writer's tip: White hat vs black hat SEO

Not all SEO is created equal. What's known as 'black hat SEO' uses deceptive tactics to attempt to trick the algorithms into a better ranking: keyword stuffing (overusing keywords) or using invisible text to include lists of keywords that only the spiders will see, posting the same content in numerous places to increase keyword count, and 'link farming' – trading links with other black hat websites.

'White hat SEO' strategies revolve around creating clear, well written content of high relevance, building a genuinely engaged community and promoting your website to relevant people in a personal way. Bloggers who know their audience well and are using site metrics to closely target their content are white hat SEO naturals.

How search works

At the moment of writing, Google was performing 40,000 searches per second. By now, that has already increased. The algorithms Google uses to search and rank the web's 60 trillion (also growing by the day) pages are constantly upgraded and changed. The latest SEO best practice has to keep up with Google's famously secretive engineers as they continuously tweak their formulas. The SEO landscape is constantly changing, and if you're serious about blogging you need to keep up to date with the latest thinking.

In a nutshell, Google uses 'spiders' to navigate the web by crawling from link to link. The pages it finds are sorted by their content and other factors, and organized into Google's index. For each search, Google uses algorithms to decide which pages in its index are relevant to the search, and rank them, using over 200 factors, some of the most important being:

• How many times does the page contain the search keywords?

- Do the words appear in the title? The URL? Directly adjacent?
- Does the page include synonyms for those words?
- What is the page's PageRank? The PageRank algorithm counts the number and quality of links to a page to determine how important the website is, on the basis that more important websites are likely to receive more links from other websites.

These formulas produce each page's overall score, which determines where it will rank in the search results. When you figure that the first five results get around 70 percent of the clicks, you start to see why SEO is the holy grail of online success. SEO pros joke: Where's the best place to hide a dead body? On the second page of Google's search results. If you're not on that first page, you might as well not exist.

Using keywords

Now that you know how important keywords are to getting good search results, what's the next step? Discovering what keywords you should focus on to make sure your audience finds you. Keyword research is vital if you want to optimize your content for SEO.

You can do this in a few basic steps, and you should do it before you start blogging, if you want your blog to go places. It might be time-consuming, but will help you immensely down the track as you plan your content strategy, build an editorial calendar and think about monetizing your blog.

1. List the 5–10 broad topics you blog about most frequently and that you want to build an audience around.

2. Underneath those topics, brainstorm the specific keywords and keyword phrases that you think your audience will be searching for.

3. Google your keywords and see what related search terms are suggested at the bottom of the page – should these be incorporated into your list?

4. Make sure you have a good mix of 'head' keywords (popular keywords with high search volume) and 'long-tail' keywords (longer, more specific phrases). While more people search head keywords, long-tail searches will deliver well-targeted clicks – readers who want exactly what you're serving up. It will be hard to rank for 'travel', but the targeted traffic you'll get from 'budget travel in Greece with children' will generally be more valuable.

A blogger's view: Pam Mandel

Pam Mandel is a travel writer whose work has been published in AFAR, *the* San Francisco Chronicle, Condé Nast Traveler, Lonely Planet *and many other places. She started blogging in 1997. Find her at www.nerdseyeview.com.*

I didn't start my blog as a portfolio site, but now, it's very much a portfolio site and a place to work out ideas. It does bring me writing gigs, I've been hired more than once by folks who said, 'I love your blog and your style'. That's the best.

I've been blogging for nearly 20 years (!!!) and many things came to me simply because I existed as a blogger. Now that everyone's got a blog many of those offers have dried up. I'm opinionated, and most brands like a blogger who will reflect their message; I'm a risk. So the things that came to me when I started, like all that coveted 'free travel', has diminished considerably over time.

I blog when I feel like it. This runs counter to so much advice you'll see, but if I don't feel like posting, I don't. I've posted once a month, I've posted five times a week, it just depends. I can tell when a blogger is phoning it in to keep a site on life support, but that's how you lose readers. As for keeping it fresh, well, writing when you've genuinely got something to say does that by default.

Well-researched, fact-checked, insightful work is not common, and hiring editors will notice that you've bothered. So many blogs fall back on the 'what I did on my summer vacation/funded junket' model, and they provide zero practical information or insight. How much does this cost? How do you get around? Why are things this way?

We love it when we come across a great travel storyteller, someone who takes us with them on the journey, does more than make us wish we were there. Pick a well-known travel blogger at random, read the post, and ask yourself, 'Who is this post written for? What does this post do? Did I learn something useful or feel anything but FOMO?' Writers who help us experience a place from our screen have our loyalty. And we love it when we get great, actionable advice, things that help us save money or have an exceptional experience. Great travel writing benefits the reader in some way.

I went to Antarctica to blog for a tour operator, I got to interview (and play music) with Chris Hadfield, the Canadian astronaut and social media phenomenon, I've been invited to teach and speak, a tourism board hired me to write their website for them. And that's before we hit the social benefits – I have made so many wonderful friends around the world simply because we read each other's stuff.

Because I've been blogging for so long, I really do know who reads my blog. Marilyn, who used to live in the British Virgin Islands, then California, and now, Montana. Sal, who was once an expat in Spain, and now lives in Chicago. Doug, an author of two travel books. I can do this all day. My readers aren't a mass, they're people with names.

I still think back to that time – it must be 15 years ago now – I got on a plane and flew to Antwerp to spend a weekend with Di (an expat from New Zealand) and her Belgian husband Gert. It's the first time I packed up to spend time with a complete stranger. I've done this dozens of times since, gone to spend time with 'strangers from the internet' and every time, it's been a complete delight. I cannot overstate the value of being able to make meaningful connections with people all over the world. That's why we travel, right?

5. See how your competitors are ranking for these keywords, either by Googling incognito or using a tool like SEMrush.

There are lots of tools out there to help you, depending on how deeply you want to get into it and how much you're prepared to outlay. Google's AdWords Keyword Planner tool is a common starting point, suggesting keywords and providing estimated search volume, as well as predicting the cost of running paid campaigns for these terms. Moz have a custom-built Keyword Explorer that helps improve keyword discovery and prioritization – it cuts out a lot of manual work and it's free to try, so worth giving a go.

Link building

To decide how your page ranks, search engines are not only looking at its content, but the links pointing to it – both the number of external websites linking to it, and the quality of those sites. When a link points to a page, it's passing some of its authority, or 'link juice' to that page. So, the more high-quality websites that link to you, the more likely you are to rank well in search results.

Link building is the process of acquiring new links to your site from external sites. It involves a mixture of marketing the content you've created to the online world, and building relationships with other bloggers and webmasters.

It's worth mentioning that there are links and links. Building low-quality links will not improve your ranking, and worse, can aggressively harm it as Google continually tweaks its algorithms against these kinds of black-hat tactics. Avoid links from sites that Google considers to be engaging in link schemes – these might be 'link farms' (sites that engage heavily in reciprocal linking), sites that contain a lot of spam comments or that are in a very spammy niche such as gambling.

The best kinds of links are natural links – links you don't actively pursue, but are freely given when someone finds a piece of your content that they like so much they want to link to it. Of course, the best way to get these links is to concentrate on the quality of your content, but you can take it a step further by experimenting with 'linkable assets' – pieces of content created for the purpose of attracting links. This might be something like an infographic, a how-to guide, a video or image gallery.

These types of content can be easier to market and create excitement about when you carry out an outreach campaign – the way you're likely to obtain most of your links. This is getting in touch with other bloggers and website owners and simply asking them if they will link to your content. It's similar to the rules of pitching a travel article – you should be clear about why each of them would be interested in your content, and be able to demonstrate that you understand their website and their audience. When you contact them, it's important that you tell them why they should care about you and your content, show that you're genuine and not a spammer, and tell them what action you'd like them to take. Use their name, refer to something specific about their content and show how your content appeals to their audience. And remember – these are relationships you want to build and foster, not one-off communications.

Social sharing

The effect of social signals like Facebook likes and Twitter follows on search rankings is one of the hottest topics in SEO-land. Google have said (as of the time of writing) that these signals, although they can be seen to indicate authority and influence, do not affect search rankings.

That's not to say that they're not important. Just because Google says

Writer's tip: Using keywords well

If you're writing appealing, useful content that's mindful of keywords and above all seeks to address the needs of your audience, you're improving your chances of ranking well. But here are a couple of extra tricks to make sure you're not missing any opportunities to make search work for you:

• Try to make sure that you include keywords in your blog headlines.
• Optimize your URLs so they're search-friendly: www.crazybudgettravel.com/budget-greece/athens-on-ten-dollars-a-day is better than www.crazybudgettravel.com/77329/s507.htm.
• Include ALT tags for images – good for accessibility as well as an opportunity to emphasize keywords.
• Caption your images with relevant keywords.

A blogger's view: Tim Leffel

Tim Leffel is an award-winning travel writer and entrepreneur – founder and editor of online travel magazine Perceptive Travel *(www.perceptivetravel. com) and publisher of www.cheapestdestinationsblog.com (since 2003), travelwriting2.com (since 2010) and www.hotel-scoop.com (since 2012). His books include* Travel Writing 2.0: Earning Money From Your Travels in the New Media Landscape.

I started before the internet came along, as a travel writer doing articles for print and trade publications. I launched a blog the same year WordPress started, in 2003. Through the years after that I started new projects, wrote other books, and kept freelancing. I strongly believe the best way to be anti-fragile and make consistent money at this pursuit is to have multiple streams of income, so I've always tried to keep moving and growing as a writer and publisher.

Bloggers now need to narrowly define who their audience is and what they can offer that's not being done by 100 or 1000 other people. Starting a blog that just says, 'Look at me, I'm traveling around the world!' might have worked six or eight years ago, but that's an incredibly tough slog now.

Focus! If you're trying to please everyone and write about everywhere, you'll never stand out. The internet is a long-tail medium, so don't be a generalist. Pick a corner of the travel world that you can own and everything will be much easier.

Then it's a matter of reaching the target audience, building on it, and growing by earning attention. There's no magic formula for that or some secret short cut. It's really a matter of writing good, unique material and then grinding it out week after week on the promotion side of things. (But without turning readers off in the process.)

The number of travel blogs keeps going up, but the number that are making money keeps going up too. I surveyed a lot of bloggers for both editions of my book and there are far more now earning $100K per year than there were in 2010. There are also a lot more making enough to fund their travels or to kick back in Goa or Chiang Mai for six months. I have no idea what the ratio is and many bloggers are just hobbyists.

It takes a year or two for most bloggers to get to the point where their earnings are more than the night's bar tab on a consistent basis. So they shouldn't quit their job and blog around the world unless they've got at least a year's worth of travel money saved up. It's a slow process even if you do everything perfectly right and get lucky on top.

I'm at the point now where I'm making a comfortable six-figure living, but I do pay out a lot to freelancers and assistants so I certainly don't feel loaded. I worked part-time for more than 10 years, and eventually when the earnings reached the point where I could take the leap, I struck out on my own and haven't looked back.

Probably half my income is direct advertising deals on my blogs and websites, next is book royalties and courses, after that a zillion other things, including freelancing.

I have a very clearly defined audience for all my sites. Perceptive Travel is the loosest – adventurous, but educated and literary. I go from budget (Cheapest Destinations Blog) to upscale (Luxury Latin America) on other sites and create content for that audience in each case. I do surveys regularly and have Quantcast on a few of my sites to make sure I'm doing this right.

I've traveled to dozens of countries on someone else's tab and I get to travel for a living, writing and posting photos about interesting places and people. It's been a very long time since I've dreaded a Monday...

that these signals don't currently impact search rankings doesn't mean they never will – social is not going away as a vital force online and search engines like Google constantly review how they work to ensure that quality content is recognized.

Social sharing brings traffic to a page and directly increases its visibility. More people visiting your content makes it more likely that it will be noticed and linked to by another blogger, journalist, or author, earning you more precious link juice. So even if there is not a direct link between social shares and ranking, the indirect benefit of getting your content out there in front of more sets of eyes increases its likelihood of ranking.

Besides, your activity on social networks is vital in building and fostering your audience. Your social profiles give you the opportunity to have conversations, to promote new content and to learn about who is reading your blog and what they think of it. They bring your blog to life and make the experience of getting to know your 'brand' more fun, engaging and personal. The web is fundamentally a social place, all about building relationships, expressing identity and sharing ideas.

Monetizing your blog

A recent ProBlogger survey found that of 1500 bloggers trying to make money from their blog, 63 percent made less than $3.50 per day. Thirteen percent made between $1000 and $10,000 per month. There is money out there, but it's not easy to get.

There is no one way to make money from blogging, and in fact most bloggers who do it successfully have a number of different simultaneous income streams – read the insights from bloggers featured in this chapter to find out how they have made it work. The key is finding the mix that works for you, through experimentation and measuring the success of what you try. The bloggers we spoke to all agree – it takes time, and it takes a lot of work. We'll cover a few of the different options here, but the possibilities are endless, limited only by your imagination and entrepreneurial drive. Spend time looking at other travel blogs and see what strategies other bloggers are making work for them.

Advertising
Many bloggers start here. Ad networks like Google AdSense act as a middleman, making it easy to run ads on your blog without needing to sell

advertising space. You'll need to have decent traffic coming to your site to start making money, but as your traffic and brand grows, advertisers will be willing to pay to get exposure to your audience.

Affiliate marketing

Affiliate promotions – when you link to a product for sale on another site and earn a commission on any sales that are made as result of that click – are the most common way for bloggers to earn money. There are many affiliate programs out there and you may need to try a few to see what works for you. Many bloggers start with one of the big ones, Google AdSense or Amazon.

While the commission on sales with a program like Amazon's Affiliate Program is small (4–8 per cent), there are also benefits – it's a trusted brand that many of your readers will already have an account with, and it offers a huge array of products that you can end up earning commission on (you earn a commission on whatever the person buys when they click through from your link, even if it's not what you sent them there for).

Writer's tip: Embrace self promotion

While link building is a key reason to reach out to other bloggers and influencers, it's not the only benefit. Promoting your blog's content also means you'll get more social shares, more loyal fans and email subscribers, more invites to interviews and opportunities for guest posts. Most successful bloggers say that they spend as much time – if not more – promoting their content as they do creating it.

As well as blogger outreach and social sharing, here are some other avenues for promoting your content:

• Think about how you can promote new content on your own site, including as 'related reading' links in already popular posts.

• Promote new content in your email newsletter (though it might seem old-school, most bloggers consider email a hugely important element of their audience engagement).

• You can buy highly targeted and inexpensive traffic to get more eyeballs on your content using the likes of Outbrain or StumbleUpon.

A blogger's view: Matthew Kepnes

Matt Kepnes started his budget travel blog (www.nomadicmatt.com) in 2008. Since then it has become one of world's most popular travel blogs. He has a range of budget travel ebooks, a New York Times *bestselling book,* How to Travel the World on $50 a Day, *and runs courses on blogging at superstarblogging.nomadicmatt.com.*

In April 2008 I'd just come home from 18 months on the road and I didn't want to go back to an office job. I wanted to become a Lonely Planet writer. I started the blog as an online résumé where I could showcase the writing I'd done and get better at it. I had no idea how to break into the industry and didn't know where to start, so I started with the shitty online publications that would pay $20 for an article, but at least someone would look over my writing, I'd get some edits and step my way up the ladder. I ended up writing my own guidebook. In a way I became my own little Lonely Planet.

There weren't a lot of travel blogs back then. I had the benefit of being one of the first. By 2010 there were tons and tons of them – since then many have gone the way of the dinosaur. I think I was always a bit more business-oriented than some of the other travel bloggers. I really focused on guest blogging and getting featured on other websites, and I think that gave me an edge.

It's such a competitive field now, that being business-orientated and self-promoting is key to the success of being a travel writer. There's such a low barrier to entry. It's important to pound your chest and toot your own horn a little bit. It's the only way you're going to get heard.

There's good money from all the sponsored content, link content, and brand deals that some travel bloggers do. I'm a believer in traditional travel writing – helping people get from A to B. When you become a mouthpiece for brands you lose that. Most travel writers start blogging for the love of travel, but after a while they realize they need to make money, and they end up selling their audience as a commodity.

If you're going to build a website that provides an income, you need to think of it like a business where you provide something to your customers. When I was doing product reviews, it felt like a betrayal of trust with my readership. And it's time intensive, so I could only make as much money as there were hours in the day. But selling books and courses – though there's a lot of work up front, it becomes passive income. The growth potential is unlimited.

If you want to be a freelance writer, having an online property can get you freelance jobs but it can also earn you income. It's not mutually exclusive – you don't have to be either one or the other. I know bloggers who earn 80 percent of their income from freelance travel writing. I don't really like freelance travel writing, I like doing my website. People come up with the mix that works for them.

Email is the lifeblood of my blog. You should always have an email list. Facebook can bury your posts, the lifecycle of a Tweet is 3 seconds... Even if you don't read an email when it hits your inbox, it's there. It can't be avoided, it can't be missed. You can make hard sales pitches and announce products in a more detailed way than on social media.

Learn to write well – the barrier to entry is so low that everybody has a blog, but not everyone has a quality blog. Never stop trying to be a better writer. Most bloggers never even start trying to be a better writer.

Writer's tip:
Social media management

Even successful bloggers admit that getting the balance right on social media can be difficult and that it requires a major time investment. When you're starting out, the places you really need to be are Twitter, Facebook and Instagram – use them to publicize each new post. As you build your blog and your presence, you can start to explore Google+, Pinterest, StumbleUpon and Snapchat; YouTube if you go down the video path. Focus on the platforms that you really enjoy and build as you go.

Remember: it's called social media. It's a conversation. The bloggers who stand out are the ones who actively seek out other bloggers' articles of interest, comment on them and share them. After all, that's what you want other bloggers to do with your posts. You need to be present on the platforms, actively responding to comments, engaging people and interacting.

Keep your content on social platforms consistent with the overall feel and theme of your blog, don't over-post or you'll start to annoy people, and use hashtags wisely. Follow people who do it well, and learn from them.

The key thing to bear in mind is that the value you have built in your blog is the trust your audience has in you. Make sure you only promote quality products that you truly believe in and that have relevance to your audience, or you can harm that trust – and destroy your blog's value.

Selling services

The travel space is full of potential for selling services. There are travel bloggers out there offering tours, personal travel advice, travel writing workshops – you name it. The limitation on this type of monetization is your time – not only to organize, but to physically be present for the activity. Think of the opportunity cost – it's time you can't spend creating or promoting content, which may end up being the more profitable activity, depending on your mix of strategies.

Selling products

For bloggers who have created a strong brand and an engaged following, selling products can become their major source of income. Ebooks and courses are popular products to sell, and some bloggers also sell merchandise like T-shirts, prints and tote bags. Guidebook products are popular among travel bloggers and for some, these can be a good source of include (see Nomadic Matt's story, pages 146–7). A big plus with this type of monetization is that it becomes a passive income stream, a source of earnings that you don't have to keep working at after the initial effort (which can be considerable).

It's also worth mentioning that there may be opportunities to repurpose content that you have already created for your blog as a paid product. Collecting together, repackaging and perhaps adding some new content to all your posts on, say, budget travel, or on Greece, you could create a 'Budget Travel Handbook' or a travel guide to Greece.

5

Life on

the road

Travel writing: the glamorous life?

There you are on the African savannah, notebook in hand, camera around your neck, bouncing through the bush in hot pursuit of the king of beasts. Later on you'll be sitting around the campfire recounting the day's exploits while sampling the local beer.

Sounds wonderful, doesn't it? But to get there, you had to fly for a day and a half, squeezed into an economy-class seat between an apprentice sumo wrestler and a man whose personal beliefs forbid bathing. You spent a skin-slapping night on a flea-infested mattress, then had your bones rearranged on a bus bounding over a potholed highway. Your stomach hadn't adjusted well to all the time and temperature changes, so you subsisted on bottled water and cookies.

And now, while others snore blissfully away, you sit in your tent scribbling into your notebook by lamplight, having cursed the flat battery in your laptop. The following afternoon, while others nap, you interview the driver and the cook. And on the day when everyone sleeps in after the late-night bush trek, you get up before sunrise to photograph the tawny dawn light.

Now, is that glamour tarnishing just a bit?

The realities of travel writing

While travel writing certainly has the reputation of being an alluring profession, 95 per cent of the job involves a lot of hard work. It's gathering minute details on hotels, bus timetables, restaurants and walking tours. It's researching which god did what, which ruler took over from whom and when, and what is signified by the curious ceremony that's performed every third Friday in May. It's waiting for planes and trains, buses and ferries, tuk-tuks and trishaws. It's swatting mosquitoes and squatting over hole-in-the-floor toilets.

It's eating alone night after night, while whispering couples glance your way with pity. It's enviously eyeing the people languorously sunning themselves on the beach and realizing that you've got six more beaches to check out before lunch.

Being a travel writer can be lonely, exhausting and depressing. You're always on the lookout for a useful anecdote or scoping an angle. You can't ever let up, because you're always working. And that's just the traveling part. After the trip you have to sell your piece – and that can be a time-consuming and energy-draining process. Even if your work has been commissioned beforehand, you have to be patient until the editor finds time to read it, and you may have to rewrite your article substantially after they've done so.

Of course there are moments when it all seems worth it, and the rewards are many. But let us give you an honest, no-holds-barred picture of the challenges you might face, as well as some advice on how to make it all work for you.

Surviving burnout

Burnout is a major factor in the travel writer's life. You grow tired of grueling travel schedules; of airports, train stations and bus depots; of late departures and late arrivals; of packing and unpacking; of trying to drum up the enthusiasm to explore some new uncomfortable corner of the world; of juggling home life and road life. You have to strive constantly to balance fickle earnings with fixed expenses in order to pay your bills and maintain ongoing accounts. You have to set aside money for unexpected expenses and, in the USA, take care of your own health care. Both personally and practically, it can feel like you're always playing catch-up.

It's important to heed the warning signals, and to structure your life accordingly. One antidote is to take a purely pleasure trip at least once a year. If you find yourself burning out in the middle of a trip, try to turn off your mental note-taking machine for a morning and just wander at will, for pleasure, or laze on the beach. Most successful travel writers ground themselves by building in a certain number of months at home between trips; they catch up on relationships and bills, write the pieces they've researched, and recharge their batteries.

Dealing with rejection

Rejection is part of the freelancer's life. To survive, you need to adopt a certain Zen attitude, and accept that your stories or proposals will often be rejected. Above all, don't be derailed by the notion that a rejection is somehow personal, a fundamental rejection of you as a writer or, worse, as a human being. Editors are inundated with stories, the vast majority of which they cannot use; they choose the very few that happen to fit into the particular edition they are currently working on. Becoming a published writer is a job, and you have to approach it with a certain steely professionalism. Prepare your work by following the tips in this book, and persevere by continuing to write and submit your proposals and stories.

If you ever do find yourself sinking into the slough of depression, remember that virtually every writer, even the most legendary, has been rejected at some point in their professional life. For example, when he was starting out as a writer, the National Book Award-winning US writer John McPhee submitted dozens of story ideas to the *New Yorker*; each one was rejected. He persevered until they finally accepted one. A few years later he was a staff writer for that renowned magazine – one of the most coveted writing jobs in the USA. Rejection is simply part of the process.

Writer's tip:
Celebrated rejections

If serial rejections start getting you down, ponder some of history's more famous bebuffs and take solace from the thought of how foolish these editors felt with the benefit of hindsight…

• Agatha Christie suffered five full years of rejection before landing a publishing deal, then went on to become history's second-biggest selling author (after William Shakespeare).
• Margaret Mitchell's *Gone with the Wind* was rejected 38 times.
• A particularly nasty editor rejected Zane Grey thus: 'You have no business being a writer and should give up.' His Westerns went on to sell over 250 million copies.
• The first Harry Potter novel was rejected 12 times before finally being published, leading JK Rowling to billionaire status.
• 'I recommend that it be buried under a stone for a thousand years,' went one of the many rejections of *Lolita*. Vladimir Nabokov persevered and the book became a classic with sales of 50 million.
For more encouragement, visit www.litrejections.com, where you can submit your own stories of woe and share the pain.

In the UK, many newspapers and magazines don't have the time or staff to send you a rejection note and so you're often left in limbo, not knowing what to do next with your unsolicited submission or proposal. To avoid this situation, it's a good idea to send a covering letter with your article or proposal saying that if you haven't received a response within one month for newspapers, or two to three months for magazines, you intend to submit it elsewhere. If you haven't heard from the publication after this amount of time, write a courtesy letter or email telling them that you will now be submitting your story or proposal to other outlets.

In the USA, rejection notes, whether from newspapers or magazines, usually come in the form of either a form rejection or a personal rejection. A form rejection is a preprinted note or templated email, thanking you for your proposal, but letting you know that it can't be used. While this method may seem very cold and impersonal, it's just a practicality for most editors. Much as they might want to add a personal note, they simply don't have the time.

A personal rejection is a printed or hand-written note, clearly addressed personally to you. The editor may write that, while they cannot use your submission, you should feel free to send in other articles, or that they liked your article but just published a piece on the same subject. Consider this to be a major victory, and follow up immediately with another submission or proposal, thanking the editor in your cover letter for the encouraging note they just sent you. If the editor opens the door a crack in this way, you need to keep pushing and open it further. Rejections can and do lead to acceptances. You just have to keep knocking – politely but persistently – on the door.

Form rejection letters are often used by book publishers, but if an editor does include any comments, you should review them carefully. Don't bury your manuscript away after the first rejection. Bear in mind that most of literature's greatest success stories were rejected by at least one publisher – and sometimes dozens – before making it into print.

Overcoming writer's block

Sometimes I get up in the morning and just can't think of anything to write, or what I do write comes out all wrong. In my early writing days when this happened, I would while away an hour staring into the void – or clean the refrigerator for the 10th time or check yet again to see if the mail had come – but over the years I've found two techniques that help get the words flowing. The first is to write about my writer's block:

'Today, for some reason, I just can't get started writing. I'm not sure why. I wonder if it's because of the pizza I ate last night, or maybe it's just because I don't know how to get where I know I need to be in my story today. The problem is bringing that village back to life. Here's what I

Writer's tip: Digital earnings

While the internet makes a career as a travel writer more viable – more and more people work as freelancers, liberated by technology from needing to report in at an office every day – the rewards are slim if you restrict your publication efforts to online publications. Overall, online writing rates overall are far lower than the rates commanded by print, and that's when they pay at all – many websites don't offer any compensation to writers at all.

It's standard practice for websites to pay a flat rate for an article rather than a per-word rate. Matador (matadornetwork.com), for example, pay $40 per story, Bootsnall (www.bootsnall.com) pay $50, The Expeditioner (www.theexpeditioner.com) pay $30. Given that websites are generally looking for first-personal travel narratives, of the type you need to put in significant time (and expense) both to research and to write, it's difficult to see how the return on investment can work.

While there are a few exceptions to this rather depressing rule (see pages 208–11 for a list of online opportunities), working purely for online publishers is very unlikely to provide anything more than the most meager income stream. But you might consider submitting your work to publications like this, if, for example, you want to build an online portfolio to help you pitch for print work, or simply to get some practice in writing for publication. It can also be useful if you're a budding internet entrepreneur, looking to grow traffic and build an audience for your own blog. If you're successful, you could join the growing ranks of travel bloggers who are making a decent living from their work.

remember…' Suddenly, I've forgotten about my writer's block and started writing my piece again.

The second technique follows the model that John Steinbeck used when he wrote *East of Eden*. He kept a notebook. In the left-hand pages of the notebook he wrote a daily diary – this was his way of warming up his writing engine. In the right-hand pages of the same book he wrote the novel itself. I have adapted a version of this. If I simply can't get going on my story, I start writing about whatever comes to mind – the Yosemite hike we did over the weekend, the Borges story I read the night before, the glistening cheesecake in the refrigerator, the Polynesian beach I wish I were lying on… I just start writing about whatever is occupying my mind, and somehow this unlocks me and liberates my imagination to get back into the story again.

Making money as a travel writer

If all the people on the planet who make a living solely from their travel writing (excluding travel guidebook writers) were brought together in one room, the room would not be crowded. Most of the guests at this globe-girdling gathering would write books for a living, and their income would be a mix of advance payments for their new books and royalties from their old ones, supplemented by a few travel magazine or newspaper pieces a year. There would be a decent handful who run a successful, profitable travel blog (although they'd have to admit they spend a relatively small proportion of their time actually writing, in among all the other promotional and entrepreneurial tasks it takes to keep a blog up and running). Only a very few would make a living exclusively from writing articles for magazines, newspapers and websites – there simply isn't enough work to go around, and it just isn't well paid enough.

In today's publishing world, many travel writers outlay their own time and money up front without any guarantee that they'll ever see any money. Even if and when their article is finally published, if they were to calculate the hours that went into the travel, research and writing of the piece, they'd need a microscope to see their hourly wage.

Another factor to consider is the lack of any freelancers' retirement fund that will squirrel money away for you and dole it out after you've stopped wandering and scribbling. You have to do that yourself. Many

A writer's view: Daisann MacLane

Daisann McLane wrote the 'Frugal Traveler' column for the New York Times *travel section for six years, and the 'Real Travel' column for* National Geographic Traveler *magazine for 11 years. She currently lives in Hong Kong where she founded and runs a food and cultural walk company, www.littleadventuresinhongkong.com*

Be prepared to cut yourself loose and go on adventures. Go to places you adore, and immerse yourself in the people and their culture. Be open and humble. If someone invites you to come home with them and sleep on their floor, go. Put yourself in vulnerable situations and then come back home (or stay out there) and write marvelous stories. Do it because you love it, not because you see it as a way to make a fortune or be famous. Do it because you want to look back in 30 or 40 years on an amazing life lived.

Learn another language. Two would be even better! Learning a foreign language is the best way to break through the wall between you and the place you are writing about. There's a quantum difference between a piece that is written by a writer fluent in the language and culture, and a piece written by someone who's just dropped in.

Living abroad for a spell is another great way of stretching your imagination, and acquiring a different point of view that will set you apart from the rest of the would-be travel writers pitching stories. Studying and becoming expert at something that is identified or connected with another culture or place — say, for example, martial arts, or yoga, or French cooking — will give you an insider's edge for an article about India, China or France.

Over 20 years of writing, I've had four, maybe five editors who really clicked with me and understood and supported my writing. The editor makes all the difference in this work. When you find a good one, keep them in your life by any means possible. Remember their birthdays. Send chocolates from Belgium, silks from Vietnam. Offer them the name of your favorite massage therapist in Thailand.

There's no security in this career, and that can be really scary. On the other hand, when you travel to so many different places, and you see how people live outside of your little bubble, you realize how ridiculous the very idea of security is, from a global perspective. Empires come and go, personal fortunes rise and fall, the river waters flood and recede, and people somehow keep going. When I catch myself freaking out about my lack of a retirement plan, I slap myself back with a reality check: most people in the world don't have anything to catch them if they fall except their will and their determination to press on.

There are very few places left on earth nowadays that are truly inaccessible, and globalization has been so thorough and pervasive that the contrast between tradition and modernity has become almost a given. Now every traveler expects to attend video nights in Kathmandu. What's more, in response to escalating numbers of tourists and the pressures of economic development, travel destinations themselves are becoming more and more faux (for example, in China, they tear down their traditional neighborhoods and move the vendors to new, Disney-like 'Old Streets').

It's going to be very interesting to see where the next generation of travel writers will find its subject in a world where, increasingly, all the urban centers are beginning to match each other – starchitect for starchitect – and where everything once marvelous has turned to faux. Here's a thought: as economies shrink, oil diminishes, and travel becomes more costly and difficult, we travel writers may end up back in our 19th-century role as the eyes and ears of the armchair wanderer.

travel writers in their fifties and sixties are only thinking about this now, and realizing that they should have started saving for this phase of life decades ago.

It's also worth saying that what was always a challenging way to make a living has become significantly more so in recent years. Money has flooded out of a travel writer's traditional markets – newspapers and magazines – towards the internet. And while that has opened up many more opportunities to get published, those opportunities are almost always very poorly paid (unless, of course, you start your own online business and make it work).

After hearing this strong dose of reality, how is your resolve to become a travel writer faring? It's harsh, but it's important that you're realistic about the amount of money you can earn if you take this path. And if you're still able and willing to try to make travel writing your primary source of income, more power to you.

And good luck!

Earnings in the UK

Pay varies enormously in the UK, and how much you can earn in a year will depend on who you write for, how often your pieces are published, and how hard you work. As the quality newspapers have a weekly or biweekly travel section, freelance travel writers often find themselves writing more pieces for newspapers than for magazines, which are normally published monthly. Pay for newspaper articles varies from £300 to £650 per 1000 words; for travel magazines the rate ranges between £250 and £700 per 1000 words (of course, well-known writers or regular contributors are paid more). However, the length of a standard destination piece in the UK is around 1000–2000 words, so this needs to be factored in when you're calculating how many articles you need to write to make a living. Sometimes you might be commissioned to write 3000 words or more, especially for a magazine, but it's rare.

Expenses are seldom paid on top of your article fee, because it is assumed you'll be negotiating 'freebies' – trips arranged for low or no cost with airlines, hotels and other travel providers in return for coverage in the article you write, usually in the fact box (or sidebar, as it is called in the USA) accompanying your story. (The attitude towards freebies is very different in the USA, see pages 98–100.) Setting up these deals with airlines and hotels can take up a prodigious amount of your time. Of course, traveling also takes up a lot of your time, and days when you're traveling are days when you are not earning – in effect, you are paid to write, not travel. This is why you need to write as many articles as you can from one trip.

Another point to consider is that many articles are commissioned 'on spec' – this means that a travel editor has said they like the idea of what you might write but will only agree to run it (and pay you) once they have seen your copy. It is also much more difficult to negotiate free travel or accommodation with an 'on spec' piece as there are no guarantees of coverage for the service provider.

Earnings in the USA

Very few US-based freelance writers make more than $100,000 a year; the vast majority earn in the vicinity of $15,000–40,000 a year. A very good scenario would see you being lucky enough to receive six assignments from major magazines in one year. If each assignment was for an article of 3000 words, and the magazines paid an average of $1.50 a word, that would come to $4500 per story and a grand total of $27,000. That would be it, and you'd still have all your life expenses to cover, from housing and food to medical costs and phone bills. Unlike the situation in the UK, you would at least be compensated for any expenses incurred, but could you possibly survive on this amount?

To be more realistic, few US magazines would pay $1.50 a word to a new writer. Top magazines would most likely start you at $1 a word for articles ranging from short pieces (250 words) published at the beginning of the magazine to longer features (4000 words) in the middle sections. Fifty cents a word would be more common. And some magazines pay dramatically less than this, down to 10 cents a word. Major newspapers pay considerably less than major magazines, with most of them paying between $200 and $500 for articles of 1000–2000 words.

Earnings in Australia

Making a living solely from travel writing is tough in a relatively small market such as the one in Australia. Most Australian newspapers pay a rate of 50 cents a word, rising to perhaps 70 cents if you're very lucky. Features range from 1500 to 3000 words, and inside pieces vary between 700 and 1000 words. Metropolitan and smaller regional newspapers can pay a set fee of as little as AU$50. Magazines vary wildly, from a set fee of AU$350 to as much as AU$1 per word from the majors. As in the UK, expenses are rarely paid, reviewers for publications such as restaurant guides being the fortunate exception.

Earnings from travel literature

If you're writing a literary travel book on contract you will at least get some money up front from the publishers – this is called an 'advance' and the publishers award it in the hope that sales of your book will recoup that sum and more. An advance for your first book from a major publisher will probably be in the region of £10,000 in the UK, $15,000 in the USA or AU$20,000 in Australia, though there are plenty of first-time writers who have published a book for much less, and smaller publishers

Writer's tip: Striking the perfect balance

While it may be disheartening to learn that following your dream career may not be compatible with a lifetime of financial security, it's also worth considering how you might be able to have your cake and eat it too – whether that be a New York cronut, a Paris millefeuille or an Istanbul baklava. While writing about travel (especially online) may be under-rewarded, other types of writing – that you can often do freelance, and remotely – are well paid, and if you're prepared to be pragmatic it's possible to put together a portfolio of jobs that allow you to earn a decent living, and still spend time doing what you love.

Rates for copywriting are generally good (up to $100 per hour), especially if you can prove your worth, and online job marketplaces like Upwork allow you to jobsearch from your sunbed or favorite cafe terrace (WiFi permitting). You can choose when – and from where – you work, meaning that you can structure your life around travel and split your time between your travel writing and your more lucrative work. Certainly, while you're starting out, it's a good way to mitigate risk and give yourself the chance to get your travel writing career off the ground.

will pay correspondingly smaller advances. Unless you have a supplemental income, this advance will have to fund your travels and your general living expenses for the length of time it takes to research and write your book – generally one to two years. Of course, if your first book is a success and you want to write a second, the financial picture can brighten considerably.

Travel guidebook earnings

Many travel guidebook authors write full-time, either for one publisher or for a variety of companies, with only one- or two-day gaps in between assignments. The formula for paying guidebook writers depends on where you are researching (for example, whether it is a cheap or expensive destination), how well the publisher calculates the book is going to sell (the author of a guide to Thailand will be paid more than the author of a book on Vanuatu), and on your reputation to deliver a sparkling manuscript to length and on time. As with newspapers and magazines, some guidebook publishers pay better than others, and some take expenses into consideration while others don't. Very roughly, a full-time guidebook writer can expect to earn between £10,000 and £25,000 per year in the UK, from $20,000 to $45,000 in the USA, and approximately AU$30,000 to AU$50,000 in Australia.

Guidebook publishers work on one of two payment models: the flat fee and the royalty. In the flat-fee model, which most major publishers have adopted, the writer receives one set fee for their work; this covers all the travel and research expenses incurred and the writer's 'salary' for the weeks or months spent on the book. This fee is usually paid out in installments – for example, 40 per cent on signing the contract, 40 per cent on submission of the manuscript, and 20 per cent on publication of the book. These fees will vary tremendously based on the writer's assigned focus and area (not just the geographical expanse but also the cost of living and traveling there). The most important thing to remember is that this fee is your total compensation for the book and so has to cover everything – your expenses on the road and your rent and meals at home – for the duration of your work on the book.

In the royalty model, the writer receives a percentage of the sales of every book. If you're receiving a royalty of five per cent for your guide to Costa Rica, for example, and the cover price of the book is $20, you'll receive $1 per sale. If the book sells 15,000 copies, you'll receive $15,000.

What the experts say: Pico Iyer

Pico Iyer is the author of Video Night in Kathmandu, The Lady and the Monk, The Global Soul *and most recently,* The Open Road, The Man Within My Head *and* The Art of Stillness. *His website is www. picoiyerjourneys.com and he tweets as @picoyer. Born and raised in England, Pico has been based in Japan since 1987.*

In travel writing, the main thing you have to address is what you can say – how you can approach Kyoto or the Pyramids or Machu Picchu as no one has ever done before, and as few could do today. What do you bring to the dialogue you conduct with these immortal places?

Maybe you're a jeweler, and so can read meanings into the lapis and coral of the inlay work at the Taj that few of the rest of us could discern; maybe you're of Islamic descent and so can see how the gardens outside the Taj reproduce the outline of the Islamic paradise; maybe you're an architect, and so can explain to the rest of us how science and craft can produce wonder.

I don't think you can presuppose that the reader is interested either in you or in the subject matter; and I think you have to remember that your enthusiasm can only be conveyed through specifics. You have to take the reader by the hand and lead them into the place you're describing, and then lead them into the wonder or terror or mixture of the two it evokes in you.

If you're going to try to write about place, I think you have to surrender at the outset any idea of doing it for the money. I have to write 10 pieces a month (on subjects other than travel) just to pay the bills; and although I've published more than 10 books now, I can still only afford to live in a two-room flat in the countryside in Japan, paying rent and without bicycle or car or printer or almost anything.

For me, part of the beauty of travel and writing about travel is that it forces you to see all material things inwardly: you're not going to get rich and comfortable doing it, but you are going to have experiences and memories and challenges that could put Bill Gates to shame.

All the rewards are inner. They have to do with coming to a better understanding of the world and of oneself, of being able to see life as a pilgrimage and journey in which no answer is ever final and one is really moving from question into deeper question, from one way station to the next.

Writing of any kind is a way of making a clearing so as to make sense and shape out of the world, and to take all the rubble of one's experiences and emotions and observations and piece them together into a kind of stained-glass whole. It is a way of removing oneself from the world, and sometimes from the self, so as to see both more clearly. But travel writing is different because it engages with the world in a very urgent and specific way, keeps (ideally) one's eyes constantly fresh, confers on life the sense of an adventure and reminds you that every moment is provisional, every perception, local, ready to be thrown over by the next epiphany.

It keeps you on the move, teaches you (enforces) alertness and makes you more attentive than when you are at home, or blurred by the familiar. As Thoreau famously said, it doesn't matter where or how far you go – the further commonly the worse – the important thing is how alive you are. Writing of every kind is a way to wake oneself up and keep as alive as when one has just fallen in love.

When this royalty model is used, the writer usually receives what's called an advance. Like the flat fee, this advance is often paid in installments – for example, half on signing the contract and half on submission of the manuscript. Remember that the advance is just that – money advanced to you based on the publisher's notion of how many copies the book will sell; it's not an 'extra' payment. So, if you received an advance of $10,000 for your Costa Rica book and the book sells 15,000 copies, you'll receive an additional $5,000 in royalties.

Does all this add up? It's a complicated equation. You have to balance the amount of money you can make, the amount of money and time you'll have to expend on the road and at home, and the experience and knowledge you'll gain. Other factors complicate the equation even more: as you're researching, can you write articles for newspapers, magazines or websites to supplement your guidebook fee? If your subject is a country where living expenses are low, can you base yourself there to save money and stretch out the cost-of-living coverage of your payment? Ultimately, the decision comes down to you and how this fits with your life and your sensibility. Even more so than other types of travel writing, being a guidebook writer is a singular kind of lifestyle – long, hectic periods of travel followed by high-pressure periods of writing. Think about whether you have the stamina, the will and the life circumstances to take it on.

In-house versus freelancing

There are two main avenues for making travel writing your career: either working as a salaried staff member for a newspaper or magazine, or working as a freelancer.

Working as a staff writer

To be brutally honest, staff-writing jobs are as elusive as the creature Peter Matthiessen seeks and never quite finds in his classic work of travel literature, *The Snow Leopard*.

There are in total perhaps three dozen full-time travel writer jobs at newspapers in the USA, the UK and Australia, and these positions are usually occupied by established journalists – long-time staffers who have cut their teeth on the city desk and the business beat, for example, before being offered the plum role of travel. As newspapers tighten their belts in tough economic times, these jobs are becoming even rarer and more precarious. They require a good deal of decidedly unglamorous desk-bound work making telephone calls and internet expeditions to research car-rental rates and single-traveler supplements for the kinds of practical pieces the staff writer is frequently called on to produce.

The picture is the same for the very few staff-writing jobs on travel magazines: the staff writers for the most part fill in the holes in the magazine's editorial jigsaw puzzle, writing news-oriented pieces, industry stories, book and product reviews and the like. Occasionally a staff writer may be allowed to take a long weekend to some nearby or far-flung locale, but those meaty middle-of-the-book stories are usually written by freelance writers.

In terms of travel and writing, probably the best gig you can hope for is to become a contributing editor (despite the name, this means someone who writes regularly for one publication; it actually has nothing to do with editing) – but these coveted spots go to people who already have a reputation (and who actually enhance the magazine's reputation by appearing on its masthead and in its pages). And while the contributing editors may be guaranteed some kind of annual stipend from a publication (usually in exchange for a specified number of articles or for enhanced rates of pay for what they do write), they do not enjoy the perks of full-time employment.

An added complication is that in-house travel writing jobs or travel desk jobs at newspapers and magazines are rarely advertised. Travel publishing is a very small world and most jobs go to internal candidates or are advertised by word of mouth to colleagues in the industry. The plain truth is that if you are just starting out as a travel writer it will be extremely difficult for you to score a staff writing job. Even if you have a few published articles under your belt, the same applies. However, if you start off as a freelance writer, become known, get a good reputation, and move in the right circles, then you may hear of a job on offer or be tapped on the shoulder.

Another way of breaking into salaried employment – and occasionally to getting your name in print – at a newspaper or magazine is to apply for unpaid work experience on the travel desk. In the USA, such work experience is called an internship and is usually offered in affiliation with an academic program. Working on a travel desk means that you are the office anchor, doing all the administration that goes along with the travel pages – answering the phone, dealing with reader queries, organizing travel arrangements, etc. It may also include some commissioning, editing and a little writing. Although a work experience intern on the travel desk is often at everyone's beck and call, it's a wonderful training ground for any would-be travel writer. If you show initiative and flair, you might be asked to do some research on a piece and to write it up – and suddenly, voilà!, your name in print. Doing unpaid work for a busy travel desk also gives you a foot in the door and means that you could be 'in the right place at the right time' when a suitable position comes along.

The benefits of a staff job, as opposed to freelance travel writing, are a steady income, health coverage (in the USA at least), the camaraderie of office life and regular publication of your work. Writing as a staffer means you avoid the frustration, uncertainty and general agony of freelance life – continually pitching to editors for work, never knowing where or if your articles will be published, never knowing when your money will come in, and hardly ever taking a holiday because it is unpaid.

So what could possibly be the downside of working in-house? There are the problems and pitfalls – the Machiavellian minutiae – of office politics. Like all other office workers, you have to go to work every day (when you're not traveling for work), and you don't have a lot of control over what you do. If you're told to write 1000 words on the history and highlights of consumer taxes, you do it. Some people thrive on working in an office; some people detest it. And if you're considering becoming a travel writer, it seems probable that the call of the open road and the promise of a life of freedom appear more compelling than the lure of the office cubicle.

However, as an in-house writer you'll have access to some fantastic travel opportunities. And more importantly, working in-house, even if it is only for a short period of time, is an invaluable way of building up your contacts if you later want to go freelance. The bottom line is that as a novice travel writer you'd be crazy to turn down a staff job if you were offered one. Take it, learn everything you possibly can, network like mad and then decide if you want to remain on staff or go freelance.

Working as a freelancer

For most writers who choose the freelance life, the freedom of setting their own schedule far outweighs the benefits and perks of a salaried position. As a freelancer you can work when you want, on what you want; you usually have the freedom to write for several publications (as long as they are non-competing), as opposed to only one; you can write all night and sleep all day if you wish. You are your own boss, and in control – and this is a rarity in the working world.

On the other hand, unless you have some sort of independent income, you're always wondering where your next payment is coming from. That is the hardest truth of the freelancer's life: the lack of certainty, stability and regularity. Even the most famous freelancers cannot assume a steady income. When Paul Theroux, perhaps the best-known travel writer in the USA, was researching his book on Africa, *Dark Star Safari*, he proposed Africa-related articles to virtually all the major magazines in the USA – and did not get one commission.

One thing you'll definitely need to develop as a full-time freelancer is fiscal discipline. You may receive one big sum in January and not get another until July, so you need to develop a system to make your money stretch through the lean periods. If you're writing a travel literature book, there's the problem of making an advance last until your royalties kick in – which they will only do if your book sells well. Similarly, if you're working on a guidebook, payments normally come in three installments, months apart: there's an up-front fee for signing the contract, a payment upon acceptance of your work and the final check upon publication.

If you're writing for newspapers and magazines (and the few websites that pay), smaller amounts of money will be coming in on a very ad hoc basis and you'll never know from one day to the next whether you'll be rich or poor that week. Some newspapers pay at the end of the month after the month of publication – so if your story appears in the first week of July, you won't see the check until September. The bottom line is that as a freelancer you need to set up an efficient article- and payment-tracking system to ensure you don't fall into a financial crevasse.

Part-time travel writing

Using travel writing as an additional occupation to supplement your earnings and career is much more common than depending on full-time travel writing work. Some part-timers teach (those long school holidays can be spent on the road) or work as tour guides or cruise-ship lecturers; others expand their specialty by writing restaurant or book reviews, personality profiles or feature stories on the arts and culture. Some write corporate copy – year-end reports, catalogue texts, corporate brochures or press releases, for example. Some of them work as editors, copy-editors or fact-checkers; some as flight attendants or booksellers.

In many ways, it makes a lot of sense to try to make travel writing a complement to the job that you depend on for your livelihood. You can research travel articles during holiday periods and on weekends. This takes the pressure off your travel writing and allows you to ease into it. It also gives you more flexibility to pursue and write the stories you really want to do, knowing that you're not relying on their sale to put bread on the table and a roof over your head.

Whether your travel writing is a full-time profession or a part-time passion, publishing is the professional pathway you'll want to follow. How do you begin to get your travel writing published? We'll explore this territory straight ahead.

Getting more out of your words

Repurposing is one of the greatest tools – and challenges – of the travel writer's job. The aim is to make as many different publishable articles as possible from one trip. The key here is having a good sense of the different markets you want to write for, and the different kinds of stories, or angles, that appeal to those markets. Think this way, and even in the planning process, you can divide your trip into likely story subjects. Your aim should be to get three or four articles from each trip.

Let's plan a one-week stay in Kyoto, Japan. With the proper planning and execution, here are four stories that could be written from that one trip.

The cultural angle

Let's say you arrange to spend two nights on a homestay with a Japanese family. Your first piece, based on this stay, describes the riches and revelations of overnighting with a family and seeing Kyoto through their eyes, living it through their lives. You sell this piece to a general-interest travel magazine that appreciates the different perspective on an oft-described destination.

The quest story

Before you went to Kyoto, a friend told you about a particular store that sells old ukiyo-e woodblock prints. He vaguely remembered that it was in the covered shopping area near the river, and said once you got there anyone could tell you the way. So you spent a day in search of the store – and as it turned out, your search led to all kinds of revealing detours and delights before, at the end of the day, a kindly kimono shopkeeper went a half-hour out of her way to walk you to the tiny woodblock-print wonderland. Your second piece describing this odyssey would capture Kyoto's venerable neighborhoods, spirit and artistic – and personal – treasures. You sell this to a high-culture magazine that specializes in coverage of the arts.

The travel how-to
On the third and fourth nights of your visit, you stayed at a traditional Japanese inn, or ryokan. There are many riches to this experience, but one of the most memorable is taking a bath the traditional Japanese way, first soaping yourself outside the tub, then sinking slowly into the steaming water and letting the cares of the day ease away. Your third piece would be a straightforward 'service' guide to taking a Japanese bath – what to do and what not to do, with recommendations on places to enjoy this unique experience, and some contextual reflections on the deep value of a good Japanese soak. You sell this to the in-flight magazine of an airline that has just recently inaugurated service to Japan.

The personal essay
The rock garden at Ryoanji Temple is one of Kyoto's most famous and sacred sites. On your second morning you went there to see what all the fuss was about. Inexplicably, unexpectedly, you felt a deep connection with the place. You returned at noon on the third day and in the late afternoon on the fifth day. Your fourth piece would be a personal essay describing the history and appearance of the rock garden, and then evoking and reflecting on the hold the place exerted on you – and the lessons in attentiveness, impermanence and wholeness that it bestowed. You sell this to a literary travel website.

Multimedia repurposing
You can also create content in multiple media from one trip. To take the subject examples above, you could keep a blog describing your homestay, augmented with a video of the family's children showing you how to put on a kimono; you could do a video or a photo portfolio recording your quest to find the ukiyo-e store and the discoveries you made on the way; you could produce a video on how to take a traditional Japanese bath;

A writer's view: Rolf Potts

Rolf Potts is the author of Vagabonding: An Uncommon Guide to the Art of Long-Term World Travel, *and* Marco Polo Didn't Go There: Stories and Revelations From One Decade as a Postmodern Travel Writer. *Based in the USA, he has written for* National Geographic Traveler, The New Yorker *and* The Atlantic, *as well as public radio and the Travel Channel. Find him at www.rolfpotts.com.*

My career started, as most do, with failure. Right after university, I saved up my money and spent eight months travelling around North America. When I got back, I decided I was going to write a book about the experience, and that this book would be the biggest thing since Kerouac's *On the Road*. The problem, of course, is that I hadn't considered my audience. What was interesting to me was not always interesting to the people who read these travel tales.

Travel a lot. Write a lot. Read a lot. Don't do it for the money, because there are better ways to make money. Don't even do it for the travel, because there are better ways to fund and facilitate travel. Do it because you love to write, and to write about travel. Do it because it's your passion and obsession. Don't do it because you think it will make you seem cool or sexy, because it will never match your expectations.

I think the most important thing as a writer is to read well. Be familiar with good writing (not just travel writing, but creative non-fiction, novels and poetry), and try to recognize what makes it work. Also, don't be afraid to fail, so long as you learn from your mistakes and always work at getting better. The best training in the world is the school of hard knocks.

The best way to get your name out there is to write in a very distinctive way. Some people do this by writing stories that are funny.

Other writers are good at evoking the human essence of the travel experience. Others become experts on certain countries, or on travel planning, or on certain types of travel, like adventure travel. If you can combine a talent for more than one of these elements, of course, you will do well.

Travel writing should never be fictional, but it should emulate the best techniques of fiction, such as character, action, plot, foreshadowing, dialogue and pay-off. Character and dialogue are especially important, since they bring the story to life. So be an extrovert as you travel, and color your story with the people you meet. Provide action and dialogue, setup and pay-off. Draw the reader into the story with these elements.

Travel writing doesn't pay well, if at all, and is often a solitary pursuit that your friends and families don't understand. I have personally come to terms with all of this; I'm just mentioning these factors for those who think there's a way around the bad pay, frequent solitude, and lack of life consistency. There isn't. But I love it just the same.

I've found that the easiest way to keep things simple and save money is to live overseas, preferably in a less expensive region, like Asia or Latin America. Not only does this save me money on day-to-day living, but it also increases my chances of getting work writing about those regions for newspapers and magazines.

It has been said that travel literature was crucial to the evolution of the modern novel, that Victorian Romanticism emerged from a 19th-century travel boom that created a fascination with faraway places. I'd like to think that travel literature in coming decades will champion a kind of Postmodern Realism – a measured-yet-optimistic sensibility that cuts through the fantasies of tourism and the alarmist hue of international news reporting to leave us with something that is essentially human and true about the rest of the world.

and you could post a photo gallery accompanied by a podcast reading of your reflections on the rock garden at Ryoanji.

The key to this kind of multimedia repurposing is to think imaginatively about the different ways of evoking a subject and the lessons of that subject, and the medium that is most appropriate to the particular qualities of the place or experience that you want to evoke. For centuries the writer's traditional tools were words, then some travel writers added images to their repertoire. Travel writers today can produce content across all different types of media, but their core skills – creating a story and making it come to life – remain the same.

Tools of the trade

In the past, serious travel journalists carried three items with them wherever they went: their journal or notebook, an audio recorder and a camera. More recently, a video camera may have been added to the list too.

Today, of course, most of these tasks are happily served by one device. A good cell phone will record audio and take photos and video of sufficient quality for note-taking purposes (and more, depending on what your need is – if you're taking short videos to share on your Instagram account, phone quality is good enough). It's a currency converter, calculator, address book, personal organizer, map of everywhere in the world, GPS, mini-computer, and many other things besides, with only more to come. Get the best phone you can afford and pay extra for more memory. If you're not already making the most of your smartphone, start now – as a travel tool, it's unbeatable.

Of course, there are downsides to consider. If you're going way off the beaten path, you may not always have phone coverage. You'll need regular access to electricity – make sure you have a power bank and that it's always charged.

If you want to expand your skill set into photography – and there are lots of good reasons to become a proficient photographer if you want a career in travel writing – a good camera is a vital piece of gear. Read more about using photography to enhance your travel writing profile, how to choose the right camera, and some tips for taking great photos, on pages 196–213.

Journal

Don't go anywhere without your journal – even if you usually prefer to tap notes into your phone, you can be sure your journal is always fully charged. It's where you record your first-hand experiences, impressions and reflections. Sometimes you will just need to jot down a word or phrase that will help you remember an experience; at other times it will be whole paragraphs of description. This is also where you'll feverishly copy down all the practical information you'll need for your travel pieces, such as restaurant or museum opening and closing times, costs and transport timetables. It's best to write down everything you want to remember while you're right there. You may think that you won't forget, but you will, and your notes will be especially important if you want to draw out a memory at a much later date.

Laptop computer

To laptop or not to laptop? In most cases you'll want to take your laptop with you when you travel. Travel writers generally do, but there are pros and cons. Whatever you decide, for whichever trip, bear in mind the sometimes life-saving ubiquity of internet cafes. If you decide to keep your laptop safe at home, you can still do some writing on the road and email it to yourself or to your editor.

If you do take your laptop, guard it with your life. Be aware that carrying it around can make you a target – be discreet. Always back up to the cloud (or save to a file-sharing site like Dropbox, or email yourself the latest draft – whatever method works for you) to ensure that even if the worst happens, at least you don't lose several weeks' worth of work.

The advantages

If your laptop is like your right arm in your normal life, you'll want to take it with you when you hit the road – unless you're doing some really tough travel (and even then you might find a way to make it work). If you're maintaining a blog while you travel, it's a no-brainer – your laptop is your most important tool.

The biggest advantage is the most obvious: you can write while you're traveling. This may sound pretty basic, but there's nothing like writing your article while you're in situ, or working on chapters of your guidebook while you're actually staying in the particular city you're updating. If you submit your article while you're on the road, you can answer any questions that may arise or gaps that may appear in your research right on the spot – plus it's a wonderful feeling to walk in your front door at the end of a trip knowing that your story is already done.

It's easier to email and keep up with your social networks on a laptop than on your phone. You can type more quickly into a laptop than on your phone, and than you can write longhand or even shorthand in a notebook, and for many writers, even their early drafts will be on their laptop. If you're snapping photos for note-taking purposes on a camera or phone, you can download them to your laptop as you go and free up memory on your phone or camera, and if you're taking more serious photos you can process them as you travel.

The disadvantages

A laptop can be a significant impediment, depending on the kind of traveling you plan to do. Hard travel, difficult environments and long periods away from electricity supplies are problematic. In this sense, a general rule of thumb is that laptops make good companions when you're on urban excursions but are probably best left at home if you're going on an adventure trip. Even though laptops are meant to be portable, the reality is that only a few are robust enough to survive life on the road. A well-traveled laptop will probably need to be replaced every year or two, depending, of course, on how you treat it.

Travel journalists are always searching for places to recharge their laptops, whether it be in hotel rooms, at restaurants or in airport lounges. You need to carry suitable plugs or adapters with you at all times, and keep track of how much time your battery has left so you don't lose any priceless prose if your laptop suddenly shuts down.

Even under favorable conditions, laptops can be a literal pain in the neck to lug around. Even the most lightweight model doesn't feel so light after you've been carrying it around on your shoulder all day. Invest in a good daypack or courier-style bag that holds your laptop and everything you need to keep it running.

Audio recorder

For many years travel journalists relied on microcassette recorders as an indispensable tool of their trade; these recorders are now often replaced by smartphones that have audio-recording applications built in. If, for whatever reason, you decide to use a separate, dedicated audio recorder, it's critical that it's hardy, portable and practical; easy to slip in a pocket; and simple to use in virtually any kind of situation. Size, weight, sound quality and ease of use are all important considerations. You might want to try a few different kinds to see which one works best for you.

If you decide to use your phone, it's a good idea to try it out before you hit the road to make sure it's going to do what you need it to. Audio files are big – does your phone have enough memory to record an hour-long interview? If you're planning on doing lots of audio recording on your phone, your laptop becomes a must-have, so you can download the files off your phone as you go.

My journal: Don George

I've been using the same particular style of journal since I discovered it in Tokyo in the late 1970s. It measures about 10 inches by 7 inches and has a durable but soft cover so that I can roll it up and stuff it in a pocket when I need to. At the same time, it's stitched so that the pages don't fall out and there's no awkward metal spine. Many travel writers use a standard reporter's notebook, roughly 5 inches by 3 inches, but their rigid cardboard covers aren't as adaptable as my soft-cover version, although it is a handy, stuff-in-your-pocket size.

Notebook entries are very powerful portals that transport you back to a place and to your experience there. Try to make time at least every other day to sit in a cafe or other suitable place and write about the world around you for an hour. The peripatetic Pico Iyer has told me that when he is traveling, he sets aside time every night before going to bed to record the most important experiences and impressions of the day. There is absolutely no substitute for words written on the day, in the place, as close to the experience as possible, so the details and your reactions and thoughts are fresh.

Use your journal as a friend and confidant, sounding board and aide-memoire, all in one. Number your notebooks and, whatever you do, make sure you don't lose them. I always write a big note on the first page of each notebook: 'If found, please return to: …', and then my name and address. When I finish a notebook, I note the dates of the first and last entries, and put it in storage with all my other notebooks.

The downside to recording audio, of course, is that you have to play back everything you've recorded and transcribe all the notes you'll need for your article. This is a major pain, requiring you to stop and start the recorder over and over and over again. (If this is something you'd be prepared to pay to outsource, you can find people willing to do this kind of task for very low rates on 'micro job' sites like Fiverr).

Being able to record audio is vital when carrying out interviews, whether informal or with officials such as museum curators or hoteliers. You might also want to record short vox pops about what locals or fellow travelers think of a certain situation, be it their reaction to a new restaurant or a new travel advisory. It's good practice to get the names of the people you interview on tape, together with any tricky spellings; you may not end up using the person's name even if you do quote them – depending on the context, it may be fine to write simply, 'A tourist from London told me that…' – but it's good to have the name in case you do need it. Recorded interviews are very helpful when you're writing up your story, and indispensable when publications ask to fact-check quotes; see the section on interviewing techniques on page 36.

It's also useful to start recording in situations in which someone is dispensing valuable information too quickly for you to take notes. This can be especially handy in a museum, for example, where a guide is talking about the history and technique of a particular painting or sculpture.

Another situation in which it's beneficial to record audio is on the guided city walks that many tourist offices or private individuals run. Using a recorder will help you capture important details that you might need later on when you're writing up – there is nothing worse than coming to a crucial spot in your writing and realizing that you've missed a particular piece of information.

It can be useful way to record thoughts in a situation where taking notes is impractical – such as bumping through the African bush on a safari, for example, when your written notes are likely to start looking like the profile of Mt Kilimanjaro. You can orally jot down words or phrases just as you normally would in your notebook – 'vast golden savannah', 'elephants running, ears flapping', 'gurgling roar of lion' – and they'll help recreate the scene when you're back in front of your computer.

You may also want to use on-the-spot sounds to augment a podcast or video you're planning. It's a good idea to record evocative background noise, if appropriate.

Career maintenance

Whatever stage you're at in your writing journey, it's always helpful to refine your art, re-evaluate your craft, and restoke your passion. Writing courses, workshops and conferences, author readings and lectures, and literary festivals are all excellent ways to meet fellow writer-travelers, swap tales, make connections and broaden your perspectives.

Networking

The world of travel is small, and knowing the right people is key to establishing yourself as a travel writer. A contact at a tourist board or PR company can be invaluable in helping you get the information or the interview you require. You also need to meet the travel editors or the publishers who might run your articles or be interested in your book.

A feast of launches, parties, dinners and lunches are held regularly by tourist boards, airlines, bookstores, publishers, travel fairs, hotel chains, travel agents and tour operators to promote anything from countries

Writer's tip: Sound memories

Sound is a powerful key that can open up all kinds of stored-away memories, and bring a place back to life.

Twenty years ago, I accompanied a tour group on a three-week journey along Pakistan's Karakoram Highway. When we stopped in Hunza, we were visited by an impromptu band of musicians. I don't know how it happened that they materialized at the moment we entered the village, but there they were, and they began to play. I quickly got out my tape recorder and stuck it into the air to capture their spontaneous performance. Even now, two decades years later, when I begin to play that tape, I am transported back to that scene: the marvelous musicians, the snow on the peaks around us, the crisp sunshine, the muddy fields, the neat stone walls and the rows of poplars all around.

to new airline routes. It's the aim of these companies to invite as many travel editors and travel journalists along to their event as possible in order to generate coverage. To begin with, you should try to attend as many of these functions as you can, since they all offer opportunities for networking. As you become better known, you'll become more discriminating and probably only attend one a month or fewer. You can receive invitations to these events by joining a company's press mailing list or by ringing up the marketing department or PR agency handling the event. Networking can be exhausting, and there's a real skill to working a room, but making the right contacts, putting a face to a name and establishing a good relationship with a wide range of travel professionals is central to building a successful travel writing career.

If a prominent travel writer comes to town, the odds are good that members of the local travel writing community will turn out to hear them speak; you can make good connections at such events. Other excellent ways to network include joining a writers' organization, taking a writing class or attending a writers' or bloggers' conference.

Finally, when you are on the road, you should consider virtually everything you do as an opportunity for networking, fact-finding and story-generating. If you're flying somewhere, talk to the ticket agents about how business is doing, and with the flight attendants about great places to see and things to do in the city you're visiting. Taxi drivers are an endless source of anecdotal entertainment and illumination. Hotel concierges and desk clerks can often give you valuable tips about special places in the neighborhood. All of these opportunities can enhance your life professionally and personally. And one way or another, they can help you distinguish and develop stories that get published.

Courses

Writing courses and workshops

Writing courses and workshops are often overlooked as tools of the trade, but they can be an invaluable means of recharging your professional batteries and refining and expanding your expertise and skills.

Travel writing classes are offered across the globe through community colleges, universities, writers' centers and independent learning organizations; they can also be held in conjunction with bookstores.

The majority of courses are for creative writing, but they shouldn't be discounted, as travel writers old and new can learn a lot from courses such as these. Some offer travel writing as a component of a more general course, while others specialize in the genre of travel writing. Attendees usually comprise a good mix of professional and amateur writers. Grants are sometimes available to help less-privileged students cover costs, so it's always worth asking the course organizers about funding opportunities.

You'll find many writing courses online, including those that are specifically for travel writing. There are also courses for writing for online, blogging and all facets of the writing profession. Don't just consider courses that focus on writing; learning how to edit, how to find and work with an agent, and how to work with editors can also be very beneficial in helping you understand the pressures and requirements of the publishing world. Mediabistro (www.mediabistro.com), a professional journalists' organization in the USA, has a strong program of writing and related courses, and MatadorU (matadoru.com) offers travel-writing specific courses. There are also increasing numbers of MOOCs (massive open online courses) offered for free by universities around the world, where you can hone your skills virtually. Try Coursera and Open2Study.

Writer's tip: Real-world blogging

If you're plunging into the world of travel blogging, you'll find a virtual community of people doing the same kind of thing as you and keen to share experiences and tips. Relationship building is a vital part of this world, and you'll need to do lots of virtual networking to establish links to your blog, grow your audience and raise your profile on social media. You'll generally find a supportive network of people to help you. But there's nothing like making a real-world connection. TBEX is the biggest travel bloggers' conference, held annually in a number of locations; there are non-specific blogging conferences held all over the world and you might want to attend one near you to meet other bloggers and exchange insights and experiences.

See the Resources chapter for listings and more details on courses offered online (page 215–16) in the UK (page 238), the USA (page 229) and Australia (page 247–8).

When you're considering a particular workshop or course, find out as much as you can about the presentations and course structure. What topics are covered? Who are the guest speakers? What are their credentials? How much interaction is there between lecturers and students? What kinds of opportunities are there for close critiquing of your work, and for one-on-one or small-group contact? Do the topics correspond to your interests? Read reviews or ask for feedback from past students, and find out what former students have gone on to achieve.

Typing and shorthand courses

Being able to touch-type at speed is an invaluable skill for any writer. When the words are coming thick and fast, your fingers need to keep up with them on the keyboard. If you can't type, or if your typing skills are poor, a typing course may be one of the best investments you make. It takes only around 40 hours to learn how to touch-type, and courses are generally inexpensive.

Before the advent of audio recorders, shorthand was an essential journalistic skill. There can still be situations when an audio recorder isn't appropriate and old-fashioned shorthand comes into its own again. It can be particularly useful when you are interviewing someone by phone or when the presence of an audio recorder is making an interviewee feel ill at ease. UK and Australian journalists use a form of shorthand called Teeline, which is based around the consonants of the alphabet and is therefore easy and fast to learn. As with typing courses, Teeline shorthand courses can usually be found wherever there's an adult-education center or secretarial college; you can try it online at www.teelineshorthand.org. Depending on how many words per minute you want to achieve, Teeline shorthand can be learned in anything from 70 to 100 hours. Most US journalists simply devise their own abbreviated note-taking method – but nearly all agree that having some way to quickly and easily jot down notes is essential.

Your home office

One of the essentials for a writer is a comfortable and compatible place to work, and ideally one that is a dedicated workspace. In the UK it is best to have your workspace as part of a room that's used for another purpose – for example, a bedroom or living room; if you set up your home workspace in a separate room, you could become liable for business tax rates (that is, non-domestic rates). In the USA and Australia it is actually a tax advantage if you can set aside a dedicated separate room as your workplace.

Wherever your workspace is, you want it to be truly your office. When you go there, even if you are simply stepping from one part of a room into another, you have to have the mindset that you are now entering your workplace. You are there to work and not to watch TV, listen to music or chat with friends by email, IM or phone. If at all possible, it should be free of all such distractions. Of course, you have to set up a schedule that works best for you, and if that means periodic TV, music or phone calls to friends, that's up to you. But to get the most out of your workplace, wherever it may be, you need to adopt it in your mind as the place where you focus on your work.

Basic administration

Once you start earning money as a freelance travel writer there are administrative and legal steps that you will need to take, such as filing taxes, keeping careful records and taking out insurance.

Taxes
Taxes in the UK
Whether you start writing full time, part time or on weekends and evenings after your 'proper' job, you will need to register with the Inland Revenue as being self-employed. You need to register within three months of receiving your first check (regardless of how small it might be), because otherwise you may incur a fine of £100. Once you become self-employed, you will have to pay your own National Insurance contributions, but only when your net travel writing income hits a certain annual threshold. While you're earning less than this, you can apply for a Certificate of Small Earnings Exception. For an overview of what you need to do when you become self-employed, see www.gov.uk/working-for-yourself.

As a self-employed writer, you will also have to pay your own tax (see www.gov.uk for more information). Each April, at the end of the tax

An editor's view: Sarah Miller

Sarah Miller is the editor of Condé Nast Traveller *magazine (UK).*

I was approached to launch the UK edition of *Condé Nast Traveller* precisely because I'm an editor and a journalist rather than a 'travel' journalist. Condé Nast wanted someone who understood that travel, rather than being a separate compartment, a section of a newspaper, is part of the mainstream, integral to everyone's lives, from the food we eat to the clothes we pack.

Pitching correctly is everything. Editors want good, original journalistic ideas which are timely and relevant to a publication and its production schedules. Also, don't muddy the pitch by also claiming to be a good photographer. Get your words accepted first.

It's better to build relationships with editors of complementary publications – a monthly travel magazine, a newspaper section, foreign publications – so that each editor doesn't feel you're writing for their direct competitors. Tailor-make your ideas to each. Don't send the same list of ideas to everyone but make each editor feel you are right for their brand. No editor wants to come second or feel that they're being offered second-hand goods.

Ideas are stories, they're not countries. Most people try to cover too much. An entire gap year is a guidebook, not an article. The best pieces are relevant, timely and finely focused. And whether you're writing for a newspaper or magazine, think about what would sell it, what is going to make the public buy it. Understanding lead times is essential. It's no good pitching a good idea if by the time it comes out, the peg has gone. Good travel writers are also acutely aware of timing and the seasons. It's no good pitching a skiing idea halfway through the season to a monthly because they are already on to their spring/summer issues.

Good writing is good writing and is usually born from experience. This notion that there are 'travel' writers is something I sometimes think was dreamed up by retailers who like to pigeonhole what they display. There are good journalism courses out there, but I would always see these as an extra to a good degree and interesting life. On the other hand, I don't know a single writer who hasn't benefited from a subbing course. Accurate, clear expression as much as evocation is the essence of being a good writer.

A common mistake writers make is talking too much about themselves, getting to a place, and a linear narrative of 'and then, and next' – if I read 'As we banked over Rio...', then the piece goes straight in the bin. Plus, while I don't recommend selling yourself as a photographer at the same time, not enough writers have a sense of what a piece could look like visually – both photographically or how it could be 'packaged' on the page.

Good travel writing shouldn't read like a dissertation. A good destination piece should make you feel you're there. I stop and listen to how a piece 'sounds', 'smells', 'looks' or whether it makes me laugh. I also look for people – too many writers deliver pieces that feel like the *Mary Celeste*. News reports should open my eyes to something I didn't know before. And the very best writing always makes me feel I want to read it again, like a good novel.

year, the Inland Revenue will send you a Self-Assessment Tax Return; if you return it to them before 30 September, the Inland Revenue will work out your tax bill. You will be required to pay your tax and National Insurance contributions in two installments, on 31 January and 31 July. If you haven't given up your day job, you will be required to pay tax on any travel writing income from the outset because your tax-free allowance will already have been used up. The tax rate of either 22 or 40 per cent will be worked out on your total earnings. If your travel writing income reaches £83,000, you'll have to register for VAT (the threshold figure changes annually; be sure you're aware what the current threshold is.)

Taxes in the USA

The situation is a bit less formalized in the USA. If freelance writing is a source of income, in addition to the 1040 standard tax form, you'll need to fill out the Schedule C tax form for self-employed individuals, 'Profit or Loss from Business'. For your freelance income, you'll use the 1099 forms

Writer's tip: Your home office away from home

With the rise of telecommuting and the 'digital nomad', startup culture and surging city rents, coworking is on the rise. At coworking spaces around the world, common in big cities and rapidly spreading (particularly to locations where get-away-from-it-all freelancers cluster) individuals or small workgroups rent a place to plug in their laptop, hook up to the Wi-Fi and get to work. Coffee and snacks might be provided, and in some cases these spaces act as social hubs and collaboration centers as well as just a place to type, code or create. Generally you can rent space casually by the day or pay a monthly fee for unlimited access.

To explore cowork spaces around you and discover more about the coworking ethos of collaboration, community building and sustainability, see wiki.coworking.org.

you have received from all the publications that have paid you to fill out the Schedule C form's earnings information.

If you are filing as a freelancer, you should also fill out a Schedule SE Self-Employment Tax form. The SE tax is a Social Security and Medicare tax primarily for people who work for themselves; it is similar to the Social Security and Medicare taxes withheld from salaried employees. Regulations and rates vary from year to year, so the best advice is to research the current rules and requirements by reading the IRS' concise and helpful Publication 334, 'Tax Guide for Small Business (For Individuals Who Use Schedule C or C-EZ)'. You can download this publication and peruse a wealth of other tax-related information on the IRS website (www.irs.gov).

Taxes in Australia

In Australia, freelance writers need to apply for an Australian Business Number (ABN), which must be included on all business-related invoices and stationery. If you do not have an ABN, any payments you receive may be subject to a Pay As You Go (PAYG) withholding tax of 48.5 per cent. If your annual income reaches or exceeds AU$75,000 you'll also need to be registered for GST, and will be required to lodge quarterly Business Activity Statements (BAS) specifying the GST payable or refund receivable, and any income tax payable or receivable. If you keep a separate office in your residence, you can claim a proportion of heating and lighting, rates, insurance and interest payable on your home loan. You can also claim for stationery, plus depreciation on your computer, printer, modem, desk and library etc. You need to be rigorous about keeping documentation such as invoices, fees, contractual agreements, purchase contracts and receipts. It's also a good idea to keep a running diary of your expenses and income, detailing your working hours and time spent using your computer for private use, and to keep track of business phone calls, emails and faxes. For more information, go to the Australian Tax Office website (www.ato.gov.au).

Hiring an accountant

It's highly recommended that you engage an accountant to prepare your taxes. An accountant can handle (and educate you about) the intricacies of your tax return, give you up-to-date advice and ensure you are not over- or underpaying income tax. A possible alternative to hiring an accountant is to use a tax software program to prepare and file your returns. The best of these feature a step-by-step 'interview' process that will record and analyze your answers and then generate the required tax forms.

However you choose to prepare your taxes, it is very important to bear in mind that you may be able to deduct many of your business-related expenses. These include your office expenses (stationery supplies, postage, phone calls, internet connection etc.) and a portion of your heating, lighting and other home expenses. You may also be able to deduct expenses for books, newspapers and magazines, as long as they are genuinely for research purposes, and of course research-related travel expenses such as transportation, accommodation, meals and some work-related entertainment expenses. Since each individual's circumstances and options are different, hiring an experienced tax accountant is a good idea to ensure that you take full advantage of your qualifying deductions.

Keeping records

Clearly, all of this means that you have to be a meticulous record-keeper. As a travel writer you'll incur a wide range of expenses – air tickets, hotel bills, car mileage, meals, equipment, entrance fees – and virtually all of these may be tax deductible. From the outset you need to make sure you understand what is an allowable expense and what isn't. In the UK, for example, you can claim travel expenses only on a work trip and not for a holiday that may also result in you writing a travel piece. In order to prove your legitimate business expenses, you need to keep all your receipts, and to have a thorough, well-organized calendar of your travels and other work-related activities during the year. You must keep all your records for six years in the UK, for seven years in the US and for five years in Australia.

With regard to expenses and deductions, you should be aware that the government will expect your business to become profitable at some stage. If you are incurring a business loss year after year, you should consult with a tax accountant because you will be permitted to lose money for only a certain number of years in a row. In the USA and Australia, for example, you must make money in any three out of five years or your travel writing will be classified as a hobby rather than a livelihood, and your travel-related expenses will be disallowed (but any travel-related earnings, of course, will still be taxable).

Record-keeping is important not only when it comes to taxes, of course. If you are traveling on assignment for a US publication, and that publication is paying your expenses, you will have to turn in a record of your expenses with related receipts in order to be reimbursed. Keep all your receipts in a safe place, and carry a blank receipt book so you can supply your own receipts in situations where the local establishment doesn't have a form.

To avoid the nightmare of sorting through dozens of scraps of paper days or even weeks after a trip, try to record all your expenses at the end of each day – you'll then have the date, the place, the reason for the expense and the amount, all ready to be categorized and submitted when you get home. It's also a good idea to keep a running tab of your expenses, because if you go over your expense limit, you'll be responsible for the difference.

Record-keeping is also fundamental when it comes to income. Having a story published doesn't automatically guarantee that a check will appear in the mail. These days most publications expect or require you to submit an invoice after your piece has been published; the invoice should include the subject of the article, the date of publication, the agreed-upon payment for the piece, your address, and your social security number (if in the USA) or ABN (if in Australia). It is also a good idea to include your phone number and/or email address so you can be contacted if necessary. And even after you've submitted your invoice, it isn't the editor's responsibility to keep track of whether you've been paid for your piece; they have far too many other balls to juggle. You are the only person who will be watching out for you – and you can be sure that at some point your payment will slip through the cracks.

Keep track of your publications and payments rigorously, and follow up on any outstanding invoices. The best practice is to create a table or spreadsheet that tracks all of your proposals and story submissions – where and when you submitted them and what responses you received, plus any commissions and deadlines, expenses submitted (if in the USA), dates of publication and payments received.

The inconvenient truth is that as a freelancer you have to be a businessperson, too. Your writing is your livelihood and you need to keep your business records up to date, as if your life depended on them – and it usually does.

Travel insurance

It's also extremely important to make sure you are covered by insurance when you travel. In the UK and Australia, you will need business travel insurance if you are traveling to research and write. Most travel writers take out annual policies so they don't have to worry about this aspect of their trip each time they go somewhere. In the USA, writers should check to see what kind of coverage they already have through their personal insurance and what kind of supplemental travel coverage they may need. Consult with your insurance agent to make sure you have protection for all of the potential hazards of your professional world-wanderings, from trip disruption or cancellation to loss of business equipment and medical emergencies.

Legal matters

As a professional, you need to be aware of the legal protections and issues pertinent to your work.

Copyright

Any original text that you write as a freelancer is your intellectual property and is automatically protected by copyright; you don't need to apply for it. As the writer, you can grant certain rights or licenses to publish your work. Copyright lasts for 70 years after your death. For more information about copyright, contact the British Copyright Council (www.britishcopyright.org), the US Copyright Office (copyright.gov) or the Australian Copyright Council (www.copyright.org.au).

Electronic rights

Electronic rights are an extremely thorny issue. When a newspaper, magazine or journal agrees to publish your article in print, they usually expect to have the right to publish your article on their website, without any further payment. This is especially true in the UK, where electronic rights are usually non-negotiable. These issues should be spelled out in your contract or on the outlet's website. Writers' groups make the compelling argument that if a print outlet posts an article on its website, it effectively takes away the writer's ability to sell that article to a web-only outlet, and that therefore the writer should be paid separately for the web posting. Most publishers, however, will try to secure all the rights they can for the lowest possible fee. If you're absolutely determined to negotiate over these matters, in the USA at least, enter into those negotiations with a clear sense of what you think your work is worth, what conditions you will accept and what offers are simply unacceptable – but you should also question whether you are hindering your career more than helping it. Each case will be different, depending on the article, the publication and the pay, but it is always best to have a good idea of your priorities and options in advance, and to know exactly what you want to get out of a negotiation.

Contracts

Most contracts, whether for newspaper or magazine articles or for books, are forbidding. They're written by lawyers and in tiny type. Your mind goes numb when you read them. But they spell out your legal obligations and opportunities, so it is extremely worth your while to plow through them slowly and to make sure you understand every clause. If it is a book publishing contract and you have an agent, they'll explain everything to you and endeavor to negotiate the best possible deal. Otherwise, you may want to consult a friend who has dealt with contracts before or, in extreme cases, a lawyer who can explain the fine print; or contact one of the associations listed below. You can also ask your editor to explain points you don't understand.

In theory at least, most UK newspapers and magazines will email you a contract before you start writing for them. Sometimes this contract will last a year or longer. If you write several articles for the same newspaper or magazine, it's rare that you'll receive a contract for each piece. However, there will be times when you won't receive anything at all because staff on the travel desk are just too busy. In the USA, magazines send contracts with each article, while most newspapers instead send annual contracts.

Most newspaper and magazine contracts are standard, and editors are usually extremely unwilling to deviate from the template. The most crucial considerations are your fee (and whether it will be paid on acceptance or on publication), your deadline, the rights they are buying and the rights you retain, and whether a kill fee will be paid if they do not publish your work. Book publishers send their authors very detailed contracts. One detail you'll want to make sure your contract specifies is the percentage of compensation you will receive if excerpts from your book are published in a newspaper, magazine or anthology.

A writer's view: Stanley Stewart

Stanley Stewart is a Fellow of the Royal Society of Literature and Contributing Editor for Condé Nast Traveller *magazine (UK). He writes about travel for publications including* The Sunday Times *and the* Financial Times *in the UK and* National Geographic Traveler *(US). Find him online at www.stanleystewart.com and on Instagram at stanleystewart.writer.*

My own start was unusual. I began with a book. I set off up the Nile for nine months, without a publishing contract, wrote an account of the journey and sold it to a publisher when it was complete. The success of the book opened doors for travel journalism which helped to feed, financially, more books.

It may sound blazingly obvious, but the best preparation for a career in travel writing is travel. Take a year off and travel round the world. When you come to pitching a story about the hot springs of Iceland, you will have the advantage of sounding like someone who knows what they are talking about. But remember that you must be able to write. And the best education for a writer is to read, as widely as possible.

Travel writers need to be able to double up – so when you are in Rome doing a story about riding a Vespa along the Appian Way for newspaper X, you are also getting the info together for a restaurant story for magazine Y and a piece on the Coliseum for newspaper Z.

Travel stories must be stories, not merely descriptions of a destination. It is not enough to enthuse about the blue seas or the difficulties of the hike or the charm of the old quarter. What you write must be able to stand as a good story when all the 'color' and atmosphere are stripped away.

Good travel writing is done by good writers who travel. It is not enough to have swum through piranha-infested waters to the source of the Amazon. You must be able to write well to convey that experience. Good travel writing needs much the same ingredients as any good story – narrative drive, characters, dialogue, atmosphere, revelation. Too many travel writers seem to believe that the journey 'makes' the story. Anyone can travel to Timbuktu, but only a few people will write about the journey well.

If you want advice on a contract, in the USA you can contact the Authors Guild (www.authorsguild.org) and the National Writers Union (nwu.org); in the UK you can ask the Society of Authors (www.societyofauthors.org) or the Writers' Guild (writersguild.org.uk); in Australia the Society of Authors (www.asauthors.org) can review a contract for you. In most cases you'll need to be a member of the organization to access this service.

6

Becoming
photog

a travel

rapher

On the most basic level, a camera can be used to make a visual record of a place you want to write about later. Use it to take photographs of particular features you may want to remember in detail, and that might figure in an article or story. When writing your piece, you can surround yourself with images of your destination or journey to help transport you back to a situation or place.

Photos can be used to record information you may want to use in your story, such as details provided in a historic plaque, temple marker or store sign, or in the printed explanatory text hung beside a work of art in a museum or gallery – quite simply, they can save you from having to take copious notes. These 'memory snaps' can be taken on any light, compact digital camera, or even on your cell phone.

Ideally, however, you want to be taking photos of publishable quality, so that if the opportunity arises you can sell both your words and your pictures to a publication. This is a very different ball game and demands rather more sophistication in terms of equipment and photography skills.

How photography helps your writing career

Photography and writing are two very different arts, requiring completely different skills. However, it does make sense to think about developing your photography skills if you are a travel writer. You are there, in situ; you know what you're going to write about and you're in a unique position to illustrate your words.

If you're writing your own travel blog, you'll probably want to use your own photos to accompany and enliven your posts; and for many online publications the expectation is that you'll supply images along with your story. If you're writing for a newspaper, having relevant photos could help you get published. Your story might be good but not so great that the editor simply has to run it; having compelling photos can sometimes push the editor into deciding to publish your package. Photographs taken by guidebook authors are sometimes published in the guidebook they're writing, particularly if they're researching a remote location or have pictures of unusual or infrequent events (festivals or rituals, for instance).

Glossy travel magazines are very photo-led, and employ a stable of professional photographers who are sent into the field to illustrate middle-of-the-book feature stories. The glossies might occasionally be interested in competent photos for front-of-the-book or back-of-the-book stories, but you have a better chance with more down-to-earth travel magazines. In fact, many tighter-budget magazines actually rely on their writers to provide photos. The better your photos, the better your chances of getting published.

Usually, selling both a story and photos to a publication is obviously more lucrative than selling the story alone. While stock libraries, photo-sharing sites and the opening up of the profession of photography to virtually anyone with a smartphone means that photography rates are not what they once were, it is a way you can potentially boost your income as a writer. If an editor requests photos, always ask if you'll be paid extra (and how much) for any photos that are used.

Choosing your gear

Flip through the pages of camera magazines and websites and it's easy to be overwhelmed by the choice of cameras. Models are updated or replaced at an alarming rate, with every new wave being spruiked as significantly better than the last. You just have to accept that the camera you buy will be superseded sooner rather than later. But it's not as bad as it sounds. Technology has reached a point where the changes are no longer as regularly dramatic as they once were, and the camera you buy today will only need to be upgraded if your interest level or requirements change.

First you'll need to decide between the four types of digital camera that are of most interest to travelers: compact, bridge, compact system cameras and digital single lens reflex (DSLR). Within these categories you'll find cameras to suit every budget and requirement level.

Compact digital cameras, also known as digicams or point-and-shoot, are ideal for taking photos with a minimum of fuss – perfect if you want to travel light. If all you need is an image to publish on your blog, a fully automatic, 12 MP compact digital camera will easily do the job.

Bridge cameras, also known as superzooms or 'all in one' cameras, sit between compacts and DSLRs in terms of style and size; the best of them have feature sets that rival mid-range DSLRs. They may appeal to people who want to take photos of a reasonable quality, but like the more compact package and aren't interested in extending their kit with additional lenses.

Compact system cameras fill the gap between compact cameras and DSLRs by combining the best features of both (including interchangeable lenses), to produce excellent image quality in a compact style. These cameras will appeal to people who always wanted the flexibility to choose different lenses, but were put off by the size and weight of DSLR systems.

Digital single lens reflex cameras (DSLRs) are the only choice if you're serious about travel photography and aiming for success across the widest range of subjects in all situations. Their versatility, the sheer number of useful features and the ability to take interchangeable lenses to suit all subjects makes this the ideal travel camera.

Other useful photographic kit

There are a few other pieces of equipment and a range of accessories that will enhance your photography experience and ensure things go smoothly on the road.

- A **tripod** helps achieve images with the finest detail, minimizes noise in low light indoors or out, maximizes depth of field and enables slow shutter speeds for creative effects.
- A **shutter-release cable**, or remote wireless switch, is needed if you mount your camera on a tripod and shoot at slow speeds so you can fire the shutter without touching the camera.
- A **flash light** (if it's not built in to your camera) is handy when it's inconvenient, impractical, prohibited or simply too dark (even for quality sensors) to set up a tripod.
- An **ultra violet (UV) or skylight filter** on every lens will protect lenses from dirt, dust, water and fingerprints.
- A **polarizer filter** eliminates unwanted reflections by cutting down glare from reflective surfaces. It intensifies colors and increases contrast.
- **Lens hoods** fitted to every lens prevent stray light entering the lens, which can cause flare, reduce sharpness and affect exposure settings. They will also protect the lenses.

Travel photography tips

As a travel photographer, what kinds of photos should you be taking? Think like an editor, and take photos that will help readers to see your story, complementing and enhancing your words. Your photos should illustrate the highlights and main points of your story – the landscapes or cafes, people or animals, ferries or tuk-tuks.

Submit a wide variety of photos, from close-up details to expansive vistas, and shoot a robust mixture of horizontal and vertical images, because you never know what size space will be available in a publication. If you're photographing a building, event or landscape that is absolutely crucial to your story, be sure to take both vertical and horizontal shots.

There is loads of information out there on how to take good photos. A couple of our favorites are Digital Photography School (digital-photography-school.com, run by Darren Rowse who also runs ProBlogger), where you'll find lots of free tips and tools as well as more in-depth paid courses; and in print, Lonely Planet's *Travel Photography* by Richard I'Anson. Read on for some of Richard's top tips.

Learn to see the light

The ability of light to transform a subject or scene from the ordinary to the extraordinary is one of the most powerful tools at the photographer's disposal. To be able to 'see' light and to understand how it translates on to the sensor and how it impacts on your compositions is the final building block in creating striking images.

There's light and there's the 'right light'. The keys to the right light are its color, quality and direction. As your eye settles on a potential subject, note where the light is falling and select a viewpoint from where the light enhances your subject. There is an optimal time of day to photograph everything, so be prepared to wait or return at another time if you can't find a viewpoint that works. However, most subjects are enhanced by the warm light created by the low angle of the sun in the one to two hours after sunrise and before sunset. At these times shadows are long and textures and shapes are accentuated. If you're serious about creating good pictures, this is the time to be out and about shooting. Given all other things are equal, it's the light in which a photographer shoots that sets images apart.

© jackie cooper / Getty Images

The 'golden hour' of light is usually one to two hours after sunrise and before sunset

© outcast85 / Getty Images

A little research and planning may enable you to capture special events in your destination

© Alan Crossland / Getty Images

It requires patience and commitment to capture a perfect moment

© Niels Busch / Getty Images

If possible, seek the permission of your subjects when photographing strangers

The rule of thirds is a principle that will help you take balanced, interesting images

© Samuel Borges Photography / Getty Images

Look for detail that can bring colour and texture to your photography

© Audrey Smithson / Getty Images

If a particular image is crucial to your story, take both portrait and landscape photos of it

Use the aperture to ensure the exposure on your finished image is correct

A higher ISO setting will increase sensitivity to light in darker conditions

A slow shutter speed (used with a tripod) will bring an ethereal blur to waterfalls

© PMatteo Colombo / Getty Images

Practice as much as possible with different compositions, equipment and light conditions

Writer's tip: Using your phone as a camera

Taking photos with your cell phone is no different from using any other type of camera. Apply the same basic principles of approach and composition as you do when you're using a camera, and in addition:

• Set the phone's camera resolution to the highest setting.

• Keep the lens clean.

• Shoot in the brightest possible light and avoid low light.

• If you have a flash, use it indoors and outdoors in low light and when your subject is backlit, but remember its range will be around 1m.

• Use the volume buttons to take the photo rather than the screen button, which will help keep the camera steady.

• Fill the frame by moving closer or pinching on-screen to zoom in.

• Keep the phone cool. As the sensor heats up the noise increases, making for inferior-quality photos.

• Transfer the images to a computer and edit them using image-editing software in exactly the same way as your camera photos. You'll be amazed at how good some of the pictures can look.

Practice, practice, practice

Once you've got the technical stuff sorted, can work efficiently with your gear and can see the light; practice. You can photograph most of the subjects you'll encounter while traveling in any town or city in the world, including your own.

Planning and executing a shoot of your own city is a great way to practice your research skills, test your camera equipment, perfect your technique, develop your eye and get a feel for changing light. Buy a guidebook, check out the postcards and souvenir books, and draw up a shot list. Treat the exercise exactly as you would if you were away from home. You'll quickly get an insight into just how much walking you can expect to do, how many locations and subjects you can expect to photograph in a day, and how manageable your equipment is.

You can then use this knowledge to plan your trips away from home a little more accurately to meet your goals. As a bonus, you'll be rewarded with a fresh insight into your home town. You're sure to see it in a different light and to discover subjects and places you didn't know about.

Research and plan

Research and planning go a long way to getting you to the right place at the right time more often than not. The more time you have, the more opportunities you give yourself to photograph subjects in the best light. Photographers demand more time in a place than the average camera-toting tourist – sometimes just a few extra minutes can make all the difference. The sun may come out or go in, the right person may stop and stand in just the right place, the rubbish-collection truck parked in front of the city's most beautiful building may move on, the people buying fruit may hand over their money. If you have days rather than minutes, you can look for new angles of well-known subjects, visit places at different times of the day, shoot in a variety of great light, and get better coverage.

Check out the dates of special events such as festivals, public holidays and weekly markets. The spectacle, color and crowds that are the hallmarks of these special days provide so many great photo opportunities that it's worth planning your trip around them.

For the most productive and enjoyable time, ensure you have an understanding of the size and layout of the city, or general area in the case of nature-based destinations, and the locations of the key sights and activities. Stay in the most central location you can (and book a room with a view). Accommodation may be cheaper on the edge of town but you'll have to spend more money on taxis, walk further, get up earlier and carry around extra bits of gear (such as a tripod) when you don't need them.

Shoot raw files

If you want to get the very best results from your digital camera, capture your images using the raw file format, an option available on advanced compacts and DSLR cameras. Often described as a digital negative, it's the format preferred by professional photographers.

Raw files are not processed by the camera's software, which compresses the data and makes adjustments that are permanently embedded in the image file. Instead, raw files are compressed using a lossless process, so they retain all the information originally captured, but are saved to the memory card quickly. Adjustments such as white balance, exposure, contrast, saturation and sharpness are made by the photographer after the image has been downloaded to a computer. Creative decisions can then be tailored to each image using the much greater functionality of image-editing software.

Be patient

So much time creating good pictures is spent not actually taking pictures but incessantly looking, either on the move or standing around; watching, waiting. Very few really good photographs are the result of random, machine-gun-fire technique or accidently being in the right place at the right time. Moreover, if you're out and about you create the opportunity to come across fleeting moments. You will not get those 'lucky' pictures from your hotel room or barstool.

When you do find a great location and the light is just right – but an element beyond your control is needed to make the picture, such as a child in a red jacket running into frame – you'll have to balance the competing desires of trying to see everything and patiently waiting for the perfect moment to create interesting pictures. If possible wait; be patient; commit to the image. Whether it's a matter of seconds for an action to occur, a couple of hours for the weather to change or revisiting a location at the best time of day, the quality of your images will improve dramatically. Commitment to the image is a key professional trait; it keeps photographers out there way beyond the time needed to simply visit a place.

Talk to strangers

Some photographers ask before shooting strangers, others don't. It's a personal decision, often decided on a case-by-case basis. Asking permission allows you to use the ideal lens, get close enough to fill the frame, and it provides the opportunity to take several shots, as well as to communicate with your subject if necessary. It also means you know you're not photographing someone against their wishes.

How you approach people will affect the outcome of your request for a photo. Simply smiling and holding your camera up is usually sufficient to get your intention across. You may choose to learn the phrase for asking permission in the local language, but it can be less effective than sign language (especially when you have to repeat the sentence 10 times to make yourself understood). Approach the person with confidence and a smile. When you get the go-ahead, shoot quickly, which will increase the possibility of capturing more spontaneous and natural images.

A good way to get started is to photograph people who provide goods or services to you. After a rickshaw ride or buying something from a market stall ask the person if you can take their photo. Very rarely will they refuse.

Adjust your exposure

Correct exposure means the sensor is exposed to just the right amount of light to record the intensity of color and details in the scene that attracted you to take the photo in the first place. Too much light and the image is overexposed and will appear too light. Not enough light and you have underexposure and the image is too dark. A good exposure is achieved through a combination of the sensor's ISO rating, the aperture setting and shutter speed:

• ISO – image sensors are light sensitive and the ISO rating is the foundation on which the variable settings of shutter speed and aperture are based. As the ISO setting is increased, the sensor becomes more sensitive to light.
• Shutter speed is the amount of time that the camera's shutter remains open to allow light on to the sensor. Shutter speeds are measured in seconds and fractions of seconds.
• Aperture is the lens opening that lets light into the camera body. The aperture is variable in size and is measured in f-stops.

These elements are known as the exposure triangle and an understanding of how they interact with each other, and the ability to quickly assess the best combination required for a specific result, is fundamental to creative photography. By varying these three elements of the exposure triangle the same scene can be portrayed quite differently.

Highlight your subject

The very first thing to consider is the subject – what is it and why are you taking a photo of it? Successful images have a point of interest: the key element around which the composition is based and that draws and holds the viewer's attention. It's probably the thing that caught your eye in the first place.

• Always focus on the point of interest. If something else is the sharpest part of the composition, the viewer's eye will rest in the wrong place.
• Aim to place the point of interest away from the center of the frame because centering the subject often makes for a static composition.
• Avoid including other elements that conflict with the main subject. Look at the space around and behind your subject and make sure nothing overpowers it in color, shape or size.

Follow the rule of thirds

As you look through your viewfinder or study the LCD screen, imagine two vertical and two horizontal lines spaced evenly, creating a grid of nine rectangular boxes. Try placing the point of interest, or other important elements, on or near the points where the lines intersect.

If you're taking a portrait, the subject is the person's face and the point of interest would be his or her eyes. In a landscape the point of interest may be a boat floating on a lake; place the boat on one of the intersections and also position the horizon near one of the horizontal lines.

One of the traps with the rule of thirds for autofocus cameras is that if the subject is not in the middle of the frame, it may not be in focus because the autofocus sensor is usually in the middle of the viewfinder. However, most compact and all DSLR cameras have a focus-lock facility, which you should be confident using. This facility allows you to produce more creative and technically better pictures by locking the focus on the main subject then recomposing without the camera automatically refocusing.

Learn to use editing software

Shooting raw files requires a considerable amount of post-capture computer time and more than a basic understanding of image-editing software. Raw files must be processed or converted before they can be opened in photo-editing programs. Cameras with raw file capture are sold with proprietary software for that purpose. Alternatively, you can use a third-party specialist raw-conversion program or most typically one that is included in your image-editing software.

As with image capture, you can use automated features to make the process quicker, but to obtain the absolute best results and produce digital files and prints that maximize the capabilities of your camera take the time to learn how to use the powerful tools in your software. Your investment in time, software and computer equipment will be rewarded with the ability to bring your images to life and to have total control over how they look.

Be your own critic

With more pictures being taken and seen than ever before (that's more pictures, not better pictures!), it's important to take some time to critique your own photos in an objective way. This is not easy. We're all emotionally attached to images we take, but if you want your pictures to stand out, a disciplined assessment of them will give them the best chance of catching people's attention and being appreciated.

The assessment and selection process is an excellent time for reflection and self-teaching. Your best pictures and worst failures will stand out clearly. Study them to see what you did wrong and what you did right. Look for patterns. Are all your best pictures taken on a tripod? Are all the out-of-focus frames taken with the zoom at its maximum focal length? Next time you can eliminate the causes of your failures and concentrate on the things that worked. Your percentage of acceptable pictures will start to rise. It's better still if you can complement your own assessment with the views of someone you respect and trust to give honest, constructive feedback. Note that this will very rarely be your family and friends. Self-critiquing is an important and never-ending process in the life of a photographer.

7

Reso

urces

Here's a handy guide to get you started and help you along the way: a collection of valuable resources online and in the USA, UK and Australia including publications, reference tools, courses, organizations and much more.

Online resources

Writing opportunities

Please bear in mind that some of these publications don't pay for stories, and most of the ones that do pay very little. In most cases you can find pitching or contributor guidelines and information about rates in the 'About us' section of their website.

About.com
www.about.com/travel
About.com uses freelance writers for its travel content. See 'Write for About' to find out which destinations they're seeking experts for.

Atlas Obscura
www.atlasobscura.com
Atlas Obscura are looking for surprising and unexpected stories, particularly about history, science, weird news, culture, and exploration. Find their editorial calendar online to help with crafting your pitch.

BBC Travel
www.bbc.com/travel
The travel feature section within BBC.com (only accessible outside the UK) commissions stories that have a new or unexpected angle and a strong, context-heavy narrative – and they pay well above the standard online rates.

BootsnAll
www.bootsnall.com
Billed as the 'ultimate resource for the independent traveller', and offering booking information, discussion groups, travel guides and traveller's resources. They accept story submissions and publish travel articles.

BudgetTravel.com

www.budgettravel.com

A resource for the budget-conscious traveler with tips and tools focused on making every destination more accessible – make sure your pitches are strongly budget-focused.

International Living

internationalliving.com

The idea behind this site is that in the right places overseas, you can live better, for less. Although targeted at retirees, they seek personal stories from anyone (not necessarily professional writers) making a living overseas or while traveling. There are also opportunities to write for their *Fund Your Life Overseas* and *Incomes Abroad* newsletters.

Matador Network

matadornetwork.com

An online travel publisher with a global network of contributors: editors, writers, photographers, and film-makers; contributions invited.

Nowhere

nowheremag.com

A literary travel magazine publishing narrative with a strong sense of place, character or time; traditional features as well as travelogues, journal excerpts, profiles, conversations, reviews, video and audio. They also run writing contests each fall and spring.

Outpost Magazine

www.outpostmagazine.com

A Canada-based website with an adventure spin, publishing longform travel journalism and comprehensive travel guides to little-seen destinations around the world.

Perceptive Travel

www.perceptivetravel.com

Online travel magazine publishing quality writing aimed at independent travelers; they only accept submissions from authors with books in print.

Roads & Kingdoms

roadsandkingdoms.com

An award-winning online magazine with an investigative journalism spin on the traditional travel story. Pitch if you have an unusual angle or you can go deep on a specific issue; make sure you read the site to understand what they're looking for.

The Expeditioner

www.theexpeditioner.com

An online travel magazine featuring articles, travel news, commentary, insights and video from bloggers around the globe.

The Wayward Post

thewaywardpost.com

An online magazine with a social conscience, looking for socially conscious trip guides, inspiring storytelling and features about using travel as a force for good throughout the world.

Transitions Abroad

www.transitionsabroad.com

Designed for people who are interested in studying or working – or simply living – abroad. It includes useful links to numerous travel writing sites and blogs. They encourage contributions and run an annual travel writing competition.

World Hum

www.worldhum.com

Publishes first-person narratives, 'rants and raves' and travel interviews. Stories published here have won Lowell Thomas Travel Journalism Awards and been included in travel anthologies including *The Best American Travel Writing*. Also provides links to travel-related journals, magazines, communities, blogs, newspaper sections, book publishers and other helpful sites.

World Travel Guide

www.worldtravelguide.net

Columbus Travel Media publishes guides to top travel destinations and loads of features, updated daily. They seek contributors for features and for travel guide updates.

Travelmag

www.travelmag.co.uk

A fiercely independent online travel magazine interested in both articles and pictures – there's no payment but it's a good way of getting your name in print.

Resources for writers

Absolute Write

www.absolutewrite.com

There's a great list of recommended resources for writers on here, loads of personal experiences and tips from published authors and a very active forum.

Allen & Unwin Writing Centre

www.allenandunwin.com/being-a-writer

'Being a Writer' gathers inspirational tips and practical advice for writers, including author interviews, useful links and competition news.

Author Network

www.author-network.com

An extensive range of resources for writers including information on festivals, courses, agents and competitions, plus tips and insights from authors.

Break into Travel Writing

breakintotravelwriting.com

A large collection of podcasts and articles covering the travel writers' life, and how to take your blog to the next level.

Copyblogger

www.copyblogger.com

Understand the basics of content marketing and how you can apply them to your blog writing.

Contently's The Freelancer

contently.net

Resources, trends and insights for the freelance writer, plus a database of freelance rates. The 'Content Strategist' blog here will help you keep up to date with trends in social media, SEO and blogging.

Fiverr

www.fiverr.com

Need someone to create a logo for your website or blog? Want to outsource some interview transcriptions? You can find someone to do almost anything for a super-cheap price here – be prepared to shop around to get quality results.

Freelance Writing

www.freelancewriting.com

A job board (you can filter your search for travel writing jobs) as well as tons of resources, tips, articles, guidelines and contests.

Goins, Writer

goinswriter.com

Jeff Goins' website and blog contain lots of resources, insights and ideas for writing professionally, maintaining your creativity and becoming an online entrepreneur.

Jane Friedman

janefriedman.com

Practical information from a publishing expert, particularly useful for keeping on top of tech and self-publishing.

Mediabistro

www.mediabistro.com/career-advice

The 'Go Freelance' section of the Mediabistro site has lots of advice on how to pitch and managing your freelance writing career.

Moz

moz.com/tools

This online marketing company is a one-stop-shop for blogging beginners with free guides to help you get your head around SEO, link building, social media and much more. Follow the blog for the latest trends and insights.

Online Newspapers
www.onlinenewspapers.com
Comprehensive list and links to thousands of international newspapers.

PublishersGlobal
www.publishersglobal.com
Links to every publisher in the world.

ProBlogger
problogger.com
The best how-to-blog site on the web – everything you need to know about setting up, writing and monetizing your blog.

SmartBlogger
smartblogger.com
Blog writing, tech tips, how to build traffic and make your blog as big as it can be.

The Write Life
thewritelife.com
A community site featuring contributors who specialize in all areas of professional writing – ebook promotion, blogging, finding an agent and much more.

The Write Practice
thewritepractice.com
This site focuses on honing your writing skills – free articles and tutorials to improve your writing as well as paid programs and a community to help you reach your creative goal.

The Writer
www.writermag.com
Articles, resources for freelancers, event and course listings and writing prompts to keep your creative juices flowing.

Travel Writing 2.0
travelwriting2.com
From where to find freelance jobs to interviews with successful travel writers to lists of resources to a blog full of insights – expert Tim Leffel's website is a treasure trove for budding travel writers.

Who Pays Writers?
whopayswriters.com
An invaluable resource: an anonymous, crowd-sourced list of which publications pay freelance writers, and how much, based on the personal experiences of the community.

wpbeginner
www.wpbeginner.com
A comprehensive how-to site to help you set up your blog in WordPress.

Writers' & Artists' Yearbook
www.writersandartists.co.uk
An 'insider's guide to the media', including loads of advice for unpublished writers, a research center, an active community of writers and a calendar of literary events.

Writer's Digest
www.writersdigest.com
'Write better, get published' – articles, tips, blogs, courses, forums, event listings and a blog on how to find a literary agent.

Zero to Travel
zerototravel.com
Articles and podcasts to help you build your life around travel, including how to get your start as a travel writer.

Online courses

Great Escape Publishing
www.greatescapepublishing.com
Travel writing, blogging and photography, but also courses covering other ways of making money while traveling like import/exporting and running tours.

MatadorU
matadoru.com
Offers courses in beginners' and advanced travel writing, travel photography and film-making.

Mediabistro
www.mediabistro.com/online-training-courses
The career site for media professionals offers courses in a wide range of writing- and freelancing-related subjects like social media marketing, SEO writing, podcasting and travel writing, among many more.

Superstar Blogging
superstarblogging.nomadicmatt.com
Travel blogger Nomadic Matt runs courses in travel writing and blogging, travel photography and taking video.

The Recipe for SEO Success
www.therecipeforseosuccess.com.au
Sydney copywriter Kate Toon's '10 Day SEO Challenge' is a great introduction to SEO; she also runs a copywriting school and blogs about all things freelance writing. Plus, she's funny.

Travel Blog Success
travelblogsuccess.com
Courses in travel blogging, Facebook marketing, freelance writing and brand partnerships, and a members-only group to help you find your way to a successful blog.

Writers Online Workshops
www.writersonlineworkshops.com
Courses to hone your writing skills – character development, description

and setting, editing and revising your work – as well as your professional skills – writing a query letter, how to market and sell your ebook, and much more.

Reference and tools

Bartleby.com
www.bartleby.com/reference
A little dated, but a good source of freely available dictionaries, quotation collections, literary encyclopedias and histories.

Dictionary.com
www.dictionary.com
Online dictionary and thesaurus.

GrammarBook.com
www.grammarbook.com
Help with all those pesky grammar and usage questions (for US English).

time and date.com
www.timeanddate.com
World time zones, meeting planner, international country codes and much more besides.

Universal Currency Converter
www.xe.com
Gives you the ability to calculate your dwindling finances online in any number of different currencies.

World Standards
www.worldstandards.eu/electricity
Useful information on the types of plugs used worldwide (plus some other world comparisons).

Travel trends and information

ABTA
www.abta.com
The Association of British Travel Agents, you can download their most recent trends reports here.

AITO
www.aito.co.uk
The Association of Independent Tour Operators; contact them for story ideas, specialist information or press trips.

ANTOR
www.antor.com
Association of National Tourist Offices in the UK; the peak body for the world's tourist offices.

ETC
www.etc-corporate.org
The European Travel Commission promotes tourism to Europe and has regular, comprehensive trends reports downloadable from their website.

Gov.UK
www.gov.uk/foreign-travel-advice
Country-by-country travel advice from the British government.

IATA
www.iata.org
The International Air Transport Association site features some useful reports, facts and figures.

Intellicast.com
www.intellicast.com
Extensive weather information to help plan outdoor and weather-sensitive activities such as golfing, sailing, hiking, skiing or relaxing at the beach. Free, accurate and up-to-date weather information and forecasts for most US and featured international destinations.

National Rail Enquiries

www.nationalrail.co.uk
Information about Britain's train services.

OAG Travel News

www.oag.com
The market and trend reports published by this air-travel intelligence company could be useful for identifying future travel trends and story ideas.

PATA

www.pata.org
Pacific Asia Travel Association is the leading authority on travel and tourism in the Asia Pacific region; some of their trend reports can be downloaded for free.

Phocuswright

www.phocuswright.com
Credible data, information and analysis on the travel, tourism and hospitality industries – detailed reports available; see the Press Room for access to events.

Skift

skift.com
A travel industry intelligence company with a technology focus, providing info and predictions on travel trends.

The Weather Channel

www.weather.com
Current worldwide conditions and forecasts, maps, weather-related news, educational material, seasonal features, and other resources for travel planning.

Thorn Tree Travel Forum

www.lonelyplanet.com/thorntree
Lonely Planet's online community of travelers gathers here to exchange information about anything and everything travel-related; you'll also find discussions about culture, literature, food, and politics.

Tnooz

www.tnooz.com

News, analysis, commentary, education and data for the travel industry focusing on travel technology, including marketing, devices, start-ups, social media and commerce.

Tourism Australia

www.tourism.australia.com

The research section includes a breakdown of visitor arrivals data and other market intelligence.

TravelMole

www.travelmole.com

Travel industry site with daily trade news reports, event listings and reference directories.

Travel Weekly

www.travelweekly.com

'The Travel Industry's Trusted Voice' in the USA provides news for travel agents, with a good section on travel trends.

Travel Weekly

www.travelweekly.com.au

The news source for Australia's travel industry, with the latest news and travel-related event listings.

US Department of State

www.state.gov/misc/list

Country-by-country travel advice from the US government.

US Department of Homeland Security: Transportation Security Administration

www.tsa.gov

Information, links, tips and requirements for air, rail, passenger vessel, highway and mass transit travel.

US Travel Association

www.ustravel.org

Research, statistics, analysis and forecasting for the US travel industry.

VisitBritain

www.visitbritain.com

The British Tourist Authority site has a comprehensive media center.

World Tourism Organization

www2.unwto.org

Look in the Media section of this site for handy factsheets, publications and trends reports.

World Travel Guide

www.worldtravelguide.net

Travel information on virtually every country in the world.

WorldTravelWatch

www.worldtravelwatch.com

'Reporting on worldwide safety issues for travelers since 1985' – from crime waves, disease outbreaks and transit strikes to political upheavals; also cultural quirks and tourism-specific news.

Ecotourism & responsible travel

ClimateCare

www.climatecare.org

The site has a carbon calculator so you can calculate and offset your travel carbon footprint; a useful resource for writing about ethical travel.

Ethical Traveler

www.ethicaltraveler.com

A non-profit organization seeking to use tourism to protect human rights as well as the environment, with lots of advice on how (and where) to travel ethically.

The International Ecotourism Society

www.ecotourism.org

The world's largest and oldest ecotourism organization, TIES is dedicated to generating and disseminating information about ecotourism and has a network of members around the world in the travel industry, development and academia.

Tourism Concern
www.tourismconcern.org.uk
Campaigning for ethical and fairly traded tourism.

Embassies, consulates & passports
US Department of State
www.travel.state.gov
Provides information to US citizens about passports and visas required to visit other countries.

UK Foreign & Commonwealth Office
www.fco.gov.uk
Provides details of all embassies and consulates in the UK, as well as travel and passport advice.

Department of Foreign Affairs & Trade (Australia)
www.dfat.gov.au
Details of overseas high commissions, embassies and consulates, as well as information on visa regulations, passport advice and the government's travel advisory service (www.smartraveller.gov.au).

Facts, figures & statistics
Australian Bureau of Statistics
www.abs.gov.au
Australia's official statistical organization publishes a range of information including national economic and social indicators, the consumer price index and papers from the 2006 census.

The British Library
www.bl.uk
Online access to one of the world's greatest collections of historical documents and materials.

CIA The World Factbook
www.cia.gov/library/publications/resources/the-world-factbook
A trustworthy reference to the must-know facts and figures for every country in the world – the travel writer's go-to source.

National Statistics Online
www.statistics.gov.uk
Easily searchable database of UK published reports, useful if you need specific numbers for a story.

The World Heritage List
whc.unesco.org
The official list of World Heritage sites, with information about why each of them makes the grade.

Health
Department of Health
www.nhs.uk/nhsengland/Healthcareabroad
Travel health advice for UK-based travelers.

Travel Health Pro
www.travelhealthpro.org.uk
Comprehensive travel health advice for every country in the world, plus factsheets, information about diseases and the latest news.

World Health Organization
www.who.int
Credible information about a variety of world health-related topics and overviews of the health status of member nations.

TripPrep.com
www.tripprep.com
A database of the immunization and vaccine requirements for destinations around the world.

US Centers for Disease Control and Prevention
www.cdc.gov/travel
Health information on specific destinations as well as comprehensive

health advice for travelers on a range of topics from counterfeit drugs to high altitudes.

Smart Traveller

smartraveller.gov.au/guide/all-travellers/health
Travel health tips and recommendations from the Australian Department of Foreign Affairs and Trade.

US resources

Travel publishers

Travel guidebooks
Avalon Travel

avalontravelbooks.com
Publishers of the Moon travel guides and Rick (and now Andy) Steves' guidebooks.

Fodor's Travel Publications

www.fodors.com
Publishers of the Fodor's guidebook series (which is owned by Penguin Random House).

The Globe Pequot Press

www.globepequot.com
Publishers of a variety of theme and destination guides.

Let's Go

www.letsgo.com
'The leaders in student travel', as a wholly-owned subsidiary of Harvard Student Agencies, employs only Harvard students.

Lonely Planet

www.lonelyplanet.com
Head office is in Franklin, Tennessee; there are also offices in London and Melbourne.

Rough Guides
www.roughguides.com
Head office is in London, there is also an office in New York City.

Sasquatch Books
www.sasquatchbooks.com
Publishers of guides to the Pacific Northwest, Alaska, California and the Southwest.

Wilderness Press
www.wildernesspress.com
Publishers of outdoor activity-oriented guides to California, Alaska, Hawaii, the US Southwest and Pacific Northwest, New England, Canada and Baja.

Frommer's
www.frommers.com
Publishers of a number of different Frommer's-branded guidebooks.

Travel literature
HarperCollins
www.harpercollins.com
HarperCollins publishes travel-related titles, particularly literary non-fiction. Manuscripts must be submitted through an agent.

Houghton Mifflin Harcourt
www.houghtonmifflinbooks.com
Publishes Paul Theroux and Jeffrey Tayler. Manuscripts must be submitted through an agent.

Knopf Doubleday
knopfdoubleday.com
Under various imprints including Vintage and Anchor, Knopf publishes top travel authors like Bill Bryson, Geoff Dyer and Peter Mayle. Manuscripts must be submitted through an agent.

Penguin Random House
www.penguinrandomhouse.com
Publishes travel narrative books; also publisher of Fodor's, Rough Guides and DK Eyewitness Travel Guides. See the FAQs under About Us for their submission guidelines.

Seal Press
www.sealpress.com
A specialist women's press (and part of the Perseus Books group) publishing travel literature by women from across the globe.

Travelers' Tales
www.travelerstales.com
Publishes anthologies and travel advice books, with more than 100 titles in print. Submissions are welcome for the annual anthology of best travel writing, and for book-length manuscripts.

Publishing industry resources
Editor & Publisher Databook
www.editorandpublisher.com/databook
Editor & Publisher release an annual report of contact information (among other data) for all US and Canadian newspapers. The print version is $389; access to the searchable online database is $995.

Jeff Herman's Guide to Book Publishers, Editors, & Literary Agents
www.jeffherman.com
A who's who for the publishing industry. Provides contact information for hundreds of top editors and agents. Published annually.

Writers' Market
www.writersmarket.com
A database of agents, publishers and publications; monthly and six-monthly subscriptions are available.

Magazines

AFAR
www.afar.com
AFAR is a literary, 'experiential' travel magazine with a focus on stories about making connections with people, experiencing their cultures, and understanding their perspectives.

American Road
www.americanroadmagazine.com
A quarterly magazine to help with planning an American road trip.

Budget Travel Magazine
http://www.budgettravel.com/magazine
For submission guidelines see www.budgettravel.com/contact-us.

Backpacker
www.backpacker.com
Nine issues a year covering destinations for backpacking, camping and hiking, plus reviews, outdoor skills information and advice.

Condé Nast Traveler
www.cntraveler.com
A monthly magazine seeking stories that appeal to upscale travellers.

Islands
www.islands.com
Focus on the Caribbean, Mexico, Hawaii, Tahiti and exotic destinations, there may be opportunities to pitch for their front-of-the-book section. Published eight times a year.

National Geographic Traveler
www.traveler.nationalgeographic.com
Find submission guidelines at: travel.nationalgeographic.com/travel/traveler-magazine/about-us/writer-guidelines

Outside
www.outsideonline.com/magazine
A monthly magazine dedicated to covering the people, sports, activities,

politics, art, literature and gear of the outdoors. Guidelines for contributors are at: www.outsideonline.com/contact-us

Travel + Leisure

www.travelandleisure.com
Monthly magazine targeting high-end, active leisure and business travelers, open to submissions.

Newspapers

Atlanta Journal-Constitution

www.ajc.com
The Sunday section publishes articles on regional, national and international destinations.

The Baltimore Sun

www.baltimoresun.com
Features a Sunday travel section; the best way to break in is by pitching regional articles.

The Boston Globe

www.bostonglobe.com
Sunday travel section.

Chicago Tribune

www.chicagotribune.com
Sunday travel section; interested in the Midwest and shorter stories.

The Christian Science Monitor

www.csmonitor.com
National paper publishing a variety of travel articles and essays.

The Dallas Morning News

www.dallasnews.com
Sunday travel section.

The Denver Post

www.denverpost.com
Sunday travel section.

Los Angeles Times

www.latimes.com

National paper with a Sunday travel section.

Miami Herald

www.miamiherald.com

Sunday travel section.

The New York Times

www.nytimes.com

A national newspaper with one of the largest travel sections in the USA covering a variety of international and domestic destinations.

The Philadelphia Inquirer

www.philly.com/inquirer

The Sunday section publishes articles on regional, national and international destinations.

The San Francisco Chronicle

www.sfchronicle.com

Sunday travel section; break in by pitching California stories.

The Seattle Times

www.seattletimes.com

NW Traveler on Sunday features articles on regional, national and international destinations.

The Washington Post

www.washingtonpost.com

National paper with a Sunday travel section featuring articles on a wide variety of international and domestic destinations.

Writers' groups & associations

You'll find an extensive list of major writers' organizations at www.writersandeditors.com.

American Society of Journalists and Authors

www.asja.org

The USA's leading organization of independent non-fiction writers. Their monthly member newsletter provides valuable information on writing markets; members can also access writer forums, a mentoring program, networking opportunities and a press card.

International Food, Wine and Travel Writers Association

www.ifwtwa.org

IFWTWA is a gathering point and resource base for professionals in the food, wine and travel industries. The association organizes conferences, regional meetings, and press trips.

National Writers Union

www.nwu.org

The NWU is a trade union for freelance writers working in print, electronic and multimedia formats who work for American publishers or employers.

North American Travel Journalists Association

www.natja.org

A professional organization of writers, photographers and editors aiming to provide educational and networking opportunities.

Poets & Writers

www.pw.org

The USA's largest non-profit organization for poets, fiction writers, and creative non-fiction writers provides information, support and guidance. They also organize writing programs and conferences.

Society of American Travel Writers

www.satw.org

The leading organization for travel writers and other travel media professionals promotes responsible journalism, provides professional support and encourages the conservation of travel resources.

Classics of US travel literature

Don George's list of top 20 works of travel literature by US authors:

Arctic Dreams by Barry Lopez
Blue Highways by William Least Heat-Moon
The Colossus of Maroussi by Henry Miller
Coming Into the Country by John McPhee
Desert Solitaire by Edward Abbey
Ghost Train to the Eastern Star by Paul Theroux
The Inland Sea by Donald Richie
The Innocents Abroad by Mark Twain
Jaguars Ripped My Flesh by Tim Cahill
Notes from a Small Island by Bill Bryson
On the Road by Jack Kerouac
Pilgrim at Tinker Creek by Annie Dillard
The Snow Leopard by Peter Matthiessen
The Solace of Open Spaces by Gretel Ehrlich
Travels with Charley by John Steinbeck
Two Towns in Provence by MFK Fisher
Video Night in Kathmandu by Pico Iyer
Walden by Henry David Thoreau
Westward Ha! by SJ Perelman
Zen and the Art of Motorcycle Maintenance by Robert M Pirsig

Writing courses

Association of Writers & Writing Programs

www.awpwriter.org

Dedicated to the promotion of writers and creative writing programs at universities in the US and Canada, with writing programs, conferences and contests.

ShawGuides' Guide to Writers Conferences and Workshops

www.writing.shawguides.com

Free access to continually updated information on almost 1500 writing conferences, writers' workshops, creative career writing programs and literary retreats.

UK resources

Travel publishers
Travel guidebooks
AA Travel Publishing

shop.theaa.com/store/leisure

Travel guides to the UK and beyond plus walking guides, restaurant and hotel guides and a range of travel narrative books.

Berlitz

www.berlitzpublishing.com

Over 130 pocket guidebooks to the world put together by the team that also produces Insight Guides.

Bradt Travel Guides

www.bradtguides.com

Bradt focuses on emerging travel destinations with its range of travel guides; it also publishes other titles in travel literature, 'slow travel' guides to British regions and wildlife guides.

Crimson Publishing

www.crimsonpublishing.co.uk

Publishes various series including Pathfinder Guides and Gap Year Guides.

Dorling Kindersley

www.dk.com

Heavily illustrated Eyewitness country, city and regional guidebooks, Top Ten guides to world cities and a family travel series. Part of Penguin Random House.

Footprint Handbooks

www.footprinttravelguides.com

Travel guides for independent and adventurous travelers.

Insight Guides

www.insightguides.com

Over 400 highly pictorial guides to the world, plus pocket guides and thematic guides.

Lonely Planet

www.lonelyplanet.com
Head office is in Franklin, Tennessee; there is also an office in London.

Rough Guides

www.roughguides.com
Guidebooks to over 120 destinations, plus music and other reference guides.

Time Out Guides

www.timeout.com
A range of themed London guides (eating and drinking, for cyclists, weekend breaks, etc), plus guides to over 40 (mostly European) cities.

Trailblazer Publications

www.trailblazer-guides.com
A range of route guides for the adventurous traveler including walking guides and rail guides.

Travel literature
Bloomsbury Publishing

www.bloomsbury.com
Bloomsbury does not have a large travel literature list but it does publish books in the 'travel and adventure' genre. Submissions must come via an agent.

Eye Books

www.eye-books.com
Small publishing house specializing in travel books about personal journeys and growth – ordinary people doing extraordinary things.

Faber and Faber

www.faber.co.uk
Publisher of Jan Morris, Simon Armitage and Lawrence Durrell.

Hachette UK

www.hachettelivre.co.uk
Hachette UK includes the publishers Hodder & Stoughton John Murray and Little, Brown Book Group who publish some travel literature titles.

The Orion Publishing Group

www.orionbooks.co.uk
Publishes travel literature by AA Gill and Michael Palin, among others.
Part of Hachette UK.

Pan Macmillan

www.panmacmillan.com
Publishes a handful of travel literature books; only manuscripts submitted
by an agent are considered.

Penguin

www.penguin.co.uk
The publishing superpower created by the merger of Penguin and Random
House (Penguin Random House) publishes Paul Theroux, Bill Bryson
and much more travel non-fiction under imprints including Transworld,
Jonathan Cape, Chatto & Windus, Vintage, Ebury and Arrow – each must
be contacted separately for submission enquiries.

Publishing industry resources

Association of Authors' Agents

agentsassoc.co.uk
Includes a directory of members.

The Booksellers Association

www.booksellers.org.uk
Contains info on events and online directories of publishers and members.

The Literary Consultancy

www.literaryconsultancy.co.uk
Offers manuscript assessment, mentoring and some other publishing-
centered services.

The Publishers Association

www.publishers.org.uk
There's a useful 'Getting Published' section here.

Writers' & Artists' Yearbook

www.writersandartists.co.uk/listings

Comprehensive listings of magazines, newspapers, book publishers, literary and artists' agents, and theatre, television and radio producers, available to buy as a book or online database.

Travel magazines

Adventure Travel Magazine

www.atmagazine.co.uk

In print for over 20 years, this bi-monthly magazine covers outdoor activities in adventurous locations – trekking, mountaineering, mountain biking, cycle touring, climbing, kayaking and snow sports.

Business Traveller

www.businesstraveller.com

Monthly magazine with business- or lifestyle-related destination features.

Condé Nast Traveller

www.cntraveller.co.uk

Glossy, monthly travel and lifestyle magazine aimed at the high end of the magazine market.

Escapism

www.escapismmagazine.com

A free monthly travel magazine available at London Underground stations with a focus on quality writing rare in freesheets.

Food & Travel Magazine

www.foodandtravel.com

The best in food and travel from around the world; monthly.

France Magazine

www.completefrance.com/our-magazines

Monthly magazine about France; also publishes *Living France* and *French Property News.*

Geographical
www.geographical.co.uk
Monthly magazine of the Royal Geographical Society.

Globe Magazine
www.globetrotters.co.uk
The bimonthly magazine of the Globetrotters Club; they don't pay for articles.

High Life & Business Life
highlife.ba.com
businesslife.ba.com
High Life is the monthly in-flight magazine for British Airways passengers. *Business Life* is carried only on short-haul flights and carries lifestyle stories with a business twist.

Holiday Which?
www.which.co.uk
Published six times a year by consumer watchdog Which?; provides independent travel features, investigative articles and hard news on all aspects of holidaying in the UK and abroad. Most articles are written by staff; freelancers are occasionally employed.

Lonely Planet Traveller
www.lonelyplanet.com/magazine
Monthly travel magazine that provides independent travel advice, inspiration and information.

National Geographic Traveller
www.natgeotraveller.co.uk
The UK edition of the US magazine, 10 annual issues focusing on authentic travel experiences and insightful storytelling. Find submission guidelines at www.natgeotraveller.co.uk/contact-us

The Sunday Times Travel Magazine
www.sundaytimestravel.co.uk
Monthly glossy newsstand magazine covering all things holiday.

TNT Magazine

www.tntmagazine.com/news/uk

A free weekly magazine for UK-based travelers, distributed in London and Edinburgh.

Travel Trade Gazette

www.ttglive.com

A weekly magazine for the travel trade.

Travel Weekly

www.travelweekly.co.uk

Free, weekly travel industry newspaper.

Traveller Magazine

www.wexas.com/traveller-magazine

Quarterly travel magazine for the Wexas travellers' club aimed at a 35+ age group.

Wanderlust Travel Magazine

www.wanderlust.co.uk

Leading magazine for independent travelers, published eight times a year. Guidelines are at: www.wanderlust.co.uk/aboutus/writers

Newspapers

The *Daily Mail*

www.dailymail.co.uk/travel

Travel section on Saturday, plus a small travel section on Wednesday. The *Mail on Sunday* also includes a travel section.

The *Daily Telegraph*

www.telegraph.co.uk/travel

Saturday travel section. The *Sunday Telegraph* also includes a travel section.

The *Guardian*

www.theguardian.com/theguardian/travel

Travel supplement on a Saturday. Sister paper The *Observer* also includes a Sunday travel section.

The *Independent*

www.independent.co.uk/travel

The *Independent* is an online-only newspaper with a big travel presence.

The Times

www.thetimes.co.uk

Saturday travel section; *The Sunday Times* also includes a travel section.

Writers' groups & associations

Arts Council England

www.artscouncil.org.uk

The national development agency for the arts supports writers through Grants for the Arts, the annual Arts Council England Writers' Awards scheme, International Fellowships and a range of literary prizes.

British Guild of Travel Writers

www.bgtw.org

The leading organization of travel media professionals organizes monthly meetings and regular networking events, plus you can get a press card. Strict membership criteria apply.

The English Centre of International PEN

www.englishpen.org

PEN campaigns to defend writers and readers in the UK and around the world whose human right to freedom of expression is at risk.

National Union of Journalists

www.nuj.org.uk

Founded in 1907, the National Union of Journalists is one of the biggest journalists' unions in the world. Find help with training, legal services, advice on what freelance writers should be paid, and much more.

Outdoor Writers & Photographers Guild

www.owpg.org.uk

Membership is open to writers, journalists, photographers, illustrators, broadcasters, film-makers, artists, publishers and editors, actively and professionally involved in sustainable activities in any outdoor setting.

Public Lending Right

www.plr.uk.com

Register your books to qualify for payment under the PLR Scheme, whereby authors receive government payments for the borrowing of their books from public libraries.

Society of Authors

www.societyofauthors.org

Benefits of joining this union include clause-by-clause contract vetting, advice on professional issues, networking opportunities and invitations to talks and seminars.

Writers' Guild of Great Britain (WGGB)

www.writersguild.org.uk

A trade union for writers working in television, radio, film, theatre, books and multimedia, offering benefits including free training, contract vetting, a pension scheme, Welfare Fund and entry to their Find A Writer directory.

Writing courses

The Arvon Foundation

www.arvon.org

This registered charity runs five-day residential creative writing courses and retreats held at beautiful rural houses. Grants are available to help with course fees.

London College of Communication

www.arts.ac.uk/lcc

Runs short courses on various subjects of interest to writers: pitching, editing, photojournalism, feature writing, copy writing and much more.

National Council for the Training of Journalists

www.nctj.com

One- to four-day courses for beginners to established journalists looking to sharpen their skills, from social media to subediting. Longer journalism courses also available.

The Open University

www.open.ac.uk

With a network of centers throughout the UK, the Open University runs several writing courses a year.

Secrets of Paris Travel Writing Workshop

www.secretsofparis.com

Five-day travel writing for beginners workshop, held in Paris and run by Paris-based authors and writers three times a year.

Travellers' Tales

www.travellerstales.org

Offers one- to two-day travel writing courses in London, as well as 'creative holidays' where you can practice your writing in locations like Andalucia and Marrakesh led by expert tutors.

Travel Writing Workshops

travelworkshops.co.uk

One-day travel writing workshops held in central London run by journalist Dea Birkett and author Rory MacLean.

University of East Anglia

www.uea.ac.uk

Offers short courses in creative writing, including specialization in travel writing. UAE's MA in Creative Writing, set up by Angus Wilson and Malcolm Bradbury, is famous.

Australian resources

Travel publishers
Allen & Unwin

www.allenandunwin.com

Publishes a wide-ranging list of 250 titles each year, including Australiana and travel writing.

Classic British travel literature

Following is a list of 20 travel literature classics by UK authors compiled with help from Lonely Planet co-founder Tony Wheeler and the staff members of Stanford Travel Bookshop, London:

Arabia Through the Looking Glass by Jonathan Raban
Arabian Sands by Wilfred Thesiger
Frontiers of Heaven by Stanley Stewart
Full Tilt by Dervla Murphy
Holy Mountain by William Dalrymple
I Came, I Saw by Norman Lewis
In Patagonia by Bruce Chatwin
Into the Heart of Borneo by Redmond O'Hanlon
Journey Into Cyprus by Colin Thubron
A Pattern of Islands by Arthur Grimble
The Road to Oxiana by Robert Byron
A Season in Heaven by David Tomory
A Short Walk in the Hindu Kush by Eric Newby
South From Granada by Gerald Brenan
The Southern Gates of Arabia by Freya Stark
Terra Incognito by Sara Wheeler
A Time of Gifts by Patrick Leigh Fermor
An Unexpected Light by Jason Elliot
Venice by Jan Morris
The Worst Journey in the World by Apsley Cherry-Garrard

Hardie Grant Books

www.hardiegrant.com.au

Publishes a healthy list of travel titles including the 'Explore Australia' series and Hide & Seek city guides.

HarperCollins Publishers

www.harpercollins.com.au

HarperCollins Australia's list of contemporary non-fiction titles includes a handful of travel and memoir titles.

Hachette Livre Australia

www.hachette.com.au

The Australian arm of Hachette Livre runs a small local publishing program.

Lonely Planet

www.lonelyplanet.com

Head office is in Franklin, Tennessee; there is also an office in Melbourne.

New Holland Publishers

au.newhollandpublishers.com

This branch of the international New Holland company focuses on non-fiction Australiana including pictorials, natural history and regional travel destinations.

Pan Macmillan Australia

www.panmacmillan.com.au

Pan Macmillan publishes and distributes a range of imprints, including Australian lifestyle and travel titles. They accept unsolicited submissions on the first Monday of each month – Manuscript Monday! See www.panmacmillan.com.au/manuscript-monday

Penguin Australia

www.penguin.com.au

The Australian arm of the Penguin Random House empire publishes non-fiction lifestyle, travel and memoir titles. Submission guidelines are at penguin.com.au/getting-published

Text Publishing Company

www.textpublishing.com.au

The publisher of prestigious Australian authors such as Murray Bail, Tim Flannery and Anna Funder publishes travel narrative titles. Submission guidelines are at www.textpublishing.com.au/manuscript-submissions

Wakefield Press

www.wakefieldpress.com.au

Small, independently owned Adelaide-based publisher interested primarily in true stories, gastronomy and culture.

Publishing industry resources
Australian Publishers Association
www.publishers.asn.au
Includes useful information for getting published as well as general trade information.

Margaret Gee's Australian Media Guide
www.connectweb.com.au
Listings and details for more than 21,000 media contacts and 4500 media outlets; around $500 for print and $1000 for online access.

The Australian Writer's Marketplace
www.awmonline.com.au
Listings directory of over 2000 opportunities for Australian writers – magazines, newspapers, publishers, literary agents, awards and courses, plus an online learning center and comprehensive listings for writers' groups and workshops. Subscription costs $25 per quarter.

Travel magazines
4x4 Trader
www.bauer-media.com.au/brands
A monthly publication focusing on off-road adventure travel in Australia and internationally.

Australian Country Magazine
www.australiancountry.net.au
Quarterly magazine focusing on country living.

Australian Geographic
www.bauer-media.com.au/brands
Bi-monthly magazine seeking to inspire, educate and connect readers to Australian landscapes, plants and animals, science, industry and people.

Australian Geographic Outdoor
www.bauer-media.com.au/brands
Bi-monthly magazine covering destinations, activities, products and services for outdoor adventurers.

Australian Gourmet Traveller
www.gourmettraveller.com.au
Monthly magazine devoted to wine, food and travel.

Australian Traveller
www.australiantraveller.com
Bi-monthly, focused on Australian domestic travel.

Get Lost
www.getlostmagazine.com
Quarterly focusing on travel lifestyles and culture, targeting the backpacker and youth markets.

Luxury Travel
www.luxurytravelmag.com.au
Quarterly magazine focusing on high-end travel.

On the Road
www.ontheroadmagazine.com.au
Bi-monthly magazine for camping, 4WD and ecotourism enthusiasts.

Spirit of Australia
www.qantas.com/travel/airlines/spirit-of-australia/global/en
Qantas' in-flight magazine is published monthly.

TNT Magazine Australia
www.tntdownunder.com
A free, fortnightly publication for independent travelers and backpackers.

Travel + Leisure Australia
www.travelandleisure.com
Monthly travel glossy, covering the globe.

Vacations & Travel Magazine
www.vacationsandtravelmag.com
Quarterly, publishing well-researched luxury, experiential and inspirational travel features.

Newspapers

The Advertiser

www.adelaidenow.com.au

The daily of South Australia's capital city carries a travel section on Saturdays and its Sunday counterpart, the *Sunday Mail*, carries the *Escape* lift-out; shares content across News Limited newspapers in other cities (see www.escape.com.au).

The Age

www.theage.com.au

Melbourne's former broadsheet (now tabloid format) carries a travel section on Saturday, which shares content with Fairfax papers in other cities (see www.traveller.com.au).

The Australian

www.theaustralian.com.au

Saturday's *Weekend Australian* includes a travel and lifestyle lift-out.

The Canberra Times

www.canberratimes.com.au

The capital's newspaper includes a Sunday travel section which shares content with Fairfax papers in other cities (see www.traveller.com.au).

The Courier Mail

www.couriermail.com.au

The Sunday Mail features the Escape travel lift-out, which shares content across News Limited newspapers in other cities (see www.escape.com.au).

The Daily Telegraph

www.dailytelegraph.com.au

This Sydney newspaper includes a travel section every Tuesday and the *Escape* lift-out in its Sunday edition; shares content across News Limited newspapers in other cities (see www.escape.com.au).

Herald Sun

www.heraldsun.com.au

Melbourne's tabloid includes a travel feature section on Friday and the *Escape* lift-out on Sunday; shares content across News Limited newspapers in other cities (see www.escape.com.au).

The Sydney Morning Herald

www.smh.com.au

Sydney's major newspaper carries a travel section on Saturdays, which shares content with Fairfax papers in other cities (see www.traveller.com. au). Its Sunday counterpart, the *Herald Sun*, also carries travel features.

The West Australian

au.news.yahoo.com/thewest

Travel features appear in Saturday's weekend edition.

Writers' groups & associations

Australian Society of Authors (ASA)

www.asauthors.org

Promotes and protects the professional interests of Australian writers. Members receive the association's journal, *Australian Author,* as well as regular newsletters.

Australian Society of Travel Writers

www.astw.org.au

The ASTW is dedicated to promoting ethical and honest travel, and the unbiased reporting of it, and organizes regular networking events for its members.

Copyright Agency

www.copyright.com.au

This not-for-profit copyright-collecting society seeks to secure fair payment for authors and publishers; membership is free.

Fellowship of Australian Writers (FAW)

www.writers.asn.au

A non-profit membership-based group dedicated to supporting, promoting and advocating the needs and interests of Australian writers.

Sydney PEN

www.pen.org.au

The local chapter of PEN International, which promotes literature and literacy and works to oppose restraints on freedom of expression.

Varuna – The Writers' House

www.varuna.com.au

Residential fellowships are offered annually to writers in all genres and of all levels of experience.

Writers' centers

Australian Capital Territory

www.actwriters.org.au

New South Wales

www.nswwc.org.au

Northern Territory

www.ntwriters.com.au

Queensland

www.qwc.asn.au

South Australia

www.sawriters.on.net

Tasmania

www.taswriters.org

Victoria

writersvictoria.org.au

Western Australia

www.writingwa.org

The various writers' centers provide support for Australian writers, including local advice and the use of resource libraries and facilities; many also offer writing and other related courses.

Writing courses

The Good Universities Guide (www.gooduniversitiesguide.com.au) is an online guide to courses at every university and training college in Australia, searchable by subject.

Centre for Adult Education

www.cae.edu.au

Offers short entry-level courses and professional-development courses in travel writing, professional and creative writing, editing and lots more.

Open Learning Institute of TAFE

www.oli.tafe.net

The short, vocationally oriented correspondence courses include freelance journalism levels I and II.

Open Universities Australia

www.open.edu.au

Australia's distance-learning university offers a range of writing, editing, publishing and journalism courses.

Aussie travel literature classics

These 10 travel literature titles reveal quite different responses to Australia and its culture, penned by both locals and visitors:

Down Under by Bill Bryson
In the Land of Oz by Howard Jacobson
One for the Road by Tony Horwitz
Sean & David's Long Drive by Sean Condon
A Secret Country by John Pilger
The Songlines by Bruce Chatwin
Thirty Days in Sydney by Peter Carey
Tracks by Robyn Davidson
Sydney by Jan Morris
The Winners' Enclosure by Annie Caulfield

University of Sydney
www.cce.usyd.edu.au
The Centre for Continuing Education offers a range of creative writing courses, including a travel writing course.

Sample paperwork

In this section we've gathered contributor guidelines from three eminent publications, to give you a good sense of the kinds of information such guidelines provide. If you're after specific guidelines for a publication you want to target, try Googling the publication's name along with 'freelance guidelines', 'writer guidelines' or 'contributor guidelines', and you'll often find their information available online.

In addition to these guidelines, we also reproduce sample model and property release forms for photographers. Get those journals and cameras ready – and good luck!

Los Angeles Times travel section

Dear Travel Writer:
Welcome to the cornerstone of what we do.
What follows on this page is the most important information contained in these several pages. The *Los Angeles Times* values honesty, fairness and truth. We understand the difficulties of the profession, but we also know that our reputation – and yours – rests on ensuring that our readers receive the best information possible.
These guidelines are from our own code of ethics, constructed over many months and with much care.

The *Los Angeles Times* ethics guidelines for freelance writers
The work of freelance journalists appears in our paper and on our website alongside staff-produced photos, articles and graphics. Freelancers must therefore approach their work without conflicts and must adhere to the same standards of professionalism that *The Times* requires of its own staff. It is the responsibility of assigning editors to inquire about a freelancer's potential conflicts of interest before making an assignment.

Conflict-of-interest provisions may apply differently to contributors to the Op-Ed pages. They are expected to bring institutional and personal perspectives to their work. They are not expected to avoid conflicts, but they are expected to disclose them.

More information about our expectations follows. If you have any questions, please call me or e-mail me.

Thank you again for your interest in and work for the *Los Angeles Times.*

Sincerely,

Catharine M. Hamm

Travel editor

Guidelines for submitting manuscripts to the *LA Times Travel* Section:

With the increasing power of the internet, it is a small world after all. We are awash in information: guidebooks, web blogs, chat rooms, travel websites, maps etc.

The *Travel* section is looking for bold, original travel features that tell a great story and are strong character-driven or first-person narratives – the more experiential the better. Stories should be sophisticated, compelling, complete and written with flair. They should evoke a strong sense of place (sounds, colors, smells, tastes), time (when did you go?), expertise and personal perspective, and they should be written with a very precise story angle in mind. We are not looking for everything you need to know about Shanghai; we are looking for the city from the vantage of its architecture or its fine arts. Find a salient angle in your story, be selective with your descriptions and historical facts and spin a tale that tells us your unique experience. We want stories that will make readers get out of their chairs and go – or at least enjoy the ride from their armchairs. We also want destination stories that reflect travel trends, stories that put us out ahead of the curve. Destinations will vary according to our needs, but stories should have a compelling reason to be told, an 'of the moment' quality that make them relevant rather than just an 'I went to Italy and did this, then I did this.'

In these stories, we require an equal emphasis – in length and in scope – on the Guidebooks sidebar that accompanies each destination feature. This nuts and bolts information is as important to readers as the ride you take them on. Be creative and be detailed about attractions, hotels, restaurants etc.

Above all, be honest. Not every trip goes well. We know that not all hotels are great and that meals are sometimes lousy. We know that tour guides aren't equally well-versed and that weather can be bad. And, more important, our readers know it too because they are travelers. So if something unpleasant happens, that's part of the story, although this isn't supposed to be carpfest either.

Freelancers must approach their work and travel arrangements without conflicts and must adhere to the same standards of professionalism that The Times requires of its staff. The *Travel* section will not consider pieces written about trips that have been subsidized in any way (even if part of a trip was not comped). We may ask for receipts.

Completed stories are considered on speculation only. Stories must be based on trips taken within the previous two years. To be considered, the story may not have run elsewhere or be pending publication elsewhere.

National Geographic Traveler
Writers guidelines

Thank you for your interest in contributing to *National Geographic Traveler*, which is published eight times a year by the National Geographic Society. *Traveler*'s publishing goals are to find the new, to showcase fresh travel opportunities, to be an advocate for travelers. *Traveler*'s tag line is 'Where the Journey Begins,' and accordingly, a *Traveler* story must capture a place's essence in a way that inspires readers to follow in the writer's footsteps – and equip them to do so with useful destination information.

What types of stories does *Traveler* publish?

Each issue of the magazine contains five or more features, roughly balanced between US and foreign subjects. Generally, we are interested in places accessible to most travelers, not just the intrepid or wealthy. The types of destinations we cover vary widely, from mainstream to adventure travel.

Traveler features are usually narrow in scope; we do not cover whole states or countries. Subjects of particular interest to us are national and state parks, historic places, cities, little-known or undiscovered places, train trips, cruises, and driving trips. Service information is generally given separately at the end of each feature in a section that includes how to get to the destination, things to see and do there, and where to obtain more information. The writer is expected to send along as much service information as possible with the manuscript to help us prepare this section.

We also publish several regular service-oriented departments, with the emphasis on meaty, practical information. Subjects include photography, food, lodgings, ecotourism, adventurous learning experiences, and short getaways. Essays offering reflections on the travel experience round out the department mix.

What kinds of proposals is *Traveler* looking for?

We accept freelance queries for most of our departments. Ideas for features are generated both by the *Traveler* staff and by freelance contributors. We do assign features to writers we have not used but only to those whose published clips demonstrate the highest level of writing skill. We don't accept phone queries from writers, and we discourage the submission of unsolicited manuscripts for feature articles. We don't accept proposals about trips that are subsidized in any way.

How should an idea be proposed?

If we have to sell readers to consume our magazine, then writers must sell us with more than just notions and place-names, so please do not send us any unfocused wish lists of multiple queries. Restrict each submission to one or two well-developed proposals that have been crafted especially for us. A carefully considered proposal combines support for doing a particular destination with some premise or hook. A good query has a headline that suggests what the story is, a deck that amplifies on that, a strong lead, and not much more than a page that clearly sets out the premise and approach of the piece. The query should represent the writer's style and should answer these questions about the story: Why now, and why in *Traveler*?

Check the *Traveler* index to make sure we have not recently run a piece on the topic you are proposing. Prospective contributors doing preliminary research for a story must avoid giving the impression that they are representing the National Geographic Society or *Traveler*. They may use the name of the magazine only if they have a definite assignment. When *Traveler* gives an assignment, the terms are clearly stated in a written contract.

How long are *Traveler* feature stories and departments?

Most *Traveler* features range from 1500 to 2500 words, depending on the subject. *Traveler* departments generally run from 750 to 1500 words. Compensation varies depending on the type of feature or department but is competitive with other national magazines. Payment is made upon acceptance. We buy all rights to manuscripts, although copyright is returned to the author 90 days after publication.

What does *Traveler* look for in writing style?
There are no limitations on style, as long as the writing is lively and interesting, although a sense of discovery should be at the heart of every *Traveler* story. We want our writers to project a curious and knowing voice that captures the experience of travel – the places and personalities, the insights and idiosyncrasies. Writers who work for us must see destinations with fresh eyes and real insight. We place a premium on surprise and good storytelling – the compelling anecdote, the colorful character, the lively quote, the telling detail. And we prefer that our readers be allowed to experience a destination directly through the words and actions of people the writer encounters, not just through the writer's narrative.

Beyond being strongly evocative of place, our articles attempt to speak to the soul of traveling. Every traveler, no matter how seasoned, wonders what awaits at a new destination. This goes beyond weather and accommodations and language and scenics and museums. There's a certain frisson of expectation: How foreign is this destination? What new experience will I have? This is travel as texture – the feel of a place, its essential differentness, its look, its flavor. We seek that texture in every story we publish.

Wanderlust
Writer guidelines
With only eight issues a year, the opportunities for getting work published in *Wanderlust* are very limited. The vast majority of our articles are commissioned specifically for the magazine, and written by experienced journalists, guidebook authors or travel experts.

Please read our guidelines carefully and note that we do not accept enquiries or proposals by telephone. Here are answers to some of the commonest queries we receive:

Should I send a manuscript or a proposal?
Please do not send us manuscripts – we simply do not have the time to read them.

If you have already completed the trip(s) you wish to write about, please contact us by email or letter with:

- A one-paragraph proposal outlining the story
- The proposed first paragraph of your story
- Brief details of how you undertook your journey, including any tour operators used
- If you have pictures, please include up to five low-resolution images to give a flavour of your trip (if emailing, your whole message should not be larger than 2MB)
- Any relevant experience you have, with links to / cuttings from previously published stories if possible

If you have not yet undertaken the trip you wish to write about – or your proposal is for a different kind of feature, please email submissions@wanderlust.co.uk, or write to us with:

- A one-paragraph proposal outlining the story
- Your proposed dates of travel
- Brief details of how you will be undertaking your journey, including any proposed tour operators
- Any relevant experience you have, with links to previously published stories if possible

Please note we cannot respond to postal contributions unless a self-addressed envelope (SAE) is enclosed, which must be stamped or accompanied by sufficient International Reply Coupons (IRCs).

I've submitted a proposal – what do I do next?

Although we endeavour to reply to proposals, at busy times this is not always possible. If we are interested, we'll respond by email, asking you for further details or a draft article for consideration. But please bear in mind that this may take several weeks. If you have not heard back from us within a month, feel free to email or write again. If you need an answer by a specific date, let us know – and if the date passes, please assume we are not interested. Please do not telephone the office to follow up submissions – if you do not hear back from us, you should assume we are unable to use your proposal.

I'm a first-timer writer – will my proposal be considered?

Yes, but you need to demonstrate writing flair and professionalism. You should also target one of our shorter regular slots, for example *Dispatches*, *Wanderlust Weekends*, or a consumer feature.

How do I know if you've already covered somewhere?

Most of our articles from the last five years are now archived on this website [www.wanderlust.co.uk], and can be searched by destination. Study a copy of the magazine before considering a submission. It is no coincidence that the majority of our contributors are regular readers.

Do you accept articles without accompanying photographs?

Yes. The photographs in the magazine come from a variety of sources – writers, professional photographers, stock libraries – and we can normally find or commission images to accompany a good article. However, if you have print-quality, professional standard images, please let us know when submitting a proposal.

What do you look for in an article?

Our mission is simple – we want to provide our readers with the best writing, the best photographs and the most authoritative facts. *Wanderlust* aims to cover all aspects of independent, semi-independent and special-interest travel. We do cover 'soft' adventure but leave the crampons and adrenalin stuff to other magazines. Off-the-beaten-track destinations, secret corners of the world and unusual angles on well-known places are always of particular interest.

We are particularly interested in local culture and try to provide more of an insight than travel articles in other publications – hence, we prefer pieces to be written by someone with an in-depth knowledge of a topic or destination. You should make yourself familiar with the style, tone and content of *Wanderlust*, and be aware of recent articles to ensure your chosen subject has not been covered in the past year or so. Most of our articles from the last five years are now archived on [our] website, and can be searched by destination.

If tackling a topical subject then do bear in mind that we plan the contents of each issue up to a year ahead. Always ask yourself what makes your article different from all the others that may have been sent to us on the same topic, and why you are qualified to advise others.

What kinds of feature / regular formats do you publish?
Wanderlust includes various features open to submissions:

I. DESTINATION FEATURES

Covering a specific destination – a country or a region – or an activity, eg, horseriding in Chile, walking in Morocco. Should be both anecdotal and informative, written in the first person and in the past tense, and between 1800–2200 words.

2. DISPATCHES

Shorter, topical pieces (1200 words) describing a recent development in a destination of interest to our readers. Recent Dispatches have included an eyewitness account of a royal wedding in Uganda, a new walking trail in the Middle East, and slum tourism in Mumbai.

3. SPECIAL INTEREST FEATURES

Do you have specialist knowledge on a travel-relevant subject? Topics covered to date include safaris, cycling holidays, New Zealand walks, family adventure trips. Must be authoritative – authors should have in-depth and regional or global knowledge.

4. CONSUMER ARTICLES

A practical guide of value to travellers. Explain how people can save money, or make their travels better and easier. The style should be direct and instructive, but easy to read and understand. Recent articles have included: finding cheap flights online; road safety abroad; making better travel videos.

What kind of articles DON'T you publish?
If your proposal falls into any of these categories, it's not for us:
- Luxury hotels, resorts or spas
- Activity holidays – golf, skiing, bungee-jumping etc. If an activity provides a unique perspective on a destination or a way of travelling through it (for example, hiking or kayaking) that's fine, but activities are not of interest in themselves.
- 'Big trip' diaries. Round-the-world odysseys, charity challenges, 'wacky races' across continents in unusual vehicles – all make great trips, but long-winded, cumbersome and often superficial articles.

- Family travel. We have a regular column on this subject but do not run full-length features.
- One-off expeditions. All journeys must be achievable by our readers.
- Trips to FCO-blacklisted destinations, for example war- or disaster-zones. We will not feature destinations the FCO advises against visiting.
- Previously published articles of any kind.

Who reads *Wanderlust*?

Our readers encompass all ages and budgets, and at least 50 percent are female. They are well educated and reasonably affluent, and are mostly active travellers, perhaps more experienced than you. Although most are British we have readers in more than 80 countries worldwide. Some travel independently, others with specialist small-group or tailor-made tour operators. Major interests include wildlife, trekking and photography. A high proportion take two to three long-haul breaks a year.

Do you commission articles purely for your website?

We rarely publish narrative travel features on the site, but we do consider interesting blogs and inspirational round-ups. To suggest an idea, please email us at website@wanderlust.co.uk.

Do you have any general advice for aspiring travel writers?

Wanderlust editors regularly contribute to travel writing training courses. We also run occasional trips with training agency Travellers Tales for those interested in improving or selling their work. Keep an eye on our website for details.

Here are some general tips:
- Your article should have a beginning, a middle and an end – do not just tail off.
- Make the opening paragraph one of your strongest, in order to pull the reader in. You do not have to tell a story in chronological order – you can open with a tense situation and then flashback to how it began.
- Ensure that your piece has a strong central theme that moves the reader forward and provides a point to it all.
- Do not try to cover too much in one article – there may be several different articles hiding inside one large piece. You should be able to sum up the contents of your article in a single sentence.

- Show the good and bad side. Disasters and tricky situations often make for a more entertaining read than harmonious, straightforward trips.
- Present an honest account – *Wanderlust* is not a travel brochure. If you hated a place, then say so (and why).
- Feature articles should have personality – though often not yours; dialogue and comment from local people add colour to a story.
- Think about how you can avoid blandness in your descriptions of a destination – recounting a seemingly unimportant incident can bring a place to life more than a detailed adjectival description of its physical appearance. And don't forget smells, sounds, flavours and even temperature or air quality as well as sights and emotions.
- Be aware of the political, environmental and social background to the places you describe – they may not be pertinent to your story, but be sure of this, especially if you are going to allude to them.
- Be aware of the consequences of what you write – for example, ecological issues such as the damaging effect that snorkellers may have on a coral reef. Be wary of endangering the subjects of your article if describing an illegal activity or political views.
- Avoid Americanisms (unless you are recounting speech or quotations from an American!), jargon, foreign terms that are not generally understood, and the numerous travel clichés that many writers fall back on – snow-capped mountains, lands of contrast, kaleidoscopes of colour and seething masses of humanity will all get the chop.
- If we have recently run an article on a particular destination or topic then it will probably be some time (perhaps several years) before we cover that area again.
- Check your facts and be wary of making generalisations that you cannot be sure of.
- It goes without saying that *Wanderlust* will not tolerate any racist, sexist or otherwise discriminatory writing, but be careful too of patronising the peoples you describe and making generalisations about characteristics that could be deemed insulting.
- We have readers in 80+ countries worldwide – try to avoid references that would confuse other nationalities.

Please do not telephone the office to follow up submissions – if you do not hear back from us, you should assume we are unable to use your proposal.

Sample release forms

Model Release

By signing this document:

I irrevocably consent to the Photographer (and its licensees and assigns) incorporating my image or likeness in photographs or illustrations in any form or media (images) and reproducing, publishing and communicating the Images in any form and media for any purpose, whether commercial or otherwise (including advertising), and to the use of my name and any other text or works in connection with the Images. I waive any right to inspect or approve the Images or any publication incorporating the Images and any right to compensation for the use of the Images by the Photographer, its licensees and assigns. I release the Photographer, its licensees and assigns from any or all claims, actions, proceedings, demands and expenses and other liabilit y that may arise in connection with the use of the Images by any person. I confirm that I am either over 18 years of age or that my parent or guardian has also agreed to these terms by signing in the space provided below.

I understand and agree to the above.

Signed: _____ Signed by parent/guardian: _____

Print name: _____ Print name: _____

Address/email/phone number: _____

Description of image: _____

_____

Date: _____

Property Release

By signing this document:

I irrevocably consent to the Photographer (and its licensees and assigns) incorporating an image or likeness of the property described below in photographs or illustrations in any form or media (images) and reproducing, publishing and communicating the Images in any form and media for any purpose, whether commercial or otherwise (including advertising). I waive any right to inspect or approve the Images or any publication incorporating the Images and any right to compensation for the use of the Images by the Photographer, its licensees and assigns. I release the Photographer, its licensees and assigns from any or all claims, actions, proceedings, demands and expenses and other liability that may arise in connection with the use of the Images by any person.

I warrant that I am the owner of the property and/or am fully authorized to enter this property release.

Signed: _____ Print name: _____

Address/email/phone number: _____

Property description: _____

Property address: _____

_____

Description of image: _____

_____

Date: _____

GLOSSARY

advance monies paid to an author in advance of actual sales, as part of a royalty-based agreement

back-of-the-book magazine section reserved for promotions, round-up pieces and classified advertisements

brief an assignment given to an author, usually indicating the subject, style and word count expected by the publication

bright a short, front-of-the-book article

byline a line in a newspaper, etc., naming the writer of the article

clips copies of a writer's previously published articles

commission an assignment given to a writer that is guaranteed to be published by a publication

contributor guidelines rules, principles and advice from a publication as to how to submit material for their consideration or publication

copy-edit to edit text by checking its grammatical and factual consistency and accuracy

embargo a contracted period of time during which the original assigning publication forbids you to reprint the story with another publication

fact box essential information to complement a travel article, such as how to get there, where to stay, where to eat

flat fee method of payment where author receives a set fee for their writing

front-of-the-book magazine section that includes short articles or 'brights'

in medias res without preamble; in the middle of

kill fee compensation given when a publication decides not to publish a commissioned or accepted article

lead introductory segment of a story

lead time amount of advance time a publication needs to plan its content and articles

lede US spelling for lead

masthead in a newspaper, etc., the section at the front of the publication or top of the editorial page where the publication's staff is listed

middle-of-the-book section of a magazine where the high-profile feature articles are published

nut graf a 'nutshell paragraph'; journalism slang for the editorial heart of the story

on spec 'on speculation'; in the hope of success but without formal agreement or instruction from a publication

peg an occasion, theme or pretext, which often forms the basis of or reason for an article

pitch a proposal for an article idea

query see *pitch*

SASE self-addressed, stamped envelope

section break a line break or graphic element (in text) that tells the reader one sequence has ended and another is beginning

sidebar see *fact box*

sub-edit see *copy-edit*

transition connecting word or phrase that acts like a bridge between parts of an article

vox pop popular opinion

About the authors

Don George

National Geographic has described Don George as 'a legendary travel writer and editor.' Don has been exploring new frontiers as an author, editor and adventurer for more than 30 years. Currently Editor at Large and Book Columnist for *National Geographic Traveler* magazine, Features Editor and blogger for Gadling.com, Editor of *Recce: Literary Journeys for the Discerning Traveler* (www.geoex.com/blog), and host of the Adventure Collection's blog, The Adventurous Traveler (www.adventurecollection.com), Don has also been Global Travel Editor for Lonely Planet, Travel Editor at the *San Francisco Examiner & Chronicle* and founder and Editor of Salon.com's Wanderlust travel site. Don's stories have been selected to appear in numerous collections, and he has edited nine travel anthologies, including Lonely Planet's acclaimed *Better Than Fiction*, *The Kindness of Strangers*, *By the Seat of My Pants*, and *Tales from Nowhere*. Don has won numerous awards for his writing and editing, including the Society of American Travel Writers' Lowell Thomas Award. His most recent book, *The Way of Wanderlust: The Best Travel Writing of Don George,* was published in 2015. See more at www.don-george.com.

Janine Eberle
Janine sat behind a desk at Lonely Planet for many years,
working as commissioning editor and publisher (amongst
other things), emerging every so often to research guidebooks
from Austria to India. Finally, she succumbed to the lure of
the wild and today she's a freelance writer and editor. She writes about
her adopted hometown at secretsofparis.com

Published in July 2017 by Lonely Planet Global Limited
CRN 554153
www.lonelyplanet.com
ISBN 978 1 7865 7866 2
© Lonely Planet 2017
Photographs © as indicated
Printed in Singapore
10 9 8 7 6 5 4 3 2
Written by Don George with Janine Eberle

Managing Director, Publishing Piers Pickard
Associate Publisher Robin Barton
Commissioning Editor Jessica Cole
Art Direction Daniel Di Paolo
Layout Designer Mariana Sameiro
Editors Janine Eberle, Lucy Doncaster
Print production Larissa Frost, Nigel Longuet

STAY IN TOUCH lonelyplanet.com/contact

AUSTRALIA The Malt Store, Level 3, 551 Swanston St, Carlton, Victoria 3053 T: 03 8379 8000

IRELAND Digital Depot, Roe Lane (off Thomas St), Digital Hub, Dublin 8, D08 TCV4

USA 124 Linden St, Oakland, CA 94607 T: 510 250 6400

UK 240 Blackfriars Rd, London SE1 8NW T: 020 3771 5100

Although the authors and Lonely Planet have taken all reasonable care in preparing this book, we make no warranty about the accuracy or completeness of its content and, to the maximum extent permitted, disclaim all liability from its use.

MIX
Paper from
responsible sources
FSC™ C021741

Paper in this book is certified against the Forest Stewardship Council™ standards. FSC™ promotes environmentally responsible, socially beneficial and economically viable management of the world's forests.